William Shakespeare: His Life and Times

Twayne's English Authors Series

Arthur F. Kinney, Editor

University of Massachusetts, Amherst

TEAS 513

William Shakespeare: His Life and Times

Dennis Kay

Lincoln College, Oxford University

Twayne Publishers • New York
Maxwell Macmillan Canada • Toronto
Maxwell Macmillan International • New York Oxford Singapore Sydney

William Shakespeare: His Life and Times
Dennis Kay

Copyright © 1995 by Twayne Publishers

Twayne Publishers
Macmillan Publishing Company
866 Third Avenue
New York, New York 10022

Maxwell Macmillan Canada, Inc.
1200 Eglinton Avenue East
Suite 200
Don Mills, Ontario M3C 3N1

Library of Congress Cataloging-in-Publication Data

Kay, Dennis.
  William Shakespeare: his life and times / Dennis Kay.
    p. cm.— (Twayne's English authors series; TEAS 513)
  Includes bibliographical references and index.
  ISBN 0-8057-7063-1 (alk. paper)
    1. Shakespeare, William, 1564–1616—Biography. 2. Shakespeare, William, 1564–1616—Contemporary England. 3. Dramatists, English—Early modern, 1500–1700—Biography. 4. Theater—England—History—16th century. 5. Theater—England—History—17th century. 6. England—Civilization—16th century. 7. England—Civilization—17th century. I. Title. II. Series.
PR2894.K33 1994
822.3'3—dc20   94-19818
                                                                        CIP

The paper used in this publication meets the minimum requirements of American National Standard for Information Sciences—Permanence of Paper for Printed Library Materials. ANSI Z39.48-1984. ∞ ™

10 9 8 7 6 5 4 3 2 1

Printed in the United States of America.

For
Stéphanie

Contents

Preface

It has sometimes been claimed that Shakespeare's life is a mystery, and that all that is known about him could be written on one side of a postcard. Such a claim fed the notion that Shakespeare was an artist uniquely removed from time, who dealt in universals, soaring above the trivial particularities of the world he lived in.

Each of these ideas needs to be questioned. To start with, a good deal is known about his life. Admittedly, we know little about his physical appearance, and of his personality only (though this is better than nothing) the suggestion of an amiable and gentle disposition. Based on the surviving records, the story of Shakespeare's life shows a man driven to develop his business interests and to preserve his estates in Stratford.

There is little evidence that Shakespeare was writing with an eye on posterity, seeking to secure a posthumous reputation through his writing. Rather, his writing was intimately bound up with the culture of his day. In particular, his talents lay in writing for the public stage, a medium whose tendency to be social and collaborative was especially marked in the culture of early modern England, where the function, value, effects, and even the existence of drama were matters of intense concern.

This book is designed to be a companion and complement to other volumes in the Shakespeare series. It is conceived primarily as a resource for students rather than as a final work of reference, as a way of raising questions rather than as an anthology of answers. It seeks to bridge the gap that can exist between the student's experience of Shakespeare and the most exciting recent research, particularly the research that has explored his works in relation to Elizabethan and Jacobean culture.

The book is organized to be read either in sequence or in sections. The first chapter deals with Shakespeare's hometown of Stratford-upon-Avon, giving an account of the town and of the career of Shakespeare's father, John. There are then sections on his family and on his own appearances in the town records. The second chapter discusses the curriculum Shakespeare probably followed at the grammar school in Stratford and then surveys the evidence the plays provide of his reading throughout his life. Chapter 3 is a survey of English history from the accession of Henry VII in 1485 to the death of James I in 1625. It consists of both a bare historical narrative and a more general essay on the culture and society of Shakespeare's England. The fourth chapter describes London, the city where Shakespeare worked for some 20 years, and records the evidence of his activities and residences. Chapter 5 is a brief survey of the theatrical industry in which Shakespeare worked, considering the playhouses, acting companies, the playgoers, and changing attitudes to the drama. The two chapters that follow are essays on, respectively, Elizabethan and Jacobean culture, with special reference to the place of drama within them. The final chapter is a brief survey of the major periods in Shakespeare's literary career. Most quotations have been modernized, except where the retention of the original seemed especially valuable to illustrate the point being made.

It would be impossible to do justice to the subjects touched on here in a volume of this length, but there are perhaps some compensating advantages in gathering together such material at a time of so much intense interest in the interactions between texts and histories. I hope that the reader will find it useful in itself and a stimulus to further investigations into the relations between Shakespeare and the culture in which he participated.

I would like to thank Oxford University for the award of a Special Lectureship that gave time for the book to be started, and the Department of English at George Washington University for their hospitality while it was being finished.

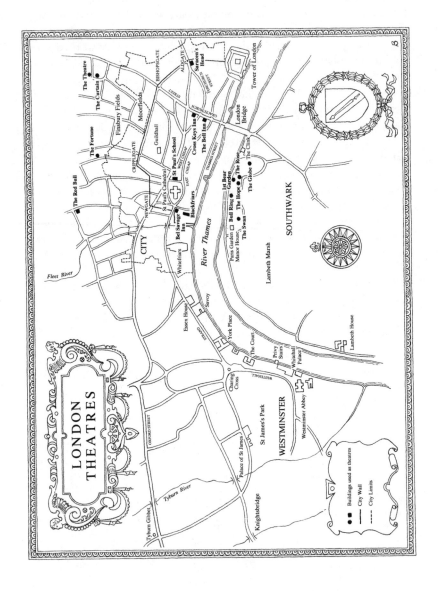

LONDON THEATRES

The Theatre
The Curtain
Finsbury Fields
Moorfields
The Fortune
CRIPPLEGATE
The Red Bull
CITY
NEWGATE
Fleet River
Whitefriars
Bel Savage Inn
St Paul's Cathedral
Blackfriars
St Paul's School
Cross Keys Inn
The Bell Inn
Guildhall
BISHOPSGATE
ALDGATE
Saracen's Head
BOROUGH STREET
LUDGATE
HOUNDSDITCH
WOOD STREET
CHEAP
EAST
THAMES STREET
London Bridge
Tower of London
River Thames

1st Bear Garden
Paris Garden
Bull Ring
Manor House
The Hope
The Swan
The Rose
The Globe
The Clink
Lambeth Marsh
SOUTHWARK

Essex House
Savoy
York Place
The Court
Charing Cross
Privy Stairs
Whitehall Palace
WHITEHALL
Lambeth House

Tyburn Gibbet
Tyburn River
OXFORD STREET
Palace of St James
St James's Park
Knightsbridge
WESTMINSTER
Westminster Abbey

Buildings used as theatres
City Wall
City Limits

13

Chronology: Historical Events

1509   Accession of Henry VIII.

1517–1521   Lutheran Reformation begins in Germany.

1525   William Tyndale's translation of the Bible published.

1531   Sir Thomas Elyot's *The Boke Named the Governour* published.

1532   Henry VIII divorces Catherine of Aragon.

1533   Pope Clement VII excommunicates Henry VIII, who marries Anne Boleyn. Elizabeth is born.

1534   Acts of Succession and Supremacy mark England's break with Rome. Anabaptists take control of Munster.

1535   Thomas More and John Fisher are executed.

1536   John Calvin's *Institutes* published in Latin.

1536–1540   Dissolution of monasteries and religious houses.

1542–1547   Henry VIII's wars in France and Scotland use up revenues from Dissolution.

1543   Copernicus's *De Revolutionibus orbum celestium* published.

1547   Henry VIII dies. Accession of Edward VI and institution of radical Protestantism.

1549   First Protestant Prayer Book published.

1552   Second Protestant Prayer Book published. Edmund Spenser is born.

1553   Edward VI dies. Accession of Mary Tudor after attempted Protestant coup involving Lady Jane Grey. Catholicism is reestablished.

1554   Mary marries Philip II of Spain. Philip Sidney (godson of Philip II) and Walter Ralegh are born.

1555   Nicholas Ridley and Hugh Latimer are executed for heresy in Oxford. The Peace of Augsburg confirms the sway of Protestantism in Germany.

1556   Thomas Cranmer is executed for heresy.

1557   *Songes and Sonnetes* ("Tottel's Miscellany") published.

1558   Mary dies. Accession of Elizabeth I, 17 November.

1559   The settlement of the Elizabethan Church is expressed in Acts of Supremacy and Uniformity.

1560   Geneva Bible published.

1562   French religious wars begin: English troops are sent into action on Protestant side and withdrawn after a year.

1563   John Foxe's *Actes and Monumentes* ("Foxe's Book of Martyrs") published.

1564   William Shakespeare and Christopher Marlowe are born.

1567–1568   Revolt in the Netherlands is suppressed by Spanish troops under the Duke of Alva.

1567   Mary Queen of Scots is deposed following the death of the Earl of Darnley and her marriage to the Earl of Bothwell; James VI succeeds her at age 13 months. Sir Henry Sidney is victorious in Ireland.

1568   Mary Queen of Scots is given refuge in England. Bishops' Bible published.

1569   Plot by the Duke of Norfolk and the revolt of the northern earls (in favor of Mary) fail.

1570   Pope Pius V excommunicates and deposes Elizabeth.

1572   French Protestants are massacred on Saint Bartholomew's Eve. John Donne and Ben Jonson are born.

1573   Henry Wriothesley (later Earl of Southampton) is born.

1575   New Poor Law. The Earl of Leicester entertains Queen Elizabeth at Kenilworth castle.

1576   Antwerp is sacked. William of Orange emerges as Dutch leader. The Theatre opens.

1577   Sir Francis Drake's fleet sets off to circumnavigate the world. The Curtain and Blackfriars theaters open.

1578   John Lyly's *Euphues: The Anatomy of Wit* published.

1579   Jesuit missions to England begin. Spenser's *The Shepheardes Calender* published.

1580   Drake returns in triumph. Lyly's *Euphues and His England* published.

1581   Anti-Catholic laws are strengthened. Edmund Campion and Robert Parsons are executed as traitors.

1583   11,000 Catholics are arrested in aftermath of foiled Throgmorton and Arden plots against Elizabeth.

1584   More Jesuits are executed. William of Orange is assassinated. Spanish Ambassador Mendoza is expelled as tension rises.

1585   Earl of Leicester leads armed force to the Netherlands. Colonists are sent to Roanoke Island, Virginia.

1586   Babington plot is foiled. Mary Queen of Scots is tried. Sir Philip Sidney is killed in the Netherlands.

1587   Mary Queen of Scots is executed. Drake attacks Cadiz. Pope Sixtus V declares crusade against England.

1588   The Spanish Armada is defeated then destroyed by storm. Leicester dies.

1589   Henri III is assassinated; Henri of Navarre becomes Henri IV. English forces support Henri IV in religious civil war in France.

1590   James VI marries Anne of Denmark. Sir Francis Walsingham dies. Philip Sidney's *Arcadia* published. Spenser's *The Faerie Queene*, books 1–3, published.

1591   The Earl of Essex leads English army in France to aid Henri IV.

1592   Ralegh is in disgrace following secret marriage. Essex is recalled from France. Drake attacks Corunna. Robert Greene dies.

1593   A plague strikes London; theaters are closed. Marlowe dies. Period of poor harvests begins (until 1597), leading to famine, high prices, and widespread disease.

1594   Plots are made against Elizabeth's life. James VI's son, Prince Henry, is born. The Earl of Tyrone leads uprising in Ulster. Lord Chamberlain's Men emerge.

1595   Ralegh sails for Guiana. Jesuit poet Robert Southwell is executed. Spenser's *Amoretti, Epithalamion, Colin Clouts Come Home Againe* published.

1596   Spanish fleet at Cadiz is severely damaged by English forces led by Essex and Frances Howard. Drake and Sir John Hawkins die in the West Indies. Spenser's *The Faerie Queene*, books 4–6; *Prothalamion*; and *Fowre Hymnes* published. Sir John Davies's *Orchestra* published. The Swan theater is built.

1597   New Poor Laws. Francis Bacon's *Essays* published. Second Blackfriars theater is built.

1598   Edict of Nantes ends French religious wars (giving limited rights to Protestants). Tyrone's rebellion. Philip II of Spain dies. William Cecil, Lord Burleigh dies. Sidney's *Works* published. The Theatre is demolished; the Globe theater is built.

1599   Essex leads expedition against Tyrone. Episcopal and governmental action against publication of satires and erotic verse: volumes of satires publicly burned. Spenser dies. Oliver Cromwell is born. The Globe opens.

1600   Essex is tried and convicted but not imprisoned. Thomas Nashe dies. Richard Hooker dies. Giordano Bruno is burnt for heresy in Rome. The Earl of Gowrie and his brother allegedly attempt to assassinate James of Scotland in August.

1601   Essex rebels and is executed. Elizabeth's thirteenth Parliament. Mountjoy defeats Spanish forces in Ireland. Southampton is imprisoned for complicity in the Essex revolt. Poor Law revised.

1602   Jesuits and other priests are ordered to leave England. The Bodleian Library is founded in Oxford.

1603   Elizabeth dies. Accession of James I, 25 March. Ralegh is convicted of treason and imprisoned in the Tower. Mountjoy is victorious in Ireland. Severe plague strikes London. John Florio's translation of Montaigne's *Essays* published.

1604   Peace treaty is signed with Spain. Hampton Court Conference. James's first Parliament; limited electoral reforms.

1605   Gunpowder Plot; capture and trial of conspirators. Bacon's *Advancement of Learning* published.

1606   Father Garnet is executed for complicity in Gunpowder Plot. Parliament resists plans for union with Scotland.

1607   Captain John Smith settles at Jamestown; unsuccessful plantation in northern Virginia (return in 1608).

1608   John Milton is born. Parliament rejects union proposals, discusses new fiscal arrangements to finance crown activities. Henry is created Prince of Wales.

1609   Moors are expelled from Spain. Truce is established between Spain and the United Provinces. Virginia Company claims Bermudas for the English crown.

1610   Talks to establish the Great Contract break down. Parliament is dissolved. Donne's *Pseudo-Martyr* published. The Puritan George Abbott becomes Archbishop of Canterbury. Henri IV is assassinated. Henry, Prince of Wales, is invested.

1611   King James Bible published. Plantations are established in Ulster, partly funded by sale of baronetcies.

1612   Prince Henry dies. The "Lancashire witches" are tried and executed. Tobacco first cultivated in Virginia.

1613   Princess Elizabeth marries Frederick, Elector Palatine, 14 February. Sir Thomas Overbury scandal. Globe theater burns down, 29 June.

1614   James summons then dismisses the "Addled" Parliament. Initial prominence of George Villiers (later Duke of Buckingham). Fulke Greville is named chancellor of the exchequer. Ralegh's *History of the World* published. King James's *Works* published.

1615   Trial of the Overbury accused: lesser participants executed, others banished. Robert Armin dies. Donne enters holy orders. Ralegh's "The Prerogative of Parliaments" published.

1616   Bacon replaces Edward Coke as lord chancellor. Prince Charles is created Prince of Wales. Miguel de Cervantes, Francis Beaumont, Richard Hakluyt, and Philip Henslowe die. Jonson's *Works* published.

Shakespeare's Family Tree

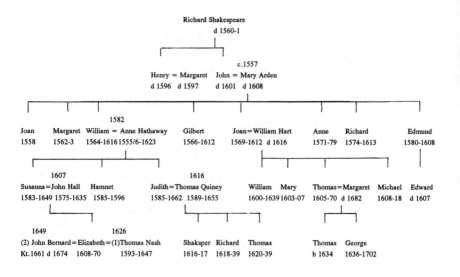

Chronology: Shakespeare's Life

1564   William Shakespeare born to John and Mary (Arden) Shakespeare.

1565   John Shakespeare is appointed alderman.

1566   Brother Gilbert born.

1568   John Shakespeare is elected bailiff.

1569   Sister Joan born.

1571   Sister Anne born.

1574   Brother Richard born.

1577   John Shakespeare suffers financial difficulties.

1579   Anne Shakespeare dies.

1580   Brother Edmund born.

1582   William marries Anne Hathaway.

1583   Daughter Susanna born.

1585   Son Hamnet and daughter Judith born.

1587   John Shakespeare is removed from Stratford Corporation.

1592   Robert Greene attacks Shakespeare in his pamphlet *Groatsworth of Wit*. John Shakespeare fails to attend church.

1593   William Shakespeare dedicates *Venus and Adonis* to the Earl of Southampton.

1594   Dedicates *Lucrece* to the Earl of Southampton. Lord Chamberlain's Men established.

1596   Is granted coat of arms. Hamnet Shakespeare dies.

1597   Purchases New Place in Stratford.

1598   Recorded as hoarding malt during corn shortage. Francis Meres's *Palladis Tamia* published. Dismantling of the Theatre; erection of the Globe.

1599   Resides on Bankside. The Globe opens in May.

1601   John Shakespeare dies. Essex Rebellion.

1602   Buys 127 acres in Old Stratford and a cottage in Chapel Lane.

1603   King's Men formed. Shakespeare sues Philip Rogers for debt.

1605   Actor Augustine Philips leaves Shakespeare gold 30 shilling piece. Shakespeare buys half-interest in tithes in Stratford area.

1607   Daughter Susanna marries John Hall. Edmund Shakespeare dies.

1608   Mary Arden Shakespeare dies. Granddaughter Elizabeth Hall born. Shakespeare sues John Addenbrooke for debt. Shakespeare is a sharer in the Second Blackfriars theater.

1610   Probably moves to Stratford.

1611   Defends his Stratford tithes in Court of Chancery.

1612   Is a witness in Stephen Belott/Christopher Mountjoy suit. Gilbert Shakespeare dies.

1613   Shakespeare purchases Blackfriars gatehouse. Makes "impreso" for Lord Rutland, in collaboration with Richard Burbage. Richard Shakespeare dies. Shakespeare is left £5 in the will of John Combe.

1614   Is involved in Welcombe enclosure controversy.

1616   Daughter Judith marries Thomas Quiney. Grandson Shakesper Quiney born. William Shakespeare dies.

1623   Anne Shakespeare dies. Registration of the First Folio.

1626   Granddaughter Elizabeth Hall marries Thomas Nash.

1635   John Hall dies.

1647   Thomas Nash dies.

1649   Elizabeth Nash marries John Bernard. Susanna Hall dies.

1662   Judith Quiney dies.

1670   Elizabeth (Hall) Bernard dies.

Note on the Publication of Shakespeare's Works

Thirteen of Shakespeare's plays, as well as his *Sonnets*, and the narrative poems *Venus and Adonis* and *Lucrece*, were published in editions that are considered reliable ("good" Quartos). The following list gives dates of subsequent reprintings:

1594	*Titus Andronicus* (rpt. 1600, 1611)
1597	*Richard II* (rpt. 1598, 1598, 1608, 1615)
	Richard III (rpt. 1598, 1602, 1605, 1612, 1622)
1598	*1 Henry IV* (rpt. 1598, 1599, 1604, 1608, 1613, 1622)
	Love's Labour's Lost
1599	*Romeo and Juliet* (rpt. 1609, 1622)
1600	*2 Henry IV*
	The Merchant of Venice (rpt. 1619)
	A Midsummer Night's Dream (rpt. 1619)
	Much Ado about Nothing
1604–1605	*Hamlet* (rpt. 1611)
1608	*King Lear* (rpt. 1619)
1609	*Troilus and Cressida*
1622	*Othello*

Other plays were published in so-called bad Quartos—texts held to represent corrupt versions of the Shakespearean "original":

1594	*The First Part of the Contention* (2 Henry VI) (rpt. 1600, 1619)
1595	*The True Tragedy of Richard Duke of York* (3 Henry VI) (rpt. 1600, 1619)
1597	*Romeo and Juliet*
1600	*Henry V*
1602	*The Merry Wives of Windsor*

| 1603 | *Hamlet* |
| 1609 | *Pericles* |

There were also Quarto editions of plays whose relation to the Shakespeare texts is evident, if highly problematic—namely,

| 1591 | *The Troublesome Reign of King John* |
| 1594 | *The Taming of a Shrew* |

The First Folio of 1623 inlcuded all the plays that had previously been published, together with 16 other works—namely (in Folio order), *The Tempest, The Two Gentlemen of Verona, Measure for Measure, The Comedy of Errors, As You Like It, All's Well That Ends Well, Twelfth Night, The Winter's Tale, 1 Henry VI, Henry VIII, Coriolanus, Timon of Athens, Julius Caesar, Macbeth, Antony and Cleopatra*, and *Cymbeline*.

Chapter One

Stratford

However grand the circles in which he moved, and however strong his ties with London and the court, William Shakespeare never lost contact with Stratford. He had family responsibilities there, and expanding property and business interests that required his presence from time to time. Many of the most reliable pieces of evidence relating to his life derive from this side of it.[1]

Stratford Life: Geography and Commerce

Stratford-upon-Avon's chief functions derive, like its name, from its location, a place where a highway (Anglo-Saxon: *stræt*) can be provided with a crossing or *ford* over a river (Welsh: *afon*). It still preserves the general shape, and some of the buildings, of the small market town where Shakespeare was born in 1564. One major difference is the disappearance of the wooden Market House, with its elaborate cupola and clock. It consisted of a large room held up in the air by four pillars, beneath which tradesmen—including Shakespeare's father, John—sold their goods at the weekly market on Thursdays (Schoenbaum 1977, 5). All that remains for the modern visitor to see is a patch of grass on a traffic island at the junction of Bridge, High, and Henley streets.

In Tudor times it was believed that the church of the Holy Trinity stood on the site of an ancient monastery established at "Stretforde" during the ascendancy of the kingdom of Mercia. Before the Reformation the town and its surrounding fields had belonged to the bishops of Worcester, who secured for the townsfolk the right to hold fairs, the longest of which lasted for 16 days. Stratford's weekly Thursday market dated from the time of Richard I. In fact, there were three markets: cattle were sold at the Rothermarket, the chief market was at the Market Cross, and dairy produce was sold outside the Guild Chapel. Over the years the occupations of the townspeople became increasingly specialized. Commerce became progressively more important as greater numbers came to the markets or passed through Stratford on their way north to Birmingham or Coventry or south to Bristol or London.

With the Reformation the population acquired responsibility for the town's administration, and the local people were compelled to establish a system of self-government. From the seventh year of Edward VI's reign (1553) the town became independent and acquired a seal and a charter. Its corporation consisted of a bailiff together with 14 aldermen who had the right to choose 14 burgesses to serve with them.

Some famous travelers recorded their impressions of Stratford in the sixteenth century. In about 1540, for example, shortly after the trauma of the dissolution of the monasteries, the antiquarian John Leland, keeper of Henry VIII's libraries, made a tour of England and recorded what he found. He noted that Stratford was a town of some fine broad streets and solid timber houses, "reasonably well builded." A generation later, William Camden, Ben Jonson's schoolmaster and one of the great scholars of the day, visited Stratford during the years of Shakespeare's early childhood. He came from the North, from Warwick, following the course of the River Avon, as he toured the country in his quest for nuggets of information to include in his *Britannia*. He commented on the contrast between woods and plain, between the forest of Arden and the fertile plain of Feldon, and he found the best vantage point from which to observe it. As he remarked, "The Feldon lieth on this side Avon southward, a plain champaign country, and being rich in corn and green grass yieldeth a right goodly and pleasant prospect to them that look down upon it from an hill which they call Edghill." To Camden, Stratford was "a fine small market town, which is indebted to two of its sons for all its glory" (Kay 1992, 28–30). Those sons were Archbishop John de Stratford and Sir Hugh Clopton, the builder of Clopton Bridge, and Shakespeare would have been brought up to admire their achievements.

John de Stratford held the high political office of chancellor of England three times in the late fourteenth century. But he also left his mark on his hometown. He provided for the expansion and augmentation of Church of the Holy Trinity, essentially to the plan as we see it today (the wooden spire Shakespeare would have known was replaced by the present structure in the eighteenth century). Stratford widened the aisles, built chapels and a chantry, and provided an endowment for five priests to sing Mass forever for him, his family, the monarch, and the Bishop of Worcester.

Hugh Clopton's is one of those rags-to-riches stories of upwardly mobile country boys so typical of fifteenth-century England. Clopton, a younger son, left Stratford to ply his trade as a mercer in London. There he became in succession alderman, sheriff, and (in 1491) lord mayor. He also was a great benefactor of Stratford. He built the handsome bridge that carries the London road. He also lavishly decorated the Guild Chapel and built for himself a fine house opposite. Eventually this house would be occupied by another Stratford man who made his fortune in London: William Shakespeare purchased the house, which had come to be known as New Place, in 1597. The stories of the three men demonstrate just how powerful and lasting was Stratford's hold over the affections of those who moved far beyond it to act out their parts on the national stage.

Shakespeare's Family

John Shakespeare

John Shakespeare, William's father, makes an undignified debut in the records of the town where he was to play such a prominent role. On 29 April 1552 he was fined (along with a group of his fellow townsmen) for making an unauthorized dunghill on Henley Street. After that, as the records show, relations between the elders of the town and the young immigrant improved markedly (Eccles, 24–37; Schoenbaum 1977, 14–22, 30–44).

The young man, probably in his early twenties, had moved to town from nearby Snitterfield. His brother Harry had evidently been content to remain farming like their father, Richard, but John found himself drawn to the nearest large town, and to a trade. He was to be a glover and "whittawer"—one who dresses white leather. He prepared the hides of sheep and goats, deer and horses and then imbued them in a solution of alum and salt. His business involved making and selling a wide range of leather goods such as gloves, bags, and belts. In Stratford-upon-Avon, the glovers had the best pitch in the market square, under the clock at the Market Cross. Glovers were also shielded from foreign competition by a protectionist act of Parliament. Presumably some personal connection helped him to be taken on as an apprentice. Richard Shakespeare had business dealings with a prominent figure in the town, Thomas Atwood, and he may have helped. Another Stratford alderman, Thomas Dickson (alias Waterman), was married to Joan, a daughter of John Townsend, a neighbor of the Shakespeares in Snitterfield. Certainly this Dickson was a glover, and he was probably John Shakespeare's master in his new craft.

On this journey from the old world of agriculture to the new age of industry, from feudal courts and tithes to capitalist enterprise, from tilling others' land and tending others' beasts to owning property, workshops, and a coat of arms, the forward-looking John Shakespeare picked up little education—he was, to all intents and purposes, illiterate. But he obviously understood and desired social status. By his choice of a wife he sought to graft the Shakespeares onto a family tree that had pretensions to gentility and antiquity.

We can follow his career fairly closely, even though there are some gaps in the records. We have seen already (thanks to the unauthorized dunghill) that by the spring of 1552—some half-dozen years before his marriage—John Shakespeare was living on Henley Street, in the western part of the large double house now known as the Birthplace. In 1556 he acquired the other half of the house (the part known as the Woolshop) and subsequently had the two parts joined together to give the appearance of a single structure. He also eventually had a rear wing built out into the garden. Further property was acquired: in 1556 he bought a house with garden and croft on Greenhill Street (now More Towns End) from a George Turner. John Shakespeare was living in Henley Street at least until 1597 (when he sold off some land at the edge of his property), and his wife shared the house with him from about 1558.

In 1553—shortly after John Shakespeare's arrival in the town—the borough of Stratford-upon-Avon received its charter of incorporation. For almost a quarter of a century the rising fortunes of the increasingly prosperous town were mirrored by those of the young man from Snitterfield.

On Richard Shakespeare's death, his eldest son might have been expected to take over his farming enterprise—and records refer to the young man as a farmer (*agricola*) at the time the will was proved. But a few months later, in October 1561, John Shakespeare was fined for failing to keep his hedges in good condition, after which no more is heard of his farming activities. It looks as though he made over the land, and sold the copyhold, well before 1574, probably to his brother-in-law Alexander Webbe, who was married to Margaret Arden, Mary Shakespeare's sister. He had plenty to keep him occupied in Stratford.

In the town records he is referred to on several occasions as a glover (as when he was unsuccessfully sued for £8 in 1556, or when he stood bail for a local itinerant tradesman in 1586) and on others (as in 1573 and 1578) as a "whittawer." Yet tradition has always maintained that Shakespeare's father was a wool trader—a tradition reinforced by the designation of his property as "the Woolshop." The Woolshop later became an inn, and its landlord told a visitor in the early years of the last century that "when he re-laid the floors of the parlour, the remnants of wool, and the refuse of wool-combing, were found under the earth of the foundations." Shakespeare's earliest biographers lined up behind the local tradition that the elder Shakespeare had been "a considerable dealer in Wool." In this century, bits and pieces of documentary evidence have been turned up to support this tradition (Schoenbaum 1977, 31).

In 1599 John Shakespeare sued John Walford, a clothier from Marlborough, in the Court of Common Pleas for failing to pay £21 for 21 tods (about 588 pounds) of wool.[2] More recent research has shown John Shakespeare was a business man on a substantial scale, and that, as well as trading in large quantities of wool, he was also involved in lending money (Kay 1992, 31–33).

The evidence consists of "informations"—accusations made by opportunist informers. Law had failed to keep up with developments in the sphere of commerce. Sixteenth-century businesses increasingly relied on credit, but they operated after 1552 in the context of an archaic piece of biblical literalism—a fundamentalist law against usury—and always ran the risk that a zealot with a relish for blackmail would bring information before the court, in the hope that the accused would be willing to buy him off in an out-of-court settlement. Those convicted of usury forfeited both loan and interest and ran the risk of further fines or imprisonment. Before 1552 interest had been permissible up to a level of 10 percent, but thereafter businessmen were faced with what was effectively a random tax on trade. Such a system obviously encourages frivolous or malicious accusations. Being an informant could be a lucrative business at the margins of legality. Indeed, one of John Shakespeare's accusers, John Langrake, was at different times fined and imprisoned for striking a deal with people he had accused before the case came to court. Yet the large sums involved in the Shakespeare accusations are indicative of the scale of John Shakespeare's enterprises.[3]

In 1569, for example, John Harrison of Evesham claimed that John Shakespeare had lent a business partner John Mussom the sum of £100 to be repaid a year later with £20 interest: such a loan would have been regarded as usury. Likewise, a similar accusation came from Langrake that same year, to the effect that Shakespeare had lent £80 and had charged £20 interest. In each accusation Shakespeare is referred to as a glover of Stratford.

Langrake also accused John Shakespeare of trading in wool contrary to a 1552 statute that restricted the buying of wool to authorized dealers. In 1571 John Shakespeare was accused of engaging in two illegal transactions. In the first he was said to have bought 200 tods (about

5,600 pounds) of wool at a price of 14 shillings per tod. In the second he was accused of buying 100 tods at the same price. Since the records say no more, it looks as though Langrake and Shakespeare came to some sort of understanding and the matter was dropped.

These transactions illuminate the scale and range of John Shakespeare's business activities. He ran a cottage industry, manufacturing leather goods and then selling them in the Stratford market. He owned in-town property that he rented out. He was in a position to advance considerable sums to business partners, and he traded in wool, a valuable local commodity. We know from other records that he dealt in timber—he sold some to the town corporation for 3 shillings—and in barley—the raw material used in the local ale- and beer-brewing industry. He probably used the Woolshop as a store for these goods. The details suggest he was a busy and enterprising man, seizing the trading opportunities presented to him, and apparently embodying in his own career—his movement from tenant farming to capitalism—the energy of the Elizabethan "middling sort." He inevitably ran a few risks, but for a quarter-century the town corporation signaled its trust by using his talents.

After 1553 the borough of Stratford was being organized to exercise the new powers acquired under the charter. John Shakespeare's first appointment, in September 1556, was as one of the two ale tasters; his chief function was to check that brewers sold beer of the proper quality at the approved price and in the prescribed manner, and that bakers made loaves of the standard weight. Twice a year the Leet, or manor court, would try offenders. As with most such offices, the duties were enforced by fines, and we know that John Shakespeare was fined in June 1557 for having missed, in his official capacity, three sittings of the court of record.

In the autumn of 1558, about the time of the birth of his first child, Joan, John Shakespeare became one of Stratford's four constables, charged with keeping the peace, confiscating weapons, stopping street brawls, enforcing local bylaws, making sure townsfolk behaved themselves during divine service, and supervising fire-fighting precautions. In 1559 he became an affeeror, the official whose job it was at the Leet to assess fines that were not laid down by statute. As he took on a range of increasingly significant responsibilities, his standing in the community was reflected first by election as one of the 14 principal burgesses in about 1561, and then by his appointment, with John Taylor, as one of the two chamberlains, who had official charge of borough finances and property.

The surviving accounts suggest that John Shakespeare had the trust of his colleagues. While the actual documents were drawn up by an official, deputy steward Richard Symons, they were endorsed by Shakespeare and Taylor and supervised by them. And even after his stint as chamberlain was over, John Shakespeare—first with Taylor (1564–65) and later alone (1565–66)—marked the accounts to show his approval (Schoenbaum 1977, 34). His deep involvement in local government—particularly his responsibility for the accurate mainte-nance of the town's financial records—cannot be matched among his contemporaries. Evidently he was a far-sighted and enterprising entre-preneur who was also enthusiastically committed to the orderly running of his adopted home.

In May 1565 the widely disliked William Bott, one of the aldermen (and owner of William Shakespeare's eventual house, New Place) was summoned to appear to answer the charge that he had claimed that "ther was never a honest man of the Councell or the body of the corpo-racyon of Stratford." Bott (called by his own son-in-law a harlot and a villain, and who may well have been a murderer) did not attend and was duly expelled (Eccles, 87–88). In his place the popular newcomer John Shakespeare was elected on 4 July and took office on 12 September. From that day on Master Shakespeare (as he would have been addressed) was entitled to wear in public the aldermanic thumb ring and black gown trimmed in fur (Schoenbaum 1977, 35–36, 233).

Still his rise continued. On the first Wednesday of September 1567, he was one of three nominees for the post of bailiff, the chief elected offi-cial of the borough. The following year he was elected, and he took office on 1 October. During his year he presided at council meetings and at sessions of the court of record as a justice of the peace. Each Thursday night he fixed the weekly price of corn—to which the prices of bread, ale, and other goods were necessarily linked. The town granted many dignities to its bailiffs. On his journey from his house to the Guild Hall sergeants bearing maces would go before him; the same officers would escort the bailiff as he took his walk of inspection through the market on Thursdays and processed with his wife to church on Sundays. In church the bailiff and his wife had a prominent pew, as they also did in the Guild Hall when sermons were given or plays were performed. Troupes of players acted in Stratford-upon-Avon toward the end of John

Shakespeare's year of office, in late summer of 1569, when the Queen's Men (who received 9 shillings for their work) and the Earl of Worcester's Men (who received just a shilling) gave shows in the Guild Hall, where John and Mary Shakespeare would have been sitting in all their finery in the front row of the audience.[4]

It was possible to hold the office of bailiff on more than one occasion: indeed, a brewer named Robert Salisbury held the post for three terms. John Shakespeare was not elected again, but he remained prominent in local affairs. In 1571, for example, he was elected chief alderman, to serve as justice of the peace alongside the new bailiff, Adrian Quiney, his Henley Street neighbor. In January 1572 the two men, granted plenipotentiary powers to proceed "according to their discretions," set off on horseback to London to try to push forward borough business in the courts and elsewhere. Clearly he was trusted by his colleagues to secure deals in the town's best interests.

Meanwhile, John Shakespeare was increasing his collection of properties in Stratford—two more houses were purchased in October 1575, as well as another 14 acres of land at Ingon. At about this time he thought about applying for a coat of arms, as his tenure of the office of bailiff entitled him to do, to the College of Heralds.

In the space of two decades John Shakespeare had established himself in the business community of his adopted home. He had become prominent in its commercial life, through his extensive manufacturing and trading operations; by offering storage space and rudimentary banking facilities; and by representing a locally based alternative for wool traders. In addition, he owned a good deal of land and a number of properties within Stratford. In the terms of the age he was evidently a modern, entrepreneurial spirit.

But the picture suddenly changes for reasons that remain obscure. After 1575 John Shakespeare bought no more property or land in Stratford or anywhere else. Corporation records indicate that, whereas he had been present at every single council meeting for which attendance is recorded from his election as bailiff through 1576, he never again attended (with exception of one meeting on 5 September 1582). Yet despite these absences, John Shakespeare's name remained on the aldermanic register for 10 more years—nobody else was so favored for so long. The corporation seems to have wanted him back, and consideration was regularly shown to him. When other absentees were fined, he was excused. When men were taxed, he was taxed at the level set for burgesses, not at the alderman's double rate. When the corporation collected for poor relief, everyone had to contribute four pence, except John Shakespeare and Robert Bratt, "who shall not be taxed to paye any thinge." At last, on 6 September 1586, two new aldermen were elected; John Wheeler was to be replaced because he had resigned, and Master Shakespeare because he "dothe not Come to the halles when they be warned nor hathe not done of Longe tyme" (Eccles, 31–35; Schoenbaum 1977, 38–43).

The likeliest explanation of John Shakespeare's decline is economic. Records of his transactions from the late 1570s and early 1580s suggest that he was selling off land and property to raise hard cash. Compared with the scale of his earlier business operations, the profits realized by these deals were frequently pitifully small. Inevitably other adversities—fines, lawsuits, arguments with neighbors—followed in the wake of his financial problems. Yet John Shakespeare's plight was unique. Throughout the West Midlands, the latter part of the sixteenth century was a period of sharp economic recession. The Stratford records tell a tale of increased disorder, drunkenness, illegitimacy, begging, and destitution. The most extraordinary statistic is that in 1601 the poor of the borough numbered some 700 people—a figure close to half its entire population.[5]

John Shakespeare's decline, though abrupt, did not plunge him into abject poverty. He was, however, one of a group of nine men who kept away from church for fear being sued for debt in the early 1590s. On the basis of nonattendance at church, he has been seen as some sort of religious nonconformist, whether Puritan or (then more usual) Catholic. The fragmentary evidence is insufficient to support either conclusion. And Stratford seems to have been a fairly tolerant place, with recognized Puritans and Catholics involved in town affairs and in local business. John Shakespeare continued after his fall to play some part in the life of the town, and he managed to hold on to his large house on Henley Street and pass it on to his son. It does not look as though he was ostracized or persecuted for heterodox religious or political views. Indeed, in 1601, Richard Quiney wrote a note naming seven men who could testify to the rights of the borough in a dispute with Sir Edward Greville, the lord of the manor. Among the small group of town officials and old men, John Shakespeare's name appeared, although he died before he had a chance to give his evidence. He was buried at Stratford on 8 September 1601 in the churchyard of Holy Trinity, having achieved the unusual age of 70 and having lived long enough to see his grandchildren, and to see his eldest son establish himself as a fashionable and successful play-wright, who bore a coat of arms and owned the biggest house in Stratford.

The Shakespeares

Shakespeare was a relatively common name—spelled in a variety of ways—in the Warwickshire and Gloucestershire areas in the later Middle Ages. In 1248, for example, a William Sakspere of Clopton in Gloucestershire was hanged for theft; in 1385 a William Shakespeare served on a coroner's jury at Balsall. Most early occurences of the name seem to derive either from the city of Coventry or from just four vil-lages—Balsall, Baddesley Clinton, Wroxhall, and Rowington—inside what was then the forest of Arden, about a dozen or so miles to the north of Stratford-upon-Avon. In more sophisticated circles the name (whose bawdily phallic implications link it with names like Shakestaff and Wagstaff) was regarded as something of an embarrassment. Perhaps it seemed indecorous for a celibate academic, for example, when one Hugh Shakespere became a fellow of Merton College, Oxford. In 1487 the college register records that he had changed his name to Hugh Sawnders. Translated from the Latin, it reads, "Hugh Sawnders, else-where called Shakespere, but this name of his has been changed, because it has such a base repute" (Schoenbaum 1977, 13, 324).

Beginning in the early sixteenth century the name is found more extensively in Warwickshire, but the furthest back William Shake-speare's line can be traced with any real confidence is to his grandfather (details from Eccles, 7–9, 14–17). Richard Shakespeare lived and farmed in a couple of manors around the village of Snitterfield as a tenant farmer from 1529 to his death in 1560 or 1561. Snitterfield occupies a low hill not far from the main road to Warwick, about four miles from the center of Stratford. Some of his land he held as a tenant of the colle-giate church of St. Mary in Warwick. This meant he was required to attend the manor court at Warwick, held annually by the deputy stew-ard at Hocktide after Easter and at Michaelmas. The penalty for nonat-tendance without good reason was a fine of two pence, and Richard Shakespeare, like many other tenants from the district, regularly opted for the fine rather than waste a day tramping six miles to Warwick, though his excuses were accepted and no fine imposed in 1532, 1538, and 1550. From the records of this manor (in which he is variously named "Shakspere," "Shakespere," "Shakkespere," "Shaxpere," and "Shakstaff") we also learn that in 1538 he was ordered to mend the hedges between his land and that farmed by one Thomas Palmer. Since no more is heard about it, presumably he did so.

Richard Shakespeare also farmed land belonging to the chief manor in the Snitterfield district, the "Warwikeslands and Spencerslands" estate, which had at one time been in the possession of the earls of Warwick. In its surviving records (now kept at the Birthplace) there are further traces of his farming enterprises. In 1535, for example, Richard Shakespeare was in trouble for overburdening the common pastureland with his animals. Twenty-five years later—in the last months of his life, as it turned out—he was fined for not yoking or ringing his pigs and for keeping his animals on the meadows. On the same day (3 October 1560) all tenants of the estate were given until the 18th of that month to make a hedge and ditch "between the end of Richard Shakespeare's lane" "and the hedge called Dawkins hedge." In the last century a "Dawkins Close" was identified on a farm on the north of a lane leading from Snitterfield to Warwick. Perhaps this was where the old man's neighbors came to help him keep his animals under control and to stop his land from flooding in the winter rains.

Richard Shakespeare was an important figure in his village; he was called on several times to value the estates of neighbors who had died. He was also known outside the village. In 1543 Thomas Atwood (alias Taylor), a prosperous alderman of the Stratford Guild, bequeathed him a team of four oxen, and when in January 1560 Thomas Lucy held an inquisition at Warwick into the estates of Sir Robert Throckmorton, "Richard Shakyspere" served on the jury. His house, on Snitterfield's High Street, had land that ran down to the stream flowing through the village. When he died his estate was valued at £38, 17 shillings; the estate of the vicar, Sir Thomas Hargrave, had been valued at £34 in 1557. His landlord was Robert Arden of Wilncote, whose daughter, Mary, was to marry Richard's son John.

Apart from John, the child of Richard Shakespeare who has left the most traces in local records is Henry, William's scapegrace uncle. Like his father, Henry was a tenant farmer and held land at Ingon, near Stratford; he was also lax about keeping his fences and ditches in good repair and declined to participate in communal road maintenance work. He spent various periods in prison for trespass and for debt and was once excommunicated for refusing to pay his tithes. In 1574 he got into a brawl with Edward Cornwell (later the second husband of Margaret Arden, sister of Mary Arden) and was fined in absentia for the attack. He was fined with two other men in 1583 for deliberately flouting the

Statute of Caps (introduced to protect the declining cap-making industry) by provocatively wearing a hat (instead of a cap) to attend church on
Sundays and holidays. The episode may have been a gesture of sympathy
with the widespread, and essentially Puritan, opposition to the statute,
but it could just have been a typical act of a man who seems to have
found authority an irritant through most of his life. He had two children
baptized in Hampton Lucy (Lettice on 10 March 1581 and James on 16
October 1585, with James being buried at the same church on 25
September 1589) and was himself buried in Snitterfield on 29 December
1596. He died with debts unpaid, and it took some time to set his affairs
in order. Still, he had his own house, a full barn, and some livestock at
his death. His wife, Margaret, survived him by less than two months
(Eccles, 9–12).

The Ardens

Mary Arden, William Shakespeare's mother, was one of the daughters of
the farmer Robert Arden of Wilmcote. Robert Arden's great grandfather
was probably Robert Arderne, who had been bailiff of Snitterfield in
1438. These Ardens claimed kinship with the ancient Arden family of
Park Hall in Castle Bromwich (now a suburb of Birmingham), who
traced their descent beyond the Norman conquest into Saxon times, to
the family of the sheriff of Warwick in the days of Edward the Confessor.
In the Domesday Book the properties of "Turchillus de Eardene" (elsewhere Turchill of Warwick) are matched by few other Englishmen in
extent or value. Even if the connection was not strong enough for them
to claim to be gentry in their own right, the farming Ardens of
Wilmcote derived prestige from an association with such a wealthy and
long-established family (Chambers 1930, 2: 18–22, 35–41; Eccles,
12–22; Schoenbaum 1977, 19–22).

Robert Arden was a successful farmer; by the time he married Agnes
Hill, the widow of another successful husbandman, he had accumulated
a sizable holding. He had also managed to father no fewer than eight
daughters (for six of whom he would be able to provide husbands), and
his new wife brought with her two sons and two daughters. The old man
and his numerous dependents lived in Wilmcote, close to the solid two-
story farmhouse in Featherbed Lane, near the village green that tourists
visit as "Mary Arden's House."[6]

Robert Arden's will is dated 24 November 1556. His daughter Mary,
slightly older than 16, was named as one of his executors. Accordingly,
she supervised the inventory made on the old man's death the following

month. In his will Robert Arden left Mary 10 marks and some valuable property—"all my lande in Willmecote cawlide Asbyes and the crop apone the grounde sowne and tyllide as hitt is." His goods were valued at £77, 11 shillings, 10 pence, and the inventory shows a well-stocked and prosperous farming operation, from the "bacon in the roof" down to the bees in the hive, from the bullocks, oxen, weaning calves, swine, and colts in the field to the implements and wood pile in the yard (Eccles, 18).

Mary Arden married John Shakespeare at some point between her father's death in late 1556 and the birth of her first child in September 1558. Robert Arden was buried in the churchyard at Aston Cantlow, and his daughter's wedding probably took place in the same parish church of St. John the Baptist (the records are not extant). She then moved in to Stratford, where she would spend the rest of her days.

The Children of John and Mary Shakespeare

The Stratford records note baptisms, not births; funerals, not deaths.[7] Therefore the precise date of Shakespeare's birth is unknown (Chambers 1930, 2: 1–2; Schoenbaum 1977, 23–26). Richard Byfield's transcript records the baptism on Wednesday, 26 April 1564, of William the son of John Shakespeare, "*Gulielmus filius Johannes Shakspere.*" The Book of Common Prayer required parents to arrange for the baptism of their child on the nearest holy day or Sunday following the birth, unless they demonstrated a "great and reasonable cause" to justify a delay. If Shakespeare was indeed born on Sunday, 23 April, the next feast day would have been St. Mark's day, on Tuesday, 25 April. There might well have been some cause, both reasonable and great, for a delay. Perhaps St. Mark's day was still held to be unlucky, as it had been before the Reformation, when altars and crucifixes used to be draped in black cloth, and when some claimed to see in the churchyard the spirits of those doomed to die in the following year—250 years later Keats would use this tradition in his poem "The Eve of St. Mark."

The Stratford archives record the harshness of the world into which Shakespeare was born. On 11 July there is a chilling note next to the entry that records the burial of Oliver Gunne, an apprentice; the note reads "*hic incepit pestis*"—on this day the plague began. Stratford was ravaged by the pestilence for the rest of the year, and only the onset of winter in December brought an end to its destruction. Some 200 people—out of a population only six or seven times that number—perished as a result of the plague during the second half of 1564. Like the elderly and the infirm, newborn children and infants were most at risk.

On Henley Street, a couple of doors from John Shakespeare's house, four of the children of the miller Roger Green died, as did two sons and a daughter of the town clerk, Richard Symons. When that August the council (including John Shakespeare) met in emergency session—in the open air to reduce the chances of infection—the most they could do was to make rudimentary provisions to relieve the hardship of the sick and dying while they waited for the healthier, cooler air of winter. John and Mary Shakespeare had already lost two children, Joan (born in 1558 and died in infancy) and Margaret (born in 1562 and died a year later). The prospects for a newborn child in the summer of 1564 were not good.

The Shakespeares' fourth child, and their second son, was christened Gilbert on 13 October 1566 at Holy Trinity. He was very probably named for Gilbert Bradley, who was, like John Shakespeare, a glover, a neighbor on Henley Street and—as of 1565—a burgess of Stratford. Like his older brother, Gilbert was to divide his time in adult life between London and Stratford. With a father and godfather prominent in local government and trade, it was no surprise that his career was that of a respected and responsible tradesman. He died, probably unmarried, in February 1612.

As was quite common practice in those times of high infant mortality, the Shakespeares named their third daughter as they had named their first. Joan Shakespeare was baptized on 15 April 1569. As with the previous Joan, she was probably named for her aunt, Joan Lambert. She was to be the longest lived of the eight Shakespeare children (she died in 1646), and the only one—apart from William—to marry and bear children. Of the next two Shakespeare offspring little is known. There was a final daughter, Anne, who was baptized on 28 September 1571 and was buried at the age of seven on 4 April 1579. A boy, Richard, was baptized on 11 March 1574 and was buried on 4 February 1613—a year and a day after the burial of his brother Gilbert.

The last of the children was Edmund (presumably named for his uncle Edmund Lambert, Joan's husband), whose life shadowed that of his oldest brother. The boy was christened on 3 May 1580. In due course he followed William to London and embarked on a career as an actor. His illegitimate child, probably called Edward, was buried at St. Giles Church outside Cripplegate on 12 August 1607. Edmund himself was buried on the last day of the same year in the great church of St. Mary Overy in Southwark, just a few yards from the Globe theater. He was not yet 30 and had made no great reputation for himself on the stage. But he had a great and expensive funeral. Whoever paid for the funeral specified the "forenoon knell of the great bell" (funerals were more normally held in the afternoon); it seems likely that the chief mourner was the young man's eldest brother and that the early funeral was arranged so that the actors could attend the interment of their fellow (Schoenbaum 1977, 28–29).

Edmund was the only one of the eight children of John and Mary Shakespeare to be buried away from Stratford-upon-Avon. The life spans of the four sons and four daughters were consistent with statistics of the time: their ages at death ranged from one to 77 years, with an average life span of just over 30, in line with the national average life expectancy of the period. As far as we can tell, Mary Shakespeare, like her husband, was essentially illiterate. The unvarnished records of her married life tell a story typical of her age, sex, and class; she bore eight children, whose births were spread over 22 years, and only three years separated the birth of her youngest child from that of her first grandchild.

The Hathaways

Because Shakespeare was a minor when he married (he was 18) he would have needed his father's approval (Chambers 1930, 2: 41–52; Eccles, 63–70; Schoenbaum 1977, 75–94). His wife, Anne Hathaway, was 26. She was pregnant at the time of the marriage in November 1582, and was to give birth the following spring to Susanna, who would be christened on Trinity Sunday, 26 May, 1583 in Stratford.

In those days there were no marriage licenses. The main legal requirement was that banns be published on three successive Sundays or holy days, to enable any objections to the match to be heard. After that it was customary for the wedding to be held in the bride's parish church before assembled families and neighbors, and obligatory for the details of the event to be recorded in the parish register. This standard procedure was not followed in Shakespeare's case.

The explanation is simple. Anne was pregnant, so the marriage needed to be arranged in haste. Banns could not be published during Advent or during the 12 days of Christmas, or indeed for a week after that (i.e., between 2 December and 13 January in 1582–83). If the plan had been to have the banns read in the normal way before this off season, the last dates available would have been the last two Sundays in November and St. Andrew's day (i.e., 18, 25, and 30 November). Because the parties involved missed this deadline, on 27 November two friends of the Hathaway family traveled the 20 miles to Worcester to attend the

Consistory Court, a body empowered to grant a marriage license even if, as in this case, the normal regulations could not be observed.

Consistory Courts had a good deal of discretion in such matters and could stipulate special conditions to meet the circumstances of particular cases. Sometimes, for instance, they could dispense with the banns altogether. But the bishop's officials would require more than mere attendance. They were to be supplied with a statement on oath of the names, addresses, and occupations of the couple and their parents; a bond; a certificate testifying to the consent of the parents or guardians on both sides when necessary; and, inevitably, a fee.

The Bishop of Worcester's register for 27 November 1582 records the granting of a license for a marriage "inter Willelmum Shaxpere et Annam whately de Temple grafton." The mistake over the woman's name is one of a series of errors made by the scribe (elsewhere he wrote "Darby" where he should have written "Bradley," for example); it is not repeated in the text of the bond, dated the next day. There we read that "William Shagspere" and "Anne hathwey of Stratford in the Dioces of Worcester maiden" have been given a license to marry after just one reading of the banns. The terms of the bond specified that the two sureties, Fulke Sandells and John Rychardson (both farmers), would be obliged to pay £40 if the requirements laid down for the marriage were not satisfied. The bond records that these requirements were that there should be no impediment (precontract, consanguinity, affinity) and no pending lawsuit relating to such matters; that if any legal action were brought against the bishop or his officials for providing the license the costs of the action would be borne by William Shakespeare; and that the marriage should not be solemnized without securing the consent of Anne's friends.

Sandells and Rychardson were friends of the bride's father; in 1581 Sandells was appointed an overseer of Richard Hathaway's will, and Rychardson witnessed the document. It seems to have been normal practice in Worcester, when the bridegroom was a minor, for friends or kinsmen of the bride to stand as surety and generally to make certain her interests were safeguarded. The Shakespeares, particularly their eldest son, would be held to their agreement.

Like Sandells and Rychardson, Richard Hathaway was a husbandman. He lived and worked at Shottery, in Hewland's Farm (known since 1795 as "Anne Hathaway's Cottage"), about a mile across the fields to the west of Stratford's Church of the Holy Trinity. In his will in 1581 Richard left to his daughter Agnes (Agnes and Anne were more or less interchangeable names at the time) the sum of 10 marks, which was to be paid to her on the day of her marriage. The will is dated 1 September 1581, not much more than a year before Anne's marriage. There is no record of Anne's birth, since baptismal records began with the new reign in 1558, and she was probably born a couple of years before that.

Although the Hathaway family house in Shottery was within the parish of Stratford, it was at the boundary, where the farmland gave way to the forest of Arden. Hathaways had lived in Shottery for some time. Anne's grandfather, John, had been a prominent figure in the life of Stratford in the early part of the sixteenth century. The muster rolls of 1536 list him as an archer, and he went on to serve as constable in 1548 and to hold a variety of responsible posts. In the subsidy of 1549–50 he was assessed on an income of £10, a considerable sum for Stratford at that time. John was succeeded by his son Richard, who continued with the farming enterprises; his holdings in the Shottery area amounted to between 50 and 90 acres (the Shakespeare holdings consisted of about 107 acres in Stratford itself).

His prosperity is demonstrated by his will, in which he refers to seven children (three daughters and four sons) who were living in 1581 and makes provisions for them. His wife, Joan, was to act as executrix and residuary legatee and was clearly expected to play an active role in the day-to-day running of the farm. Meanwhile, his eldest son, Bartholomew, was left to carry on the farming business, and the will expresses the hope that the young man "shalbe a guyde unto my saide wife in her husbandrie, And also a Comforte unto his Bretherne and Sisters to his power."[8] Of the other children, the youngest son, William, was to receive £10, and the remaining five were to receive 10 marks: the boys Thomas and John at once, Margaret when she was 17, Agnes (Anne) and Catherine on the day of their marriage. The phrasing of the will suggests that Anne was the oldest of Richard Hathaway's children, and she was a good deal older than her husband.

"O spite," as Hermia says in *A Midsummer Night's Dream*, "too old to be engaged to young" (1.1.138). There are several passages in Shakespeare's plays that refer regretfully to lovers "misgraffed in respect of years" (137). The most celebrated is in *Twelfth Night*, where Duke Orsino, sick of love-melancholy, offers advice to what he thinks is a young man (actually the cross-dressed Viola):

> . . . Let still the woman take
> An elder than herself; so wears she to him,

So sways she level in her husband's heart.
For, boy, however we do praise ourselves,
Our fancies are more giddy and unfirm,
More longing, wavering, sooner lost and won,
Than women's are. . . .
. . . let thy love be younger than thyself,
Or thy affections cannot hold the bent;
For women are as roses, whose fair flow'r
Being once display'd doth fall the very hour. (2.4.29–39)

Some biographers have suggested that Shakespeare felt trapped by his marriage, conscious of having to pay for his youthful folly with a woman already moving rapidly out of the marriageable range. There were no further children after the birth of the twins Hamnet and Judith in January 1585. Had Shakespeare thought in 1582 of trying to escape his responsibilities, the presence of Sandells and Rychardson, with their friends associated with recreational archery and part-time policing, would have argued otherwise.

More positively, the way Anne was left to look after the Stratford end of Shakespeare's business may actually suggest she proved a competent manager, as her mother had been—someone who could be relied on to act as steward during her husband's absence. Just as both William Shakespeare and his father married into a degree of social pretension, they also married into farming, enlisting partners who had been brought up to manage the land. The big house on Henley Street was a bank, a warehouse, a showroom, a workshop, and the center of a small farming business. It would have been crammed with dependents, children, workers, servants, and others. The busy community, the extended family, was governed on a daily basis not by the preoccupied, upwardly mobile Shakespeare men but rather by Mary and Anne, whose upbringing had trained them for such responsibilities (Kay 1992, 56–57).

Shakespeare and His Family in the Stratford Records

Family Affairs

William Shakespeare begins to appear in the Stratford records in the late 1590s. He was by this time a prosperous man and was restoring the family's fortunes (Schoenbaum 1977, 227–37). He secured a coat of arms in the latter part of 1596 and in 1597 acquired from William

Underhill the largest house in the town, New Place, once the house of Sir Hugh Clopton and more recently occupied by the notorious William Bott, whom John Shakespeare had replaced as alderman in 1565. The transaction was completed in May, for the bargain price of £60. John Shakespeare's rehabilitation was complete. He must have enjoyed being able to sell off to the council in 1598 a load of stone for the repair of Clopton Bridge.[9]

Shakespeare had become a man his father's cronies could do business with. It occurred to them that after his recent successes he might be looking for an investment opportunity. John Shakespeare's friend and neighbor Adrian Quiney—fined with him in 1552 for the dunghill— suggested to Abraham Sturley (an educated man, formerly of Queens College in Cambridge and recent bailiff of Stratford) that the younger Shakespeare might be interested in buying some land. So on 24 January 1598 Sturley wrote to Quiney's son Richard, then in London,

> This is one special remembrance from your father's motion. It seemeth by him that our countryman Master Shaksper, is willing to disburse some money upon some odd yardland or other at Shottery or near about us; he thinketh it a very fit pattern to move him to deal in the matter of our tithes. By the instructions you can give him thereof, and by the friends he can make therefore, we think it a fair mark for him to shoot at, and not unpossible to hit. It obtained would advance him in deed, and would do us much good. (Chambers 1930, 2: 101–102; Schoenbaum 1977, 237)

Nothing came of this first approach. Later that year Quiney was sent to London again to request the Privy Council's assistance for Stratford in the aftermath of two serious fires that aggravated the crisis caused by chronic bad weather and the severe economic recession. Quiney had to wait in London for several months, complaining about the council's slowness and incurring ever greater expenses. Eventually, on 25 October, he addressed a letter "To my Loveinge good ffrend & contreymann Mr Wm. Shackespere" from his lodgings, the Bell Inn, in Carter Lane (just south of St. Paul's Cathedral). The letter is a request for a loan of £30 to tide him over. Quiney writes like a man at the end of his tether. Idling in the big city, awaiting a summons from the council while cooped up in an inn with a group of men in the pay of Sir Edward Greville (lord mayor of Stratford), cannot have been an ideal way for a sober (possibly Puritan) burgher to spend the autumn months. His companions, Greville's men, had criminal records for brawling and drunkenness. In 1602 Quiney was to die from wounds received in a fight started by these men in Stratford. He finished the note to Shakespeare by declaring he was off to the court again to see if he could achieve anything.

The letter has survived because it was never sent; it wound up instead among Quiney's papers in Stratford. It is the only surviving letter addressed to Shakespeare by someone who knew him. Here it is, with spelling modernized:

> Loving Countryman, I am bold of you as of a Friend, craving your help with xxxll. [£30] upon Mr. Bushell's and my security or Mr. Mytton's with me. Mr. Rosswell is not come to London as yet and I have especial cause. You shall Friend me much in helping me out of all the debts I owe in London, I thank God, and much quiet my mind which would not be indebted. I am now toward the Court in hope of answer for the dispatch of my Business. You shall neither lose credit nor money by me, the Lord willing, and now but persuade yourself so as I hope and you shall not need to fear but with all hearty thankfulness I will hold my time and content your Friend, and if we Bargain farther you shall be the paymaster yourself. My time bids me hasten to an end and so I commit this [to] your care and hope of your help. I fear I shall not be back this night from the Court. Haste. The Lord be with you and with us all Amen. From the Bell in Carter Lane the 25 October 1598. Yours in all kindness. Ryc. Quyney. (Chambers 1930, 2: 102–106; Schoenbaum 1977, 238–39; *Riverside Shakespeare*, Appendix B, Document 4)

Was the letter not sent because Shakespeare turned up in person? Perhaps Quiney decided to make his approach directly. The older Quiney had already written to Richard and assumed that there would be no trouble in borrowing quite a substantial sum. The old man advises, "If you bargain with Mr Sha., or receive money therefore, bring your money home if you maye, I see how knit stockings are sold, there is great buying of them at Evesham"—in other words, anything left over after settling the expenses was to be used to stock up their shop with stockings from Evesham market. In the old man's words, "I think you may do good, if you can have money" (Chambers, 2: 102–103).

On 4 November, Sturley wrote to Quiney, replying to a letter written later on 25 October. Evidently Shakespeare had verbally promised to help Quiney, whereupon Quiney wrote to reassure his partner. Sturley's reply starts by expressing a wish for hard cash rather than the personal assurance Quiney described in "which imported . . . that our countryman Mr Wm. Shak. would procure us money, which I will like of as I shall hear when, and where, and how." But he proceeds to resurrect the idea of persuading their wealthy neighbor to consider an investment back home—there must have been some bargains available in the depressed borough—"I pray you let not go that occasion if it may sort to any indifferent conditions. Also that if money might be had for 30 or £40, a lease, etc., might be procured." Later in the month Quiney received another letter from Stratford, from Daniel Baker, who wrote, "My aunt Quiney telleth me that you are to receive £20 or £30 in London, and that you will pay some money for me if need be; and in that respect I have lent her some money already to serve her occasions" (Chambers 1930, 2: 103). The story ended happily. Stratford's suit to the queen was successful, and Quiney's expenses were met by the exchequer.[10]

The records note that Shakespeare's only son, Hamnet, had died in 1596 (buried 11 August). His father, John Shakespeare, was buried 8 September 1601. Shakespeare continued to consolidate his status and reinforce his estate. In 1602 there is the record of the conveyance (on 1 May) of 127 acres of land in Old Stratford to Shakespeare by John Combe in the large sum of £320. On 28 September of that year Shakespeare bought a small plot of land behind New Place. It was about a quarter of an acre in extent and included a cottage that faced onto New Place's garden. Shakespeare's continuing ownership is recorded in 1604 and 1606. It passed to his daughter Susanna in 1617.

In the summer of 1605, while part of his mind was occupied with the fate of a foolish king who divided his kingdom, Shakespeare was engaged in some empire-building of his own. On 24 July he purchased, for the substantial sum of £440, a half share in the tithes of "corn, grain, blade, and hay" from Old Stratford, Welcombe, and Bishopton, and in the tithes of "wool, lamb, and other small and privy tithes" within the parish of Stratford itself. The vendor was Ralph Hubaud from Ipsley. As a result of this investment, Shakespeare would have received, even after paying rents, some £60 per annum from the tithes. The detailed management of the business was left to Anthony Nash. His son, Thomas, would marry Shakespeare's granddaughter Elizabeth.

Like many of his contemporaries, Shakespeare seems to have enjoyed litigation. Records of two cases from this period survive. The first concerns Philip Rogers, an apothecary licensed to sell ale, tobacco, and drugs. The Shakespeares, like other households, brewed their own ale. If they followed the normal pattern of their class, Anne Shakespeare would have supervised her maidservants once a month in brewing the household's supply. The stock of malt kept at New Place was sometimes greater than needed for this purpose, and the surplus was then sold off. Between March and May 1604 Philip Rogers bought 20 bushels of malt from the Shakespeares, and on 25 June he borrowed 2 shillings from them. Of this total debt of some £2 he repaid only 6 shillings, so Shakespeare sued him in the fortnightly court of record and demanded a further 10 shillings in damages. Since no more is heard of the case, Rogers presumably paid up. In the summer of 1608 Shakespeare tried to recover a debt of £6 from John Addenbrooke, a gentleman. The case dragged on from August to 7 June of the following year, and it involved Addenbrooke's arrest. But by the time the court found in Shakespeare's favor, awarding him costs plus damages, Addenbrooke had fled the district (Chambers 1930, 2: 113–18; Eccles, 91–92, 207).

Susanna Shakespeare, like her grandfather and great-uncle, makes her debut in the records in a disciplinary context. In the spring of 1606 (when she was 23) her name appears on a list of people who had failed to receive Communion during the Easter season. In the wake of the Gunpowder Plot of 1605 there was widespread anti-Catholic feeling, and special vigilance in maintaining church discipline. The Stratford list includes the names of some Catholics and some Catholic sympathizers. Those failing their duty for other reasons could avoid heavy fines by taking Communion. Ten on the list did so, including Susanna (Schoenbaum 1977, 286–87).[11]

She married just a year later, on 5 June 1607. Her husband was the unequivocally Protestant Dr. John Hall, who was about eight years her senior. He had settled in Stratford at about the turn of the century and had quickly developed a successful practice. A dedicated physician and a man of principle, he turned down a knighthood and displayed a scorn of earthly glory. In his later years he became cantankerous and was expelled from the council for repeatedly disturbing its deliberations. His patients came from far and wide and included the celebrated poet Michael Drayton. His case notes were eventually published as *Select Observations on English Bodies* (1657). Hall died at about 60 and was buried on 26 November 1635, having lived at New Place from 1616 (maybe earlier) until his death. Of Susanna Hall, who survived her husband by some 14 years, little is known. Hall's monument refers to her as *fidissima conjux*— most faithful wife. They had one child, Elizabeth, baptized on 21 February 1608 (she would marry into the gentry and die in about 1670 as Lady Bernard). Susanna was praised in her epitaph for being "witty above her sex" and "wise to salvation"; it was said there was "something of Shakespeare" in her personality. She may have been literate to some degree.[12] Shakespeare's mother died later in 1608 (buried 9 September 1608), having lived long enough to see her great-grandchild.

In 1610 Shakespeare was recorded as the leaseholder of a barn in Henley Street, probably inherited from his father. About this time he probably returned to Stratford to live. In the following year he joined with others to defend his Stratford tithes in the Court of Chancery. His brother Gilbert died in 1612 (buried on 3 February). In 1613 Shakespeare was left £5 in the will of John Combe. His brother Richard died and was buried on 4 February.

If his last years were touched with sadness as his parents and brothers died, Shakespeare had some compensation in the proximity of his children. Indeed, the only house in Stratford where we know the Halls lived is New Place, although there is a local tradition that they lived in a handsome house just a few yards away, known for the last hundred years or so as "Hall's Croft." They were certainly living in New Place after Shakespeare's death in 1616, and perhaps they moved in before that date. Of their lives we know precious little. But there was one major disturbance in 1613 of which record has survived (Schoenbaum 1977, 288–90). On 15 July 1613 Susanna Hall brought suit for defamation in the Consistory Court at Worcester Cathedral against John Lane. Lane (1590–1640) was a ne'er-do-well, descended from the local gentry, who got himself into a variety of scrapes. He was, for instance, presented by the church wardens as a drunkard and was sued in Star Chamber in 1619 for misbehavior and libels against the vicar and other pillars of the Stratford community.

Mistress Hall claimed that, some five weeks prior to the hearing, Lane had "reported that the plaintiff had the runinge of the raynes & had bin naught with Rafe Smith at John Palmer"—in other words that she suffered from gonorrhea and had slept with Rafe Smith. Smith (1577–1621), a nephew of Hamnet Sadler, was a haberdasher who had married in 1605 and who is noted as an associate of Lane's in later documents. Representing Mistress Hall was Robert Whatcott, who would two years later witness her father's will; Lane did not show his face to answer the charges, and was accordingly excommunicated on 27 July. Only a week before the case at Worcester, on 9 July 1613, Susanna Hall's husband was appointed a trustee for the children of Richard Lane, the uncle of John, the man who had slandered his wife.

In 1614 the chamberlain's account book records, sometime between 21 March and 30 June of that year, the visit of a preacher to the town and his entertainment by Shakespeare at New Place. The account notes, "Item for one quart of sack and one quart of claret wine given to a preacher at the New Place, xxd. [20 pence]." The preacher was probably an official visitor, invited to preach one of the three annual foundation sermons to the bailiff and council in the Guild Chapel.[13] New Place, just across the street from the chapel, would have been a natural place for the preacher to stay, with the council picking up the bill. After Shakespeare's death the Halls continued to provide such hospitality.

The Welcombe Enclosures

During Shakespeare's lifetime Stratford was several times devastated by fire. The town suffered especially from two conflagrations in 1594 and 1595, each of which occurred on Sunday. Two Puritan preachers claimed the fires were God's punishment for breaking the Sabbath.[14] A further blaze (on a Saturday this time) occurred on 9 July 1614. This "sudden and terrible" fire, fanned by strong winds, threatened the total destruction of the town. In the event it destroyed 54 houses and other property to the value of £8,000. The fire brought personal tragedies, and had a catastrophic effect on the local economy. The relief operation was slow and probably corrupt.[15] As winter approached the emotional temperature in the shattered town rose. Investors, as much as paupers, became nervous about the future.

Some saw the chaotic circumstances as an opportunity for modernization. In seventeenth-century terms, this meant only one thing: enclosures. Enclosures tended to benefit the larger landowners at the expense of the smaller, and to the impoverishment of laborers, who would lose their jobs. Those who owned tithes of small parcels of land would find their income sharply reduced as their land was used for sheep rather than for hay or grain.

An earlier enclosure scheme had failed, despite the support of the local grandee Sir Edward Greville. This time the plan was sponsored by the young Thomas Combe; Arthur Mainwaring, steward of Lord Chancellor Ellesmere; and William Replingham, a lawyer who was Mainwaring's cousin. They were determined to succeed.[16] Local opposition was organized by Shakespeare's friend Thomas Greene, who drew up a list of "Ancient freeholders" in the district (Chambers 1930, 2: 141). As Master Shakespeare is noted as the owner of four small plots within the scheme, he was unlikely to be much affected. Nevertheless, he found himself in the middle of a major and hot-tempered dispute. The council was alarmed at the likely economic and social impact of the plan on a town already on its knees. Reduced income, increased homelessness and vagrancy were just a few of their worries. On 23 September Greene got unanimous backing from the council for his opposition. He was motivated in part by the fact that he had just invested £300 into a half-interest in a group of tithes: the other half was held by Shakespeare himself, and these lands were being eyed by the enclosers.

Meanwhile, Shakespeare was in touch with the other side. On 28 October, Replingham privately agreed to compensate Shakespeare for any losses he might incur in the short term by the enclosure of his land (Chambers 1930, 2: 141–42). He also wrote to Greene with the same offer. The enclosers' strategy was to try to strike separate deals with each of the landowners.

Greene tried to maintain solidarity, but the Shakespeare/Replingham agreement was clearly a major embarrassment. He set off for London to try to resolve the problem and speak face-to-face with Thomas Combe. Combe was not available, so Greene called on his partner Shakespeare. Greene wrote a note of the meeting: it seems that Shakespeare tried to calm him down, saying that the scheme would take a long time to be finalized and would probably fail anyway. Greene wrote,

> 17 November. At my cousin Shakespeare: coming yesterday to town, I went to see him how he did. He told me that they assured him they meant to enclose no further than to Gospel Bush, and so up straight (leaving out part of the dingles to the field) to the gate in Clopton hedge, and take in Salisbury's piece. And that they mean in April to survey the land, and then to give satisfaction and not before. And he and Master Hall say they think there will be nothing done at all. (Chambers 1930, 2: 142–43)

Had Shakespeare been duped? Or was he secretly on Mainwaring's side? At the very moment he was speaking to Greene, the survey he said was scheduled for April was actually under way. When Greene got home to Stratford he found "that the survey there was passed." On 10 December he was chasing around Stratford looking for Replingham, who was presumably drawing up documents based on the survey and who he suspected might be at Shakespeare's house. Greene bumped into Combe, who smoothly claimed to be just a junior partner, but he added that Greene would be foolish to antagonize someone as well-connected as Mainwaring.[17]

Greene maintained his composure and kept the council busy and united. On 23 December he persuaded "almost all" of them to sign two letters. One was to Mainwaring, the other to Shakespeare. Greene also recorded, "I also writ of myself to my cousin Shakespeare the copies of all our oathes made then. Also a note of the inconveniences [that] would grow by the enclosure." On the same day the council wrote to seek support from major landowners in the district. As a further step two councillors, William Walford and William Chandler, were persuaded to buy some of the threatened land on 6 January 1615. These two businessmen, in their new guise as peasant farmers, boldly set out with shovels to fill in the ditch—300 yards long—that Combe's men had already dug.

The ensuing struggle was unequal. Combe rode over to the ditch, accompanied by some laborers. A crowd gathered. While Combe observed from horseback, the two councillors were thrown into the ditch. Combe mocked the town dignitaries as "puritan knaves"; he "sat laughing on his horseback and said they were good football players." This was partly bluster, because Combe was actually worried. He tried to bribe Greene with an inducement of £10 to start negotiations. Replingham treated Greene to supper and held up the Shakespeare deal as an example of what could be his if he agreed to settle. But the tide was moving against the enclosers. The next day a troop of women and children defied the laborers and filled in the ditches (Eccles, 137–38).

That was the end of work for the winter. The council secured an order from Warwick assizes restraining Combe from acting until his plan had been tested in court. They treated separately with Replingham and Mainwaring, and soon Combe had become isolated. He was not looking for compromise. He questioned the authority of the chief justice, Sir Edward Coke, to order a stay of the enclosure. Combe started beating his tenants at Welcombe and depopulated the entire village, leaving only his own household behind. He threatened that his sheep would devour any crops planted in the neighboring fields. He became a man to avoid in daily business in Stratford.

There is an enigmatic little note from September 1615 in which Greene wrote, "W. Shakespeare's telling J. Greene [Thomas's brother John] that I was not able to bear the enclosing of Welcombe." Perhaps "I" should read "he"; perhaps "bear" should read "bar" (Greene originally wrote "he . . ." but then crossed it out [Chambers 1930, 2: 143; Eccles, 138; Schoenbaum 1977, 284–85]). Maybe Shakespeare was confiding to John Greene that Thomas's imvolvement had become obsessive, and was explaining why he had kept out of it, and had in fact acted in their best interests throughout, whatever it looked like. He certainly had some explaining to do.

Finally, in the spring of 1616 the staying order was confirmed at the Court of King's Bench. Combe bounced back with a new, less ambitious scheme, which he offered to the council in a newly friendly spirit, calling them "loving friends." Unsurprisingly they resisted, not least because he had surreptitiously carried out some small scale enclosures. Eventually in 1619 he was told by the court to drop his plan and to return all the enclosed lands to their former owners.[18] By then Greene had left Stratford, and William Shakespeare was dead.

This extraordinary sequence of events leaves us little wiser about Shakespeare the man. Was he disinterested, or was he a schemer? Was he naive or duplicitous? Did he really believe the survey would take place in April? We can never know. Shakespeare and his son-in-law were ultimately proved correct. In the end, they said, the Court of King's Bench would never allow the scheme. They were right.

Shakespeare's Last Year

In the spring of 1615 there was an attempt by several owners of property in the Blackfriars complex (where Shakespeare owned the gatehouse) to tidy up some of the tangled legal interrelationships in the rabbit warren of buildings. The owners petitioned the Court of Chancery to grant Mathias Bacon (Anne's heir) authority to surrender certain deeds and patents. The group consisted of Sir Thomas Bendish, Edward Newport, William Thorseby, Robert Dormer, and his wife, Mary, William Shakespeare, and Richard Bacon, and the documents in the uncontentious case are dated 26 April, 5 May, and 22 May 1615. On 10 February 1618, after Shakespeare's death, the three trustees conveyed the gatehouse to John Greene of Clement's Inn and William Morris of Stratford as their final act "in performance of the confidence and trust in them reposed by William Shakespeare . . . and . . . according to the true intent and meaning of the last will and testament of the said William Shakespeare."[19]

Susanna Shakespeare had followed her father's advice by taking a husband older than herself. His other daughter Judith (who may well have been illiterate; she endorsed documents with a mark) did not. Her life was to differ markedly from the orderly and prosperous lives of the righteous Halls. She was 31 when on 10 February 1615/1616 she married Thomas Quiney, then age 27. The couple were soon in trouble with the ecclesiastical authorities for failing to obtain a license to permit a wedding at this time (the season when weddings were not usually permitted ran that year from 28 January to 7 April). As a result Thomas was excommunicated at the Consistory Court at Worcester, and perhaps Judith suffered the same fate.[20] By 23 November of 1615/16, however, they were both in attendance when their first child, a boy named Shakespeare after his recently deceased grandfather, was christened.

More serious was a hearing much closer to home. Quiney was summoned to appear before the church court presided over by the vicar at Stratford (the so-called bawdy court) on 26 March of 1616. Some months before his marriage to Judith Shakespeare he had impregnated Margaret Wheeler, and he had proceeded with his marriage (with irregular haste) despite the fact that his child by another woman was about to be born. This sorry episode took a tragic turn when Margaret Wheeler died in March, either in childbirth (along with the child) or very shortly thereafter. Both she and her infant were buried on 15 March. In court Quiney admitted having had carnal knowledge of Wheeler and was duly sentenced. John Rogers, the vicar, initially decreed that Quiney must appear before the congregation on three successive Sundays, swathed in a white sheet. For some reason the sentence was reduced to a less public humiliation for Judith and her husband. Quiney was fined 5 shillings and was obliged to attend the little chapel at Bishopton (within the parish of Stratford, and set in fields that Shakespeare owned) and make public and sincere admission of his misdemeanor. He was to perform this duty dressed not in a white sheet but rather in his own clothes.[21]

The Quineys had three children. The first, Shakespeare, died in the first year of his life, in May 1617. Richard was born in February 1618; Thomas in January of 1620. The two young men died only a few weeks apart in 1639. The surviving records of the lives of Judith and Thomas Quiney are easily summarized. By 1608 Quiney seems to have been effectively in charge of his mother's business, and was selling wine to the Stratford corporation. In 1611 he took on the lease of the tavern next door to his mother's house on High Street, before he and his wife moved to a new inn, the Cage, in July of 1616, just a couple of months after William Shakespeare's death. The Cage occupied a site at the corner of Bridge and High streets, and from these premises Quiney sold wine and tobacco. Over the years he held a number of middle-ranking local offices (burgess in 1617, chamberlain in 1621 and 1622) but was never made an alderman, and he features in the records of several small court cases. His business did not thrive, and in 1633 the lease of the Cage was assumed by Dr. Hall; Richard Watts, the vicar of Harbury; and Thomas

Nash, Hall's son-in-law. Eventually Richard Quiney—now a prosperous grocer in London—took over, and on Richard's death Thomas had an allowance of £12 per year. He probably died as late as 1662–63. His wife, Judith, died at age 77 in 1661–62.

Shakespeare's Will

Shakespeare's will is a much-studied and much-debated document.[22] Shakespeare took time and trouble over it, working through several drafts. The first draft was drawn up in January 1616, by the lawyer Francis Collins. A second draft was drawn up on 25 March, the day before Quiney's court appearance. There was clearly a need for numerous revisions in light of the scandal involving Judith's husband, Thomas. Each sheet of the will—in Collins's hand—was signed by Shakespeare, and on the last page appears, in a frail scrawl, the phrase "By me William Shakspere." These signatures were the work of a dying man, though he was able still to declare himself, as law required, "in perfect health and memory."[23]

Shakespeare's was a conventional will, with no emotional references to family and friends. Perhaps Collins wanted to keep his client to the well-tried formulae because of the poet's failing health. Indeed, the famous interlineations may have been necessitated by the solicitor's unwillingness to depart from his model when working at speed. The unsuitability of the model, designed primarily for Jacobean men of property, is made obvious by its failure to mention what must have been one of Shakespeare's most treasured possessions—namely, his library. Obviously his dramatic scripts had passed into the possession of the King's Men, and we can only speculate on the existence of other manuscript works hoarded with his papers in Stratford. But the printed books must have existed, and we can only assume that they passed into Hall's library on Shakespeare's death, since the will is silent about them. In 1635, as part of a legal dispute with the Halls, Baldwin Brooks (who later became the town's bailiff) broke into New Place, and, according to Susanna, made off with "goods of great value," including "divers books."[24]

And yet there are some clear signs of Shakespeare's personal intervention. His amendments to the first draft were designed to safeguard the interests of the newly married Judith and to make her as independent as possible from her disgraced husband. The draft reference to "my son in law" is crossed out and replaced with "my daughter Judith," for example. He left her £100 for her marriage portion (dowry) plus a further £50 if she gave up her claim on the Chapel Lane cottage. If she or any "children of her body" were still living three years after the will, they would receive a further £150 to divide. As long as she remained married, she would receive £10 per annum interest rather than the capital sum. Quiney could only get access to this money if he settled land of an equal value on Judith or her children. If Judith and all her children died, the money would be divided between Shakespeare's granddaughter Elizabeth Hall and his sister Joan Hart and her children. In another addition Judith was left "my broad silver and gilt bowl."

The bulk of the estate went to the Halls: all the houses and lands, including New Place, were left to Susanna. She and her husband were appointed executors, and she was also left the London property, including the shares in the Globe and Blackfriars theaters. To his sister Joan, Shakespeare left all his clothes and £20, and he willed that she be permitted to live the rest of her life in the Henley Street property, paying 1 shilling rent. He left £5 apiece to Joan's boys William, Michael, and Thomas, and his silver to Elizabeth Hall. Joan's grandson Thomas eventually inherited both Henley Street houses. Shakespeare left £10 for the relief of the poor, his sword to Thomas Combe, 20 marks to Francis Collins, and £5 to Thomas Russell. He left money for the purchase of memorial rings by some of his oldest Stratford friends—Hamnet Sadler, William Reynolds, and Anthony and John Nash. Then follows another late addition—"& to my Fellowes John Hemminge, Richard Burbage & Henry Cundell xxvjs viijd [26 shillings and 8 pence] A peece to buy them Ringes." They would cherish his memory more effectively than he could have imagined as he lay dying in Stratford that spring.

The final addition has caused the most speculation. In a passage tidying up small bequests and making administrative dispositions, there appears the famous passage—"Item I gyve vnto my wief my second best bed with furniture." "Furniture" included mattress, linen, and decorative wall hangings. This is the only reference to Anne in the will, and its tone has puzzled scholars. It could be a callous and derisive bequest, or perhaps touchingly affectionate. If the best bed had been reserved for guests, and was probably built for New Place, then the "second-best bed" would be the marital bed. In nearby Leamington in 1573 a man called William Palmer had left his wife their "second best featherbed" in the context of a will that is extremely generous to the wife (Eccles, 164–65; Schoenbaum 1977, 302–033).

It is striking that Anne—then about 60—appears so little in the will. Perhaps this means that her treatment would depend on local customs that were so well known they did not need to be spelled out. But what the custom was—what the Stratford "widow's portion" was—is unknown. In Shakespeare's London a wife was entitled to a life interest in a third of the husband's estate, plus security of tenure in the family home. Similar conventions in Stratford would have ensured that Anne would have been handsomely provided for and would have seen out the rest of her days in New Place. She died in the summer of 1623 (the year of the First Folio), and was buried next to her husband on 8 August, just below the monument. She was 67.

Collins and Thomas Russell were appointed overseers of the will, and the last sheet was signed by Collins, July Shaw, John Robinson, Hamnet Sadler, and Robert Whatcott. Shaw was a gentleman, a local business-man trading in wool and malt, who lived nearby in Chapel Street. His father had been a friend of John Shakespeare. Robinson was a laborer who worked for the Shakespeare-Hall household; Whatcott was proba-bly another employee. Sadler was one of William's oldest friends and godfather to the little boy who had borne his name.

The nature of Shakespeare's final illness is unknown, although he seems to have been in failing health for some time before his death. He died less than a month after Quiney's court case, on 23 April. He was buried two days later in the chancel of Holy Trinity. A few days earlier his brother-in-law William Hart had died (buried on 17 April). Shakespeare left money to provide for a monument to be carved by Gheerart Janssen, one of the sons of Gheerart Janssen the elder, whose stonemason's yard was close to the Globe in Southwark.[25]

Chapter Two
"Small Latine, and Lesse Greeke"

Education

Nobody has seriously questioned the assumption that Shakespeare attended the grammar school at Stratford; it would have been natural for a boy of his social class to do so. Traders and businessmen all over England were setting up new schools to educate young men to meet the challenges posed by a period of rapid social, economic, and technological change. The burgesses of Stratford were no exception. They took education extremely seriously. In the 1553 charter it was decreed that the Stratford schoolmaster should live rent-free and be paid a stipend of £20 per annum, to include £4 for repairs, maintenance, and the salary of the usher (who taught the junior boys). This was a generous arrangement (financially better than those at Eton at the time), so Stratford was able to attract well qualified teachers.

From 1565 to 1567 the Stratford schoolmaster was John Brownsword, a native of Cheshire. Brownsword was a friend (and probably a former pupil) of the vicar, John Bretchgirdle; when he left Stratford he moved north to Macclesfield. His Latin verses were to be published in 1590. Brownsword was succeeded for a short time by John Acton, a scholar of Brasenose, Oxford, before the post went to a more eminent man, Walter Roche, a fellow of Corpus Christi College, Oxford, in 1559. Roche was another northerner, a Lancastrian, and took on the duties of rector of Droitwich at about the same time as he started work in Stratford in 1569. Schoolmastering was only a brief interlude in his career; he held on to the Droitwich position after giving up his teaching in 1571 and moving into law.[1]

Shakespeare was presumably taught for a while by the next master, Simon Hunt, who worked at the grammar school from 1571 to 1575. We know from records that Simon Hunt received his license from the Bishop of Worcester on 29 October 1571, paid toward the repair of windows in 1573, and paid rent for a room for a year beginning at Michaelmas 1574. Unfortunately for scholars there were two Simon

Hunts living in Stratford at the time, and it is not known which was the schoolmaster. One was a Catholic who matriculated in 1575 at the University at Douai, the intellectual center of émigré English Catholic life; became a Jesuit in 1578; and held high office at St. Peter's in Rome, where he died in 1585. The second Simon Hunt lived a less public life, spending most of it in Stratford, where he died in about 1598, leaving an estate valued at £100. We do not know why, if he continued to live in Stratford for more than 20 years, he gave up teaching when he did.

The next master, Thomas Jenkins, held the post from 1575 to 1579, when Shakespeare was 11 to 14 years old. Jenkins was not, as used to be supposed, from Wales but was born to a poor family in London, the son of an old servant of Sir Thomas White, founder of St. John's College, Oxford. Jenkins was evidently a bright young man: he earned a B.A. in 1566 and then an M.A. in 1570 at St. John's, and held a fellowship there from 1566 to 1572. It seems that Jenkins had an abiding interest in teaching—Sir Thomas White asked the college to grant him leave in 1566 so that he could learn the craft. He took up a teaching post at Warwick, and in 1575 he transferred to Stratford. In 1579 Jenkins amicably parted company with Stratford, having lined up a successor in John Cottom, an Oxford graduate (from Brasenose College). Cottom's younger brother Thomas was a Jesuit who was sent from Europe on a mission to minister to Catholics in England: he was arrested in June 1580, arraigned (along with Edmund Campion) on 14 November 1581, and subjected to the hideous death prescribed for traitors on 13 May 1582. John Cottom resigned from his teaching position in the winter of 1581 (presumably at about the time of his brother's trial). He retired in 1582 to Tarnacre, Lancashire, where his family had some land that he eventually inherited and administered, living openly as a Catholic and paying his recusant fines until his death in 1616.[2] The next master was Alexander Aspinall (in the post from 1582 to 1624), who arrrived too late to teach Shakespeare.[3]

The curriculum would have been the standard fare of the time.[4] Boys (the system was closed to girls) normally began at the so-called petty school at the age of four or five, where the pupils would work under the guidance of the usher or an abecedarius (named for the importance placed on learning the alphabet). Each boy brought to school a "hornbook," a sheet of paper or parchment with a protective cover of transparent horn. The paper showed the alphabet, the Lord's Prayer, and some guides to spelling. When the hornbook was learned, boys moved on to *The ABC with the Catechism*, which added to the hornbook page a set of graces to be said before and after meals and the catechism from the Book of Common Prayer.

The school day was long, beginning and ending with prayers. The children started work at six or seven in the morning, and their first session (with a short pause for breakfast) lasted until eleven. They would return from dinner at one and work through (with a 15-minute break) to five. Most of the time was spent on Latin grammar, using the official textbook, William Lily's *Short Introduction of Grammar*. Learning conjugations and declensions by rote was the main activity. Shakespeare remembered this well, judging by the scene in *The Merry Wives of Windsor* (4.1) in which a schoolboy (named William) is comically interrogated by a Welsh schoolmaster-parson.

The educational system was designed ultimately to encourage fluency and eloquence in writing Latin. The student would begin with the principles and structures of grammar from Lily. He would then be introduced to collections of proverbs or short moral tales (such as Cato in the edition of Erasmus, or the fables of Aesop). The most famous and influential collection was Erasmus's anthology called *De Copia*. Stocked with such material, the student would eventually be able to imitate, improvise, and invent spoken Latin of a high order. We should remember that for scholars like Sir Francis Bacon and John Milton—indeed, up to the time of Sir Isaac Newton—Latin was the preferred language for learned discourse. It was, among other things, the international language of science.

After a couple of years on grammar and proverbs, the pupil would encounter other forms of writing. Erasmus instructed teachers on how they should present the comedies of Plautus and Terence, for instance. In some schools there was a tradition of performing such plays and for making English versions of them for the boys to act. The audience of *The Comedy of Errors*, for example, would have recognized at once that it was a virtuoso doubling of the complications of the plot of an already complicated Plautus play, *Menaechmi*.

At the age of nine or ten, in the third form (so in 1573–74 in Shakespeare's case), pupils read some more modern authors.[5] They would be trained to enrich their vocabulary by learning lists of words and definitions and would be given passages from the Geneva Bible to translate into Latin. Latin conversation was studied through dialogues and colloquies—essentially brief dramas exploring an idea or a situation or illustrating contrasting attitudes.

After this work, supervised by the usher, boys moved into the care of the master. In the upper school the training in rhetoric continued, and students also began to study elementary logic. The boys would read some Cicero and Quintilian as well as Erasmus. They were set increasingly complicated compositions to perform: in their final year they might be asked to invent speeches on particular occasions, or to imagine what some famous person might or should have said at a crucial moment in history. The older boys also read some Virgil and Horace and perhaps the satires of Juvenal and Persius. They studied history though Caesar and Sallust and started to explore moral philosophy by means of Cicero's *De Officiis*. Those chosen to start Greek would begin with the Greek text of the New Testament. Traces of all these writers have been found in Shakespeare's works. Judged from its almost ubiquitous influence on their writings, however, by far the most important literary text for Shakespeare as for most of his contemporaries was the *Metamorphoses* of Ovid.[6]

Such, in brief, was the formal education available to Shakespeare in Stratford. Had he progressed further, to the universities or to the Inns of Court, he would have found those institutions geared to train men for the professions—the church, law, medicine—or prepare them to serve as administrators or to run their estates.[7] As with many other writers of the period, he had been acquainted by his school with a wide range of authors and kinds of writing.[8] What is more, an understanding of the Elizabethan grammar school suggests that there are profound connections between an educational program that prized eloquence and verbal inventiveness, that was based on dialogue, colloquy, and imagined speeches, and the golden age of drama.[9]

The role of drama in Elizabethan education requires further comment. Of the Stratford schoolmasters listed above, Richard Jenkins and John Cottom were those most likely to have taught Shakespeare. Cottom was recommended to the town by Jenkins, and it seems likely that they saw eye to eye on educational practice—part of which involved drama. As I have noted, Jenkins was a protégé of Sir Thomas White, the founder of St. John's College, Oxford, and a benefactor of the Merchant Taylors' School, which Jenkins presumably attended. The school was led by one of the Elizabethan era's great teachers, Richard Mulcaster, the famous champion of the English language ("I love Rome, but London better. I favour Italy, but England more. I honour the Latin, but I worship the English").[10] He believed that his pupils would learn good pronunciation and develop audacity if they were taught to act. They regularly put on plays before the queen and the nobility and gentry. The system produced the greatest poet of the age, Edmund Spenser, and it trained Shakespeare's schoolmasters. It would be surprising, then, if acting played no part in the education Shakespeare received at the grammar school.

There was drama of several kinds in Stratford. At Pentecost in 1583, when Shakespeare was 19 and married for less than a year, the corporation paid 13 shillings and 4 pence "to Davi Johnes and his company for his pastime." Perhaps Jones's performance or a similar one lies behind the moment in *The Two Gentlemen of Verona* when the disguised Julia reminisces on her dramatic triumphs (Eccles, 83; Schoenbaum 1977, 111–12):

> at Pentecost,
> When all our pageants of delight were play'd,
> Our youth got me to play the womans part,
> And I was trimm'd in Madam Julia's gown,
> Which served me as fit, by all men's judgements,
> As if the garment had been made for me;
> . . . at that time I made her weep agood,
> For I did play a lamentable part.
> Madam, 'twas Ariadne passioning
> For Theseus' perjury and unjust flight;
> Which I so lively acted with my tears
> That my poor mistress, moved therewithal,
> Wept bitterly. (4.4.158–71)

The Stratford records show that troupes of actors played in the Guild Hall during John Shakespeare's year of office as bailiff (1569, when William was five years old). From then on the town was regularly visited by touring companies.[11] Some scholars speculate that Shakespeare's career began by his joining such a company to replace an actor who dropped out (Schoenbaum 1977, 116–17).

Other experiences with drama might have been available to Shakespeare in his second decade. In 1575 the Earl of Leicester entertained Queen Elizabeth at Kenilworth castle, just over 10 miles northeast of Stratford. Large crowds of local people thronged the castle precincts to see the extraordinary spectacles and pageants. Leicester was lord of the manor of Stratford; did Alderman Shakespeare attend? Did he take his 11-year-old son?

Scholars have noted passages in Shakespeare's plays that could relate to the shows of 18 July 1575. An eyewitnesss of the show, Robert Laneham, described the event as follows (spelling regularized):

> *Arion* that excellent and famous musician, in [at]tire and appointment strange well seeming to his person, riding aloft on his old friend the Dolphin . . . and swimmed hard by these islands: herewith Arion . . . after a few well couched words to her Majesty . . . began a delectable ditty of a song well apted to melodious noise, compounded of six several instruments all covert, casting sound from the Dolphin's belly within, *Arion* the seventh sitting thus singing (as I say) without.[12]

The Captain in *Twelfth Night* describes how Sebastian was delivered from shipwreck by riding "like Arion on the dolphin's back" (1.2.15). In *A Midsummer Night's Dream* Oberon reminds Puck that he once "sat upon a promontory, / And heard a mermaid on a dolphin's back / Uttering such dulcet and harmonious breath / That the rude sea grew civil at her song" (2.1.149–52). And perhaps Oberon's reference to stars that "shot madly from their spheres, / To hear the sea-maid's music" (153–54) is an allusion to the extraordinary aquatic fireworks with which Leicester astonished the spectators.

We may think of the mystery plays as an exclusively medieval, Catholic phenomenon that disappeared with the Reformation, but there were some later revivals. One took place at Coventry, just a few miles from Stratford, as late as 1579, when Shakespeare was 15. A historian born as late as 1605 recorded that Coventry

> was very famous for the *Pageants* that were play'd therein, upon *Corpus-Christi*-day, which occasioning very great confluence of people thither from far and near, was of no small benefit thereto: which *Pageants* being acted with mighty state and reverence . . . had Theatres for the severall Scenes, very large and high, placed upon wheels, and drawn to all the eminent parts of the City, for the better advantage of Spectators: And contained the story of the New-Testament, composed into old English Rithme. . . . I have been told by some old people, who in their younger years were eye-witnesses . . . that the yearly confluence of people to see that shew was extraordinary great, and yielded no small advantage to the city.[13]

The city fathers were clearly torn between uneasiness at staging such a manifestly Catholic show (they had already torn down maypoles) and enthusiasm for the city's chief tourist attraction. Soon they commissioned different sorts of play. They chose history (as in a play about the wars against the Vikings) and Scripture (in 1584 they staged *The Destruction of Jerusalem*). It is certainly tempting to see Shakespeare's own history plays as similar secular successors of the mystery plays, featuring a comparable interplay of broad, providential sweep and intense local and personal details.

The evidence that Shakespeare knew the mysteries is largely impressionistic, except for one tiny nugget. In *Richard II* the titular king, while being deposed, notes the silence of his former followers and asks, "Did they not sometime cry 'All hail!' to me? / So Judas did to Christ." In none of the versions of the Bible Shakespeare knew does Judas say anything of the sort. He does, however, say it in the York play of *The Agony in Gethsemane*; and perhaps Shakespeare used the same phrase in the lost Coventry play on the same subject. Of course this is just a speculation; still, it is hard to believe that the imagination that created *Richard III* and the three *Henry VI* plays had not been fed by the mystery plays in some way (Schoenbaum 1977, 58).

Of course nothing studied, discussed, experienced, wondered at, or understood by Shakespeare or his schoolmates existed outside a Christian context. From his childhood Shakespeare was brought up in a community that conducted its religious life according to the prescriptions of the state church. Before evensong on Sundays and holy days he would have been instructed in the catechism by the parish priest. He would have been expected to attend matins and evensong and, later, to take Communion at least three times annually. The Book of Common Prayer contained sermons that were to be read in churches, so he would have heard them. After 1570 these homilies included two especially significant works: the three-part *Exhortation to Obedience* and the six-part *Against Disobedience and Wilful Rebellion*. Traces of these sermons have been found in the plays, as have many echoes of the Book of Common Prayer (including its version of the Psalms) and of the catechism.

Shakespeare seems to have derived a good general knowledge of Scripture from church and school. Scholars have found allusions to or quotations from more than 40 books of the Bible, including the Apocrypha, in his works.[14] Closer study suggests he knew the first three chapters of Genesis almost by heart, and that he was particularly well acquainted with Ecclesiastes and the Book of Job. The biblical story that surfaces most frequently is the narrative of Cain and Abel, which is referred to on more than 25 occasions (Schoenbaum 1977, 56–62). The version of the Bible he knew was almost certainly the so-called Geneva Bible, an enduringly popular translation that featured helpful annotations in the margins. Throughout his career, however, he showed an awareness of other versions of the Bible and of the problems of translation and interpretation.

Shakespeare's religious beliefs continue to be a source of intense speculation. He has been held to be an orthodox Anglican, a secret Catholic, a Montaignean skeptic, or an agnostic. Even leaving aside interpretations of the plays that find sympathy for the old religion, some evidence for Catholic inclinations exists, but it is not conclusive.[15] For example, in an Oxford manuscript of the 1660s a man named Richard Davies of Corpus Christi College declares of Shakespeare that "He dyed a papist" (Kay 1992, 60–61; Chambers 1930, 2: 255). Davies's reliability (and sobriety) have been questioned (Schoenbaum 1977, 55, 98). At least one, possibly two, of Shakespeare's schoolmasters was Catholic: Cottom, as I have mentioned, and Hunt, perhaps a senior Jesuit official. It has been argued that Cottom secured Shakespeare employment as a teacher in the Lancashire household of a Catholic family (Honigmann 1985, 40–49, 114–34), and a dubious document, purporting to be a Catholic spiritual last will and testament of John Shakespeare, was discovered in the eighteenth century. The circumstances of its discovery were suspicious, and it was for many years dismissed as a forgery, particularly since the original was lost and therefore not available for close scrutiny. Similar documents have recently come to light, which suggests that the form of the "testament" may be genuine. It appears that thousands of such forms were brought to England by Jesuits from France and the Low Countries in the early 1580s. Its connection with John Shakespeare, however, remains unproved (Schoenbaum 1977, 45–54). Of Shakespeare himself, it has been said that "he is self-effacing to the point of anonymity on matters of faith" (Dutton 1989, 9).

Reading

The culture from which Shakespeare sprang was newly literate.[16] There were privy councillors like the Earl of Pembroke (d. 1570) who could sign their names, but no more. Shakespeare's father was hardly more accomplished, and his mother (like his daughters) left no evidence of literacy.

Shakespeare's education was not confined to the school room or the church. Traditionally, learning and experience had been passed on orally, in the fields or around a warm hearth. The bake house, the ale house, and the wash house were places where older men and (especially) women would tell their stories to the children left in their care. Shakespeare stages such events at the end of many of his plays, where the speakers decide to gather to tell their stories, pooling their experiences. From *The Comedy of Errors* to *The Tempest* Shakespeare's use of the device preserves an important feature of early modern culture, which served to stress continuities between generations and to support a sense of community. An example is Mistress Page's words at the end of *The Merry Wives of Windsor*: "Let us every one go home, / And laugh these sports o'er by a country fire" (5.5.241–42).

Alongside the accounts of furnishings left to Shakespeare's mother, Mary Arden, by her father, we learn that the house boasted no fewer than 11 wall hangings of painted cloth (Eccles, 17–18; Schoenbaum 1977, 21). These were canvas strips on which were depicted scenes from legend or from the Bible, sometimes with an appropriate caption or motto underneath to interpret the image. In *The Rape of Lucrece* William Shakespeare would refer to the way simple people could be "kept in awe" by such hangings (244–45). And in *As You Like It*, when Orlando and Jacques bandy clichés with each other, Jacques scornfully asks if Orlando has been studying sentimental mottoes inscribed on the inside of rings; Orlando replies in the same vein: "Not so, but I answer you right painted cloth, from whence you have studied your questions" (3.2.273–75). These simple mottoes would have been an important part of the education received by Shakespeare's mother. They would have typified the rural mental world from which his grammar school training was rapidly separating him.

Some Renaissance writers, like Ben Jonson, display their learning as part of laying claim to the status of author. Others, like Christopher Marlowe or Philip Sidney or Edmund Spenser, are casually allusive. Still others, like François Rabelais or Thomas Nashe, seem to start from a sophisticated seriocomic attitude to knowledge and experience. It has even been possible to reconstruct the libraries of some writers, like William Drummond or John Donne.

Shakespeare falls into none of these categories. Like many Renaissance readers, he must have derived a good deal of material from published anthologies of proverbs, sententiae, and commonplaces. It was normal for writers and intellectuals to carry around notebooks, like Hamlet's "tables," to collect new words, ideas, and phrases as they cropped up. There is therefore always the possibility that an apparent quotation or allusion to another author in a Shakespeare text may derive not from the earlier text itself but from some collection of sayings. We cannot automatically assume that Shakespeare was familiar with the context of the original.

Yet even a casual examination of the footnotes to scholarly editions, or of the list of sources proposed in the Riverside edition (48–56), or of a guide like Kenneth Muir's *Shakespeare's Sources* (1977) or of Geoffrey Bullough's seven-volume *Narrative and Dramatic Sources of Shakespeare* (1957–73) indicates that Shakespeare read both widely and closely. His knowledge of the Bible, of the Psalms and of the Book of Common Prayer (including its sermons) has already been noted. We have seen that his school training would have introduced him to dramatists such as Plautus, Terence, and perhaps Seneca, and that his lifelong fascination with the works of Ovid would have begun in the grammar school.

On the evidence of his plays, it is clear that there were several texts to which Shakespeare repeatedly returned for dramatic material. Those most frequently quarried are Raphael Holinshed's *Chronicles* and Plutarch's *Lives* in the translation by Thomas North (1579). Shakespeare used throughout his writing career the 1587 second edition of Holinshed's *Chronicles of England, Scotland and Ireland*; it was the source of the English histories, of *King Lear*, of *Macbeth*, and of *Cymbeline* and *Henry VIII*. His reading in history beyond these texts was copious. He read the medieval chronicles of Geoffrey of Monmouth and Jean Froissart and later historical works such as those of Robert Fabyan (1559), Richard Grafton (1569), and John Stow (1580), as well as such staples of the newly literate urban Protestant culture as John Foxe's *Actes and Monumentes* (he probably used the 1570 edition) and *The Mirror for Magistrates* (he knew the editions of 1559, 1578, 1587, and 1610).

From the time of the opening of the Globe theater in 1599 Shakespeare embarked on a series of classical plays, with material derived from Plutarch's *Lives of the Noble Grecians and Romans*, first published in England in 1579. Holinshed structured his chronicles in terms of narratives of the reigns of individual monarchs and presented them as part of a providential pattern. So, too, did Edward Hall in his account of the Wars of the Roses: his very title, *The Union of the Two Noble . . . Houses of York and Lancaster* (1548), exemplifies this. Plutarch's method in the *Lives* was to write moralized biographical essays, usually grouped in Greek/Roman pairs (Alexander and Julius Caesar, Alcibiades and

Coriolanus), followed by a comparative assessment and judgment.[17] Shakespeare was acquainted with all of these texts, and his changing conception of history can also be traced to Samuel Daniel's *Civil Wars* (1595), whose influence on Shakespeare can be seen from *Richard II* on. There are also indications of Shakespeare's use of Tacitus, Livy, and Machiavelli from the late 1590s.

Shakespeare's histories and tragedies almost always claim at some level to be true, to be based on real events. Even the apparent exceptions, *Romeo and Juliet* and *Othello*, were almost certainly believed to be based on fact. Comedies, on the other hand, often stress their own fictionality, and proclaim their relation to literary traditions. Shakespeare's comic sources were correspondingly various and eclectic. In addition to ancient comedy he also knew modern versions of the form, such as George Gascoigne's brilliant *Supposes* (1566).

His reading in modern English romance and fiction was fairly extensive. There are echoes of Spenser's *The Faerie Queene* throughout the canon, and it is a major source of *Much Ado about Nothing* and of *Venus and Adonis*. Sidney was by far the most celebrated English author of his generation. His literary reputation was essentially posthumous, following upon the celebration of his life and death as a paragon of knightly virtue and a national hero. He died in 1586, and his works began to appear in printed editions a few years later, just as Shakespeare was beginning his career. To his audiences, Sidney dignified the profession of writer: if a hero like Sidney could write and still be admired, so any writer could aspire to be treated with respect.[18] Sidney also was held to have established three genres relevant to Shakespeare's writings—namely, the sonnet sequence (with *Astrophil and Stella*) and the linked forms of tragicomedy and romance (in the *Arcadia*). Shakespeare's first, experimental tragicomedy coincides with the publication of the collected works of Sidney (including a hybrid, mixed-genre version of *Arcadia*) in 1598. Shakespeare also seems to have known Sidney's *Defence of Poetry* (Kay 1992, 185–90, 262–63).

Shakespeare knew and used popular collections of stories such as William Painter's *The Palace of Pleasure* (1566–67) (*All's Well That Ends Well*) and George Whetstone's *Heptameron of Civil Discourses* (1582) (*Measure for Measure*). He used Greene's *Pandosto* (1588) as the source for *The Winter's Tale* and Thomas Lodge's Lylian romance *Rosalynde* (1590) as the basis for *As You Like It*. He also knew and used John Lyly's hugely influential *Euphues* (*The Two Gentlemen of Verona*, *A Midsummer Night's Dream*, and several others), as well as Barnabe Riche's *Farewell to Military*

Profession (1581) (the chief source for *Twelfth Night*). Shakespeare's writings preserve elements of other popular literary forms of the day, such as the sonnet, the Ovidian romance, books of conduct and travel, and the masque. There is evidence of his reading in the spheres of new learning and science, as in his use of Timothy Bright's *Treatise of Melancholy* (1586) in *Hamlet* or the references to William Gilbert's *De Magnete* (1600) in *Troilus and Cressida*.

He was familiar with ancient romance, such as Apuleius's *Golden Ass* (translated by Adlington, 1566; used in *A Midsummer Night's Dream* and elsewhere), and with medieval romances like *Houn of Bordeaux* (translated by Lord Berners, ca. 1533–42) and with the writings of William Caxton (*The Ancient History of the Destruction of Troy* [1596], a source for *Troilus and Cressida*), John Gower (*Confessio Amantis* is the chief source of *Pericles* and also a source for *The Comedy of Errors*), and John Lydgate (*The Ancient History and Only True Chronicle of the Wars* [1555] is a source for *Troilus and Cressida*).

Shakespeare seems to have had some knowledge of Italian: he clearly knew Giraldi Cinthio's *Hecatommithi* (1565), a source for *Othello* and for *Measure for Measure*, as well as also Giovanni Fiorentino's *Il Pecorino* and Masuccio of Salerno's *Il Novellino*, sources for *The Merchant of Venice*, and Matteo Bandello's collection of *Novelle* (1554). No contemporary English translation of these works, or indeed of Giovanni Boccaccio's *Decameron* (source for *Cymbeline*) or the anonymous *Gl'Ingannati* (1531) (source of *Twelfth Night*) would have been available to him.

Some of his most important and formative influences, such as the Bible and Montaigne's *Essays*, are not sources at all, though evidence of their use can be widely found. In the case of Montaigne, Shakespeare seems to have had access to a text before the appearance of John Florio's translation in 1603. Since Florio was the secretary of the Earl of Southampton, Shakespeare's patron, Shakespeare might have had access to a manuscript copy.

Although it is difficult in a survey such as this to chart dramatic sources as easily as narrative ones, Shakespeare's imagination was manifestly stirred by a wide range of theatrical models, such as the mystery plays, ancient drama (whether encountered firsthand or in translation or in "modern" humanist versions) and the drama of the generations immediately preceeding him.[19] Wherever we look in the canon there is clear evidence of Shakespeare's response to the writings of his contemporaries, such as the echoes of Greene's *Orlando Furioso* (1590) in *As You Like It* and of George Whetstone's *Promos and Cassandra* (1578) in *Measure for*

Measure. Elsewhere he quarries anonymous plays, such as *The True Tragedy of Richard III* (ca. 1591) and *King Leir* (1604). His engagement with the plays of Lyly and Marlowe is especially significant at the beginning of his career; in the middle of his career his works respond to the "war of the theaters" and the satires of George Chapman, Jonson, and John Marston; later, in both comedy and tragedy, he locks horns with Jonson again.

Shakespeare's final plays show both his lifelong engagement with a few favored works and his capacity for innovation. *Henry VIII* is drawn from Holinshed and Foxe as well as a new (1610) edition of *The Mirror for Magistrates*; *The Two Noble Kinsmen* is based on *The Knight's Tale* of Chaucer (Chaucer had been a source for *Troilus and Cressida* and parts of *A Midsummer Night's Dream*) but also includes a dance from a recent court masque. Shakespeare's lost play *Cardenio* (1613) was based on the recently translated *Don Quixote*.

Ultimately, perhaps Shakespeare's most important source was his own writing. We may find that we can learn more about his art by comparing *Much Ado about Nothing* with *Othello*, *Macbeth* with *Antony and Cleopatra*, and *The Comedy of Errors* with *The Tempest*.[20]

Chapter Three

"This fortress built by nature for herself"

Shakespeare's England—that is, England during the reigns of Elizabeth I and James I—has often been described as stable, prosperous, and vital, as a golden age. Certainly great turbulence preceded and followed it. Before the Tudors the nation had endured generations of civil war—the Wars of the Roses that ended with the accession of Henry VII in 1485. Before Elizabeth came to the throne England was racked with the upheavals of the Reformation. When Charles I succeeded James I in 1625, he presided over an increasingly precarious situation. The country would see a Civil War, the institution of a republic, and eventually the king's execution after a public trial in January 1649.

History, of course, tends to be written by victors. So the high self-esteem of the Tudors was rarely challenged. Nor, for many years, was the "parliamentarian" view of Stuart history, which saw the Civil War as part of an inevitable progress from Jacobean absolutism toward parliamentary government under a constitutional monarchy. In recent years these asssumptions have been increasingly questioned. In particular, historians have reexamined the rose-tinted picture of Elizabethan and Jacobean England. They have shown that there was dissent, for example, and that the power of the monarchy was neither as absolute nor as uneqivocally supported as used to be thought. The regimes of Elizabeth and James often had to struggle for survival and work hard to keep their populations from rebellion.[1] Recent years have also seen an increased awareness of what has been called "the historicity of texts and the textuality of history," the way the discourses of "history" and "literature" inform, shape, and comment on each other.[2]

England's Rulers, 1485–1625[3]

Henry VII, 1485–1509

Henry Tudor's forces defeated those of the Yorkist King Richard III at the battle of Bosworth Field in 1485 and brought an end to the wars that had raged between the descendants of Edward III, the houses of York and Lancaster. Henry Tudor was a Lancastrian. His marriage to Elizabeth of York, daughter of Edward IV (Richard III's brother), represented a union of the houses and brought an end to the Wars of the Roses.[4] He and his family held on to the throne jealously, removing rival claimants and progressively concentrating power in the central authority of the crown. Henry sought to curb the power of the great feudal barons—a process continued by his successors. With his officials, he strengthened the central bureaucracy and substantially increased the revenues of the crown. He became a diplomat on the European stage, playing the game of dynastic marriages. His eldest son, Arthur, married Catherine of Aragon, daughter of the King of Spain, and his daughter Margaret married King James IV of Scotland. In his later years his rule became more personal, more centered on the person of the monarch, but his council and advisers were men of ability, chosen for their competence rather than their family or political affiliations. When Prince Arthur died in 1502, a papal dispensation was sought to enable Catherine of Aragon to be married to the new heir, Prince Henry. After complicated diplomatic wrangles, the young prince married his brother's widow shortly after Henry VII's death in 1509.

Printing had been introduced to Britain in the 1470s, with William Caxton and Wynkyn de Worde. It was during Henry's reign that the press began to play a really important cultural and social role. Henry appointed the first royal printer in 1504, and an ever-increasing amount of material was produced for a rapidly growing readership, as the records show. Between 1476 and 1491 Caxton printed 107 titles. The 1520s saw 550 publications; the 1530s, 739; the 1540s, 928; and the 1550s, 1,040. Such a spread of knowledge, information, and opinion changed society profoundly. It also established an obvious tension between the centralizing, controlling impulses of Tudor government and the power of the written word to challenge, even to check, such impulses. The consequences were immense. In the words of a recent historian, "a more demanding, individualistic, and better informed culture was created."[5]

Henry VIII, 1509–1547

Henry VIII was clearly a complex and enigmatic man. Given the highly personalized system of government he inherited, his personal disposition often shaped policy to the exclusion of other considerations. Nevertheless, he was served by some remarkable ministers, notably

Thomas Wolsey and Thomas Cromwell, each of whom wielded considerable power. Henry had been a great supporter of the papacy, and had written powerfully against the ideas of German reformers. To this day British coins proclaim the monarch as *Fidei Defensor*, "Defender of the Faith," a title bestowed on Henry by a grateful Pope Leo X in 1521. Yet Henry's quest for a male heir led him to divorce one wife, execute another, declare himself head of the church in England, and break with Rome.

The great argument with Pope Clement VII ended the influence of Wolsey, who had tried to secure agreement between the parties. His successor as chief minister, Thomas Cromwell, was at the forefront of the Tudor "revolution" in government and administration. He also masterminded the dismantling of the power, wealth, and influence of the Church. Religious houses were closed down, and church properties were taken over by the crown and sold to raise revenue.

Henry strove to make a mark in foreign affairs and became embroiled in policy disputes with the Holy Roman Empire, the Papacy, France, Spain, and Scotland at different times. This ambition had cultural consequences, since Henry wished to create a court that could compete for magnificence with those of his great European rivals, such as Charles V, François I, and the popes. He himself was a musician and poet of some skill, and several of his courtiers and advisers, such as Thomas More and Sir Thomas Wyatt, also displayed considerable literary accomplishment.[6]

Henry was a conservative revolutionary. In his argument with the Pope, he used biblical language and images to defend his concept of kingship. Slogans used on his behalf included "Truth as revealed in Scripture" and "We must rather obey God than men." Although he was from time to time strongly influenced by committed reformers, he was never a radical Protestant and considered himself a Catholic.

Like other Tudor monarchs, Henry VIII had neither a permanent army nor an established local bureaucracy. Yet in his propaganda campaign to justify and support the break with Rome, Thomas Cromwell showed a shrewd awareness of the power of the press and of the pulpit. Cromwell's success showed how the newly emerging technologies could be used to secure a nation's compliance to hitherto unthinkable changes.

Having divorced Catherine of Aragon in 1533, Henry was distressed at Anne Boleyn's failure to produce a male heir. He decided that he now knew his second marriage to be a disaster, that it had been cursed, and that he had been bewitched. From that it was a short step to the execution of Anne on charges of adultery in 1536. Her successor, Jane Seymour, came from the radical Protestant faction and gave Henry the

male heir he desired. She died as a result of the caesarean section performed on her (1537). Henry's fourth marriage, to Anne of Cleves
(1540), was a victim of shifting alliances in European politics. When the
match was arranged, Cromwell argued that it was essential to England's
safety. The subsequent rift between France and Spain made that consideration irrelevant. Nor did it help that Cromwell had exaggerated the
physical appeal of the woman Henry called "the Flanders mare." Even
worse for Cromwell was the fact that Henry's choice for his fifth wife was
the young Catherine Howard, niece to Cromwell's deadly enemy, the
Duke of Norfolk.

Not long after he secured Cromwell's execution, Norfolk had to move
rapidly to avoid involvement in the next scandal—the discovery of
Catherine Howard's adulteries. She and her alleged lovers were beheaded
(1541), and Henry embarked on a series of vigorous foreign initiatives,
one of which led to the disastrous sinking of his flagship, the *Mary Rose*,
whose wreck was recovered from the sea in 1980.[7]

Henry's final wife, Catherine Parr (they married in 1543), was a person of noted piety and a literary figure in her own right. She edited
Prayers Stirring the Mind unto Heavenly Meditation (1545) and was patron
of the English version of Erasmus's *Paraphrases on the New Testament*. She
was involved in the major religious controversies of the latter years of
Henry's reign. This was a period that saw numerous attempts to define
religious orthodoxy, to strike a balance between reform and tradition,
and to make clear what a loyal member of the Church of England should
be prepared to say he or she believed in.

In the 1540s Parliament debated an Act for the Advancement of True
Religion. One of its chief purposes was to limit access to Scripture. This
represented a reversal of the original Lutheran belief in liberating
Scripture from ecclesiastical control and placing the Bible in the hands of
every person. But the king and his advisors had identified 99 places in
the Great Bible where they were unhappy about the translation, and the
question was referred to the universities. While in principle Henry wanted the Bible to be made available, and to be expounded in sermons
throughout the country, he was distressed at the possibility of misinter-
pretation, or of passages taken out of context. Parliament noted that
lower-class subjects had "increased in divers naughty and erroneous
opinions." It therefore ordered that "no women nor artificers, prentices,
journeymen, serving men of the degrees of yeomen or under, husband-
men or labourers" were to be allowed to read the Bible on pain of
imprisonment. Exception was made for women of the highest social

classes, who could read Scripture in private. Apart from that, upper-class males alone could read the Bible.

Inevitably, the issue of the succession was of burning interest in Henry's last years. A new act was passed, which restored Mary and Elizabeth to the succession (thereby acknowledging their legitimacy, which earlier acts had denied). Because Edward was so young, there was much jockeying for position to become part of the regency council that was to act during the boy's minority.

Edward VI, 1547–1553

The short reign of Edward VI, who died at the age of 13, was marked by the dominance of radical and aggressive Protestantism. England was effectively ruled by a group of fiercely Protestant nobles, initially led by Lord Protector Somerset, who devoted much of their energies to intrigue and plots against each other for control of the young monarch. The rivalries of the last years of Henry VIII were replayed with renewed force and for higher stakes, especially as the young king's health proved to be poor.

Somerset's aggressive Protestantism—which involved the destruction of chantry chapels, the smashing of windows, and the breaking of statues—may have been in tune with the mood of the more radical parts of England, notably London. But he aroused great discontent elsewhere, not least among the clergy. At one point all preaching was banned, and clergy were instructed to read to their congregations 12 officially approved sermons or homilies. A further cause of discontent was Somerset's economic policy, which permitted an inflation that was felt with great severity among the poor and encouraged enclosure of common land. The riots and marches of 1549 were widespread and involved large numbers of men and women, often desperate individuals with little or nothing to lose. Armies were raised and foreign mercenaries hired to fight pitched battles with the larger rebel groups. Thousands were killed in conflicts that featured savage class hatred. Some rebels proclaimed, "Kill the gentlemen and we will have the Six Articles . . . and ceremonies as they were in King Henry VIII's time."

After a power struggle Somerset was removed and later beheaded (1552). The Duke of Northumberland, who turned out to be a more vigorous and single-minded proponent of religious changes, then took to himself similarly extensive powers. In the final years of the young king's reign, the new Protestant Prayer Book was published, the printing presses were active in the Protestant cause, and the Act of Uniformity was passed. This act required "every person" in England to attend church on Sundays, on pain of life imprisonment after a third offense.

Mary, 1553–1558

The accession of Mary was initially challenged by those loyal to the old regime. There was an attempted Protestant coup that sought to place the young Lady Jane Grey on the throne and safeguard the Protestant revolution. In the event the rebellion failed, and Mary attempted to reverse the actions of the previous reign. The three chief policies of Mary's reign were her marriage, the reestablishment of union with Rome, and her wish to declare war on France. In 1554 she married Philip II of Spain, despite widespread popular hostility to the idea of a foreign, Catholic king. The marriage provoked several uprisings, notably "Wyatt's rebellion," which started in Kent and reached London before being fiercely suppressed. Reformation laws (such as the Act of Uniformity and the permission for clergy to marry) were repealed, and ancient heresy legislation from the days of Richard II and Henry V was brought back to deal with Protestants. Some leading Protestant reformers (notably Hugh Latimer, Nicholas Ridley, and Thomas Cranmer) were executed, and hundreds of their followers were burned at Smithfield and in other places around the country.

Yet Mary lost the propaganda war: she alienated many intellectuals, who fled to Europe and became an intellectual establishment in exile. She did not understand the power of the printing press as the Protestants did. And the burnings did not endear her to the population. The most famous book of the period is John Foxe's *Acts and Monumentes*, known as "Foxe's Book of Martyrs," which preserved a hostile image of "Bloody Mary" and her reign for centuries to come. Mary's relations with her husband were not good, and there was no child of the marriage. She also managed to find herself in conflict with Pope Paul IV by the end of her life.

Indeed, her final years were a period of great tension. There was widespread disease—an influenza outbreak killed 200,000 people in the years after 1556. There was famine, malnutrition, and hardships of many kinds. Protestants interpreted such things as signs of divine displeasure. In addition, Mary involved England in wars in support of Spain, on the Continent, and in Scotland. The result was the loss of Calais, held by the English for centuries, and a series of expensive and inconclusive conflicts. When Mary died in 1558 she left her country in a state of depression and uncertainty.

Elizabeth I, 1558–1603

Elizabeth was unmarried when she came to the throne, and for much of her reign it was assumed that she intended to marry. Suitors from near and far were proposed, ranging from courtiers who were part of her entourage to monarchs of remote countries. The possibility of the queen's marriage was held tantalizingly before her people and her ministers for many years. It proved to be a way of securing a measure of control. There was a particular urgency about the question of the succession on several occasions, such as in 1562, when the queen had smallpox; in 1572, when she suffered from a severe fever; and in 1584, after the assassination of William of Orange. But right to the end she kept her own counsel and never publicly acknowledged a successor.

Elizabeth's approach to the divisive questions of religion that had racked the country under her brother and sister was cautious rather than ideological. In general terms, she sought to define Anglicanism as the national church under the sovereign, pursuing a *via media* between Puritanism and Catholicism.[8] Nevertheless, she began by reasserting the royal supremacy. An Act of Uniformity came into effect in 1559, and former church lands were to remain in the possession of the laity; a revised version of the 1552 Protestant Prayer Book was published, and every parish "minister" ("priest" being deemed a Catholic title) was ordered to use its forms.

Mary's bishops declined to accept this new situation and were duly replaced, often by radical protestants who had spent years in exile in Europe. Such men tended to be impatient at Elizabeth's pragmatism and at the ideological diversity of their ministers, many of whom had been ordained in Mary's time. Reporting systems were set up to check on observances, and to identify and fine Catholics. In every church there was to be a pulpit, a Bible, and Erasmus's *Paraphrases*. Preachers had to be licensed. The commissioners sent to enforce these regulations were frequently zealous, and there was a sustained campaign of iconoclasm that lasted for over a decade. The walls inside many churches were limewashed and painted with the Royal Arms and the Ten Commandments. Stratford's Church of the Holy Trinity was defaced in 1563.[9] John Shakespeare was acting chamberlain at the time and recorded the expenditure of 2 shillings "paid for defacing images in the chapel" (Schoenbaum 1977, 54). Also, a great deal of energy was spent in trying to trace absentees from the services. It is notable that the most strenuous efforts were reserved for periods of political crisis, where church attendance was as much a token of political loyalty as religious obedience.

Such matters became increasingly contentious as the queen's relations with the papacy and Catholic Europe deteriorated. Elizabeth was excommunicated and "deposed" by Pope Pius V in 1570, and English Catholics were placed in a very difficult position. They were faced with a test of loyalty from both secular and religious authorities. After 1581, when an "Act to Retain the Queen's Majesty's Subjects in their Due Obedience" became law, it became a treasonable offense to preach Catholicism and a criminal offense to say Mass. A priest faced a fine of £133 and a year in prison; each member of the congregation could be fined half as much and imprisoned for the same period. Jesuits were regarded as spies and risked death. Where Mary had burned heretics at Smithfield, Elizabeth had Catholic spies and traitors hanged, drawn (disemboweled while still alive), and quartered (arms, legs, and head severed from the torso) at Tyburn, the site of the modern Marble Arch in London.

The presence of Mary Queen of Scots as a prisoner in England from 1568 until her execution in 1587 provided a focus for Catholic dissidence and plotting. It also stimulated the development of a secret intelligence service that monitored the movements and correspondence of Catholics and acquired further intelligence by penetrating Catholic groups at home and abroad, acting as agents provocateurs and employing other now-familar techniques of countersubversion.[10]

Many of Elizabeth's supporters regarded her as indecisive in dealing with her imprisoned rival Mary Queen of Scots. Yet the queen's reluctance to act reflected more than a mere temperamental caution. It also sprang from an ingrained belief in the sanctity of the royal person allied to a determination to keep England as neutral as possible in the religious and dynastic wars that were sweeping the Continent and beginning to spread to the New World.

Shortly before Queen Mary's death English troops had been committed on the Protestant side in the wars in the Netherlands, and from that time on there was regular warfare. Here, too, Elizabeth was often criticized for being unwilling to deploy sufficient forces or even to sufficiently arm and supply those she did send. At the same time it proved ever more difficult to raise troops for these operations. Despite the extraordinary, almost miraculous, victory over the great Armada sent by Spain in 1588, there was no guarantee that a second attempt would not follow, and nobody could predict how a Catholic invasion would be greeted by the population as a whole.

There was also a certain amount of organized unrest in England; it tended to result from economic and social discontents, from famine, enclosures, corruption of various kinds. There was a series of uprisings from the late 1580s on, and it is easy to see why. Economic historians have calculated that during the economic crisis of the 1590s some 40 percent of the population was living below subsistence levels. On a historical scale, real wages were lower in 1597 than at any time between 1260 and 1950. There were riots in the country, where families dispossessed by enclosures had no means of making a living. There were riots in the cities, directed against hoarders and speculators. It took periods of concerted action by the propertied classes to control the rebellions and to organize interim poor relief. The maintenance of social order was a challenge throughout Elizabeth's reign.[11]

It should be noted that Elizabeth's last favorite, Robert Devereux, earl of Essex, staged an uprising in 1601. He was in disgrace at the time and faced charges of treason. His attempt was, despite all the instability and discontent within the country, almost laughably inadequate. He found himself unable to seize the queen and denounce her councillors, and when he tried to gain the support of the city he was emphatically rejected. His style of rebellion and its motivation were an anachronism: they belonged in the faction-ridden, pre-Tudor England.[12] Elizabeth's final victory signaled that she was leaving the country in a more governable state than she had found it. But her successes had been hard-won and would prove impossible to sustain.

James I (James VI of Scotland), 1603–1625

In keeping with the tone set by the relatively trouble-free defeat of the Essex rebellion, the accession of King James was stable and orderly. Contemporary accounts note the tranquility of London when the proclamation was made. Most importantly, James inherited the loyalty and hard work of Robert Cecil, who was in effective control of the administration of government until his death in 1612.

James presented himself to his new Kingdom as *Rex Pacificus*, "Peacemaker King." On arriving in England—the country in which his mother, Mary Queen of Scots, had been executed—he summoned the Hampton Court Conference, designed to establish the religious settlement for his reign. Like Elizabeth, he sought to achieve balance between the more extreme Puritan and neo-Catholic (sometimes known as Arminian) wings of the Anglican church, and he was in large measure successful. Some historians argue that the unsatisfactory nature of some of the compromises merely stored up difficulties for James's successor.

But James managed to produce a new version of the Book of Common Prayer, secure a powerful Recusancy Act (in the aftermath of the Gunpowder Plot in 1605, when a group of Catholics were apprehended as they were about to blow up the king during the state opening of Parliament), and lay the foundations for the great translation of the Bible still known as the Authorized Version (published in 1611).

James began his conduct of foreign affairs by concluding a treaty with Spain. At the same time he removed Sir Walter Ralegh from office and imprisoned him. He negotiated with both Protestant and Catholic powers in Europe to establish a peace, and he tried, in the face of parliamentary opposition, to bring about the union of England and Scotland. As his children grew older, he attempted to deploy them in the extension of his policy, seeking to marry the fiercely Puritan Henry to a Catholic princess and his daughter Elizabeth to Frederick, the Protestant Elector Palatine.

In contrast with Elizabeth's tacit encouragement of piracy designed to harass the Spanish treasure fleets and engage in random sabotage of their war effort, James and Henry encouraged the establishment of colonies and the development of overseas trade. Their impact on the Jacobean economy was small. None of the English colonies was as copiously stored with gold and precious stones for plunder as their backers hoped and proclaimed when trying to raise money and volunteers. Nevertheless, the foundation of the colonies, which were intended to be self-sufficient communities (unlike, say, the all-male fur stations and Jesuit missions introduced by the French into the northern parts of the North American continent), obviously had enormous long-term significance.

The death of Prince Henry at the early age of 18 in 1612, followed by the marriage of Princess Elizabeth in February 1613, marks the end of an era in many ways. James, without his son and without the advice of Salisbury, was increasingly susceptible to poor advice from his favorites. For a variety of reasons, the same period sees the end of some literary careers: Shakespeare, who now lived almost exclusively in Stratford; Ralegh, who was forced to abandon his *History of the World* (which Henry had supported); and John Donne, who entered holy orders, are just the most famous. Marston, Chapman, and several other writers effectively retired at around that time.

From this point on James enjoyed less success. He was forced to accede to the disgrace of his favorite Robert Carr and to the condemnation of Sir Francis Bacon. He had Ralegh executed in 1618 to appease the Spanish, and he refused to become embroiled in the Thirty Years' War in Europe, despite the urgent request for assistance from his daughter and son-in-law.

Many of James's difficultites may be related to his complex personality. He was, for instance, given to mood swings and remarkable inconsistencies and self-contradictions. His treatment of Catholics was marked by its frequent unpredictability. He was at times driven by obsessions, as with his frenzied hatred of witchcraft (large-scale witch-burning began in 1614) and violent dislike of tobacco.

But James faced many problems that were not of his own making. He had, for example, been well placed to mediate between France and Spain during the reign of the Protestant Henri of Navarre. Henri's death in 1610 disrupted the delicate balance, and James found his influence much reduced.

In the domestic economy James inherited the problems of Elizabethan England—indeed, he arrived in England at a time of severe plague. Famine was a regular fact of life for the poor. There are stories of men reduced to eating dogs and decaying horsemeat in Lincolnshire in the 1620s. And the numbers of the poor were immense: still between 30 and 40 percent of the population. Despite the check of plague, the population continued to increase throughout the period, as did inflation, which reduced the real value of wages. At the same time agricultural rents were on a rising trend, so landowners enjoyed success—a fact permanently recorded in the numerous great stone manor houses that are one of the most abiding relics of Jacobean England. The gap between rich and poor seemed to grow ever wider, and there were numerous riots, as there had been under Elizabeth. We have already seen both how Shakespeare's personal fortunes blossomed at this time and how he was embroiled in the disputes and discontents that arose from enclosures and widespread rural poverty.

Early Modern England

Every age can be interpreted as a period of transition. Almost every period of postmedieval English history has been connected with "the rise of the middle class." The development of individualism and of "modern" ideas of identity are alleged to have started in any one of a series of epochs. Even given such reservations, however, the century that began in the late 1580s—at the time of the Armada and Shakespeare's arrival in

London—saw extraordinary changes in society, in social organization, and in the ways in which individuals understood their relation to the world, to the universe, and to the supernatural.[13]

Although the population was increasing rapidly (by 50 percent between 1540 and 1600), there were fewer people in England in 1600 than there had been in 1300 before the Black Death. London was the site of the most spectacular increase in numbers, but other parts of England were sparsely populated in comparison with earlier centuries.[14] While London grew above 215,000 by 1603, no Tudor provincial town ever had a population greater than 20,000.[15] It was rare for the population of a major city (Norwich, Bristol, Exeter, York, Coventry, Salisbury, King's Lynn) to exceed 10,000.[16] Almost 90 percent of the population lived in the countryside.

The average life expectancy in Shakespeare's England was about 32 years. His own family exemplifies this. The average age at death of the children of John and Mary Shakespeare was 31.[17] Averages can be misleading, of course. There was high infant mortality, and many women died in or after childbirth: those who survived such critical times were often hardy individuals, some capable of living well into old age.

According to contemporary commentators, Elizabethan society consisted of four classes, and the evidence suggests that in the first years of King James's reign those class divisions were reinforced by an economic polarization.[18] The classes were, in descending order of wealth, as follows: nobles and gentlemen; citizens and burgesses; rural smallholders or yeomen; laborers or artisans.[19] The rapidly growing metropolis saw the rise of a cash economy and was part of a significant conversion of wealth from land to more portable forms of property. This facilitated upward and downward mobility and began to transform relations between the classes. John Shakespeare's acquisition of a coat of arms in 1596 exemplifies the process. William Shakespeare was instrumental in securing the honor for his father. He presumably read Harrison's disdainful account in Holinshed's *Chronicles*, which describes a man who "can live without manuell labour, and thereto is able and will beare the port, charge, and countenance of a gentleman." Such a man "shall for monie have a cote and armes bestowed upon him by heralds . . . and thereunto being made so good cheape be called master . . . and reputed for a gentleman ever after."[20] These accounts of social structures were based on property. Hence their silence about the poor and about women, although as noted elsewhere, the phenomenon of the "masterless woman" was necessitating some revision of attitudes.[21]

More generally, it has become clear that the new economic, social, and political arrangements of the early modern period were deeply involved with—sometimes influencing, sometimes influenced by—relations between the sexes.[22] No less clear is that many men expressed concern that the unprecedented "liberty" of women represented a profound threat to the social and natural order. Of course there was the example of Queen Elizabeth, and of a number of prominent aristocratic women; at the local level, however, women who were felt to be "a visible threat to the patriarchal system" found themselves faced with a hostile and vindictive legal system.[23] Accusations of witchcraft were merely the crudest form of this response. As far as the drama is concerned, it seems to be a given that social and sexual relations are inseparable. The critique and renegotiation of the one implies the critique and renegotiation of the other.[24] Whether the drama was an instrument for social transformation or a safety valve that confined turbulent gender and social relations to a licensed space is central to the containment/subversion debate.

Similar social and political considerations have informed studies of individualism and identity in this period. There was an obvious tension between the Renaissance impulse to forge a self, to construct a unique identity, and the centralizing, controlling urges of the early modern state. The state considered itself justified in taking an interest in the inner lives of its subjects (British people are still subjects rather than citizens), with particular reference to their religious beliefs and their loyalty to the crown. A substantial bureaucracy was established to monitor the population. And yet the sonnet, the soliloquy, amd the long interior monologues given to male and female speakers in romances and fictions all attest to the force of the drive to selfhood.[25] Such questions are closely involved with the theory and practice of education in the period. There were arguments about the scope and content of education and about who should receive it. There was widespread concern about the possible consequences of unfettered literacy, but commercial and other consideratons facilitated its spread. It is striking, for example, how rapidly female readership is identified as significant for the marketing of romance.[26] And the activities of women as patrons and then, increasingly, as authors, whether published or in the hidden world of manuscript culture, attest to a remarkable growth in the education of those hitherto wholly excluded from written culture.[27]

One of the features of Renaissance culture is the increased specialization and compartmentalization of knowledge. The greatest scholars of the Middle Ages could suppose they knew everything there was to know, or at least that they had access to all the greatest wisdom that existed. The great discoveries and upheavals, as well as the changes in social organization, of early modern Europe put an end to that.

The professions began to define themselves, partly on the model of the medieval guild system. Systems of thought and knowledge grew up, each with its own specialized vocabulary and code of behavior. The most obvious examples are the practice of medicine and law. In the case of medicine, for instance, the Royal College of Surgeons was founded in Henry VIII's reign. Medicine became an increasingly male-dominated profession, and the extensive activities of women in the healing process were steadily marginalized (as in midwifery) or in some cases demonized (as in witchcraft rituals).[28] Many of the unfortunate women burned as witches in Renaissance England were punished for the practice of ancient folk remedies.[29] If their treatment failed, they were scorned as impotent demons; if it was succesful, it merely proved how forceful their magic was. In either case they were doomed.[30]

As for the practice of law, the role of local magistrates and Justices was still important and an integral part of the implementation of government policy. These men were frequently untrained, but as time went by it became more normal for them at least to have spent time at one of the Inns of Court in London and to have acquired some specialized knowledge, particularly in the areas of law most relevant to their later lives. These justices were advised by the new breed of professional lawyers, whose influence spread throughout the kingdom. Most of the leading active politicians were lawyers, and they set the tone for a litigious age. Like medicine, the profession was a male preserve, although Queen Elizabeth's role as the fount of justice enabled her to draw on a series of powerful images and icons, such as the rusty sword she is said to have taken with her to show her latent power.[31] Shakespeare's Portia in *The Merchant of Venice* is a rare exception, and she is shown to provoke a certain amount of unease among those who see her in action.

As far as beliefs are concerned, historians continue to debate the condition of pre-Reformation Christianity in England.[32] The victorious, Protestant view was that the Catholic Church had been lazy, worldly, corrupt, and grasping, but this model is now disputed. There is not space here to go into such questions in detail, although for the student of the culture its attitudes to images, to representation, and to allegory are obviously important.

The Reformation redefined the individual's sense of self in two important ways that are connected with the development of vernacular literature in Tudor England. Medieval Catholicism has been characterized as "a cult of the living in the service of the dead." It was believed that those alive on earth (the Church Militant) could use their prayers to speed the progress of those in purgatory (the Church Suffering) so that they could join the happy souls in heaven (the Church Triumphant). With the Reformation, all that changed. Individuals were now solely responsible for an inventory of their sins and good deeds: nothing could either help or hinder them after their death. Funerals that had been attended by whole communities, and especially by the oldest members and children, became increasingly events for the family and friends of the deceased. And the mourning was directed much more to the grief of the survivors than to the fate of the immortal soul of the deceased.

With the Reformation, the organic link connecting the present to the past, the living to the dead, was severed. An individual man or woman was no longer directly implicated in the spiritual fate of his or her predecessor.[33] In this sense the Reformation brought both spiritual liberation and a sense of spiritual isolation. Individual men and women were on their own. It was the responsibility of each to make an account of his or her life to God.

The disappearance of penance and the sacrament of confession had a similar set of consequences. The late Middle Ages had developed an elaborate psychology of sin and repentance. In particular, the faithful were trained to examine their consciences, to scrutinize their actions and motives in order to present them for comment and punishment in the confessional. The language of introspection, whether in religious or secular contexts, was drawn from this practice. When it ceased, it became necessary for men and women to find secular alternatives, other forms of words, other mental disciplines. The secularization of introspection was intimately connected with the development of literature. We need only think of the soliloquy or the sonnet sequence or the essay to see how literary forms grew up in response to this new need. On a more sinister level, the technological means to encourage confession were used more in Elizabeth's reign than at any time before or since in England. There was a formalized bureaucracy of torture, based after 1589 on the Bridewell prison. Official permission was required before torture could be used, and the main purpose was to acquire names of accomplices. The usual victims were Jesuit priests and suspected Catholic conspirators. The threat of torture was frequently all that was required to stimulate the memory of the accused.[34]

The mapping and exploration of the self were paralleled by external acts and voyages. They were also shadowed by further metaphors of exploration. Thus the frontispieces of Bacon's scientific works draw on the iconography of empire. They showed the great pillars (used by both Spanish and British imperial claimants) giving onto an ocean of intellectual inquiry on which Bacon's mental vessel sailed to the distant horizon.[35] During Shakespeare's lifetime colonial enterprises in Ireland and then in North America were marked more by defeat, failure, and division than by the unfolding of a providential scheme of world conquest. Yet there was evidently a powerful sense of nationhood and an impulse to control, to enclose, to define, and to monitor Britain itself (Helgerson 1992). The first road maps began to appear in the 1590s—before that maps recorded places, sometimes estates, and major geographical features. It is salutary to recall that the English Civil War was fought almost entirely without the benefit of road maps. Jeffrey Knapp has argued in *An Empire Nowhere* (1992) that the English came to rejoice in their comparative failures, to contrast their performance with the gross materialism of Spain; for them the colonial project was ennobled by its lack of worldly rewards, as it became a victory of values, of a national spirit and character, rather than arms.[36]

Chapter Four

Shakespeare's London

A Journey to London

Shakespeare had a choice of routes to take him from Stratford to London: over the years he seems to have used both of them. The two routes diverged then, as they diverge today, on the far side of Clopton Bridge—the road to the right leading to Oxford, that to the left to Banbury. The modern motor roads follow those Shakespeare knew fairly closely.[1] By either route the trip would have taken at least four days on foot, assuming both a daily average trek of about 25 miles and good conditions underfoot. Doubtless he would have hired a horse if the means had been available to him, as they certainly were within a few years of his arrival in London; but his first journey was probably by foot.

The Banbury route (today the A422) starts with a straight six miles down to the junction with the ancient Roman road, the Fosse Way, at Ettington. It then goes on through wooded countryside toward the forbidding slope of Edge Hill, close to what would be the site of the opening battle in the Civil War more than half a century later. Then the track went along the ridge through Wroxton and down into the prosperous (and Puritan) market town of Banbury. Carrying on to the east, the road passed through Brackley and then followed the valley of the Great Ouse for seven or eight miles to Buckingham before turning south, through Winslow and on to Aylesbury (today's A413). From Aylesbury the traveler had to make the steep ascent of the Chiltern Hills, probably above Wendover, and then pass down through Great Missenden, Amersham, Chalfont St. Giles, Chalfont St. Peter, to Uxbridge, and so into London.

The Oxford route was, and is, shorter. In winter and spring it would have been wetter, colder, and vulnerable to snowfall. It took the traveler directly south along the banks of the Stour through Atherstone and Newbold (today's A34), across the Fosse Way, to Shipston on Stour. The road then moved up into the Cotswolds, along the bleak ridge that runs from the prehistoric and mysterious Rollright stones, then through the market town of Chipping Norton and on along the ancient Saltway (some stretches of which still survive as unpaved grass tracks) through the eastern edge of Wychwood down into the royal park of Woodstock, before dropping down into the Cherwell valley on the approach to the city of Oxford. Out of Oxford (on a line close to that of the modern A40), the road passed over Headington Hill and on through Wheatley, Tetsworth, Stokenchurch, over the Chilterns, and down into High Wycombe. From there the trail led through Beaconsfield and Gerrards Cross to Uxbridge.

The approach to London from Uxbridge, shared by both routes, was a weary trudge of a dozen miles or so, enlivened perhaps by an occasional glimpse of St. Paul's Cathedral. Even by 1580 the pall of smoke that was to hang over the city until the late 1950s would have been noticeable, and a thing of wonder to a traveler from a small provincial town. The road (close to today's A4020) led through Shepherd's Bush and on past the gallows at Tyburn (modern Marble Arch), through pleasant fields and clusters of houses along the Oxford Road, ignoring the Tottenham Court Road to the left and the lane down through St. Martin's Fields to the right. The road changed its name to St. Giles High Street as it passed through the village of St. Giles in the Fields (bounded on the south by the Reading Road, now known as Shaftesbury Avenue), and then, passing a walled track to the right (modern Drury Lane), it led south into Holborn, a broad street with substantial and imposing buildings (including Gray's Inn, where *The Comedy of Errors* would be performed at Christmas in 1594), across Ely Place, over the Fleet River by means of Holborn Bridge and then via Snow Hill to enter the city at Newgate.[2]

Contemporary accounts show that the scale, bustle, pride, and prosperity of the city astonished even well-traveled foreign visitors.[3] It must have been a remarkable experience for a young man from a town of not much more than 1,000, where close ties of kinship, business, and friendship bound neighbors to one another. His awe might have been tempered by noticing the recently established suburban brothels in St. Giles (relocated away from the city in response to the syphilis "epidemic"). And he would have seen the notorious filth and squalor of the Fleet River: periodic official attempts to restore the channel's navigability proved feeble in the losing battle against the city's ability to generate waste.

If Shakespeare entered the city by way of Newgate, he would have experienced the press and bustle of the crowds and seen the limbs of executed criminals displayed on poles above his head. Elizabethan London was a walled city, whose inhabitants (in theory at least) were still regularly drilled in the use of weapons well into the 1590s. Although the most recent seige had been during Wyatt's rebellion in 1554, there were extensive preparations for defense against the Armada in 1588. The city walls, like those of the Tower, so it was said, were bound together with a mortar that included human blood, and their legendary strength derived from this grisly paste. Tudor Londoners were nourished on the myth that the city had been founded by Brutus (hence "British") and other survivors of the destruction of Troy. And when the invading Romans named the inhabitants of this region the *Trinovantes*, they had been garbling the "real" name of the city—Troy Novant, or New Troy.

The walls of London contained several substantial forts, numerous turrets and bastions, and ran more than two miles around the city on the northern side. Although the walls are gone now, their route can still be traced, most easily by following the sites of the former city gates. Even in Shakespeare's time, the southern stretch of the wall, along the shore of the Thames, had fallen into disuse and crumbled into the water. An exception was Baynard's castle, next to Puddle Wharf, which still dominated the waterfront. The castle, rebuilt in 1428 by Henry V's brother Humfrey, duke of Gloucester, was where Richard III had been offered the crown, and in Elizabeth's time it was the London residence of the earls of Pembroke.

Newgate, as its name implied, was one of the more recent gates to be constructed. The original four gates had been Aldgate in the East, Aldersgate in the north, Ludgate in the west, and the Bridgegate over the Thames to the south. By the reign of Henry II (1133–89) three further gates had been permitted: Newgate, the Postern (immediately to the north of the Tower on Tower Hill), and Bishopsgate to the north. Other less substantial breeches in the wall in the form of posterns had been created, such as those at Moorgate, at Christ's Hospital (near Smithfield), and at Cripplegate.

Shakespeare's London was, to a considerable degree, the city Chaucer would have known 200 years before. It was the city in which so many of the events Shakespeare would dramatize in the English history plays had taken place. The monastic houses were gone, of course, and great nobles and merchants now created their mansions and apartments in them.[4] There were few major new constructions: as the population grew, spaces were filled with improvised structures and gardens were replaced by houses and alleys. Much of the walled city was a rabbit warren of narrow, twisting lanes, thronged with people and animals, carts and carriages. It was literally bursting at the seams with the likes of street vendors and shoppers, vagabonds and beggars.

London's population was some hundred times greater than that of Stratford. It dwarfed all other English cities. In 1550, for example, when no English city had more than 5,000 inhabitants, London had something like 120,000. By 1600 that figure had grown to about 200,000, and by 1650 to 375,000. Shakespeare's time in London coincided with rapid growth and with the final bursting out of the city walls, when the suburbs to the north and west and on the south bank of the Thames expanded at an unprecedented rate.[5]

This population increase had numerous physical and economic consequences. It posed a massive logistical problem for the civic administration. Citizens had to be housed, fed, and employed; they and their horses needed to be watered in the summer and kept warm in winter; they needed to be induced to obey the law, cared for when they were ill, and buried when they died. For new migrants like Shakespeare, the city must have rocked the foundations of their understanding of themselves, of the world, and of social relations. In the countryside, the environment where most of them were brought up, Elizabethans lived communally but also relatively spaciously, with plenty of room for each individual. The overall population was still some way short of the levels of pre–Black Death England 200 years before. In London, however, personal space was at a premium. The population was so dense that the boundaries of privacy and identity had to be redrawn. Tenements were constantly thrown up, and houses, rooms, and apartments squeezed into ever narrower spaces.

Research shows that London households did not just have less living space: they were also considerably larger (on average by some 50 pecent) than rural or urban households elsewhere. And this was not because there were different patterns of family composition in the metropolis. If anything, as a result of exceptionally high infant mortality in London and because some families sent their offspring into the countryside to be nursed, the number of resident children was lower there than elsewhere. London households were bigger because they contained more servants and lodgers (Beier and Findlay, 46–47). Given the importance attached to family and local ties, many migrants found lodgings with members of their extended family or with households connected in some way with the same provincial town or village—just as, a generation earlier, John Shakespeare had migrated into Stratford from Snitterfield. No doubt William Shakespeare had at least some names and addresses to look up when he arrived in London. New citizens thus found some familiar values, customs, and dialect in which to root their new urban identity. But all around them the entire city was embarking on an involuntary experiment in urban living, both as individuals and as a community.

London was a mercantile city. One of its few large-scale modern buildings was Sir Thomas Gresham's Royal Exchange, built at Cornhill in 1566–67 on the model of the Burse at Antwerp. It had a spacious courtyard and a distinctly cosmopolitan ambience.[6] Within the city the Guildhall stood as the focus of the local civic administration. The growing power of trade and commerce was embodied in the numerous halls of the various livery companies (successors of the medieval guilds); there may have been up to 50 of them, many custom-built. Surviving maps show the handsome turreted hall of the Drapers, which stood in Throgmorton Street, and halls of the Mercers in Cheapside, and of the Fishmongers near London Bridge. Down by the river they show docks and warehouses, quays and cranes, giving concrete expression to the city's commercial foundation. Their names (Hay Wharf, Timberhithe, Fish Wharf, Salt Wharf, Vintry Wharf) record the trades that took place there.

The West Midlands had seen the beginnings of an industrial revolution, and perhaps Shakespeare had come across some industrial processes on a grander scale than that of the local brewers in Stratford, or of his father's leatherworks. But London's industrial operations were huge in comparison. The maps show us few of the numerous factories that we know existed at the time, but they do show gun foundries, for example, one of which was at the corner of Thames Street and Water Lane. There was another, larger factory north of Aldgate on the other side of Houndsditch. John Stow reports that the noise generated by a group of iron foundries at Lothbury was "loathsome . . . to the by-passers." It is also possible to make out brick kilns—smoke would have poured out of their lofty chimneys. One is in the fields near Islington, another in Scotland Yard, from which smoke—depending on the prevailing wind— would have belched out over the adjacent palaces and mansions in Westminster and along the Strand.[7]

For Londoners, the "silver streaming Themmes" was their commercial lifeblood, their link with the ever-expanding world of Europe, the Indies, Africa, and America. And it was a highway, connecting the city with Westminster by means of barges and other small vessels. Unfortunately, they also depended on the Thames more literally: although the river was a fetid sewer, they ate its fish and drank its water. Professional water-bearers took their pack ponies down to the Thames and loaded them with great wooden "cans" for delivery to individual houses. Some water was piped in from wells and springs in the suburbs, and the carriers would also take supplies to their customers from the city's many conduits and pumps.

The huge population bought its food at the numerous markets. Some were specialized: meat at Smithfield, fish and meat at the Stocks Market (on the site of the present Mansion House), poultry at Leadenhall. Others, like Newgate market or that at Cheapside, sold a wide range of goods. But for any wide-eyed migrant from the country in those days there would have been two marketplaces above all to visit: each was a building designed for other purposes, each was a massive structure that dominated the skyline, and each was a center of exchange and commerce. One was London Bridge, the other St. Paul's Cathedral.

London Bridge was one of the wonders of the kingdom, a sight all tourists came to see. It was the only bridge across the Thames, and the only direct access to the city from the south. Its southern gate was decorated with the heads of criminals whose limbs were displayed on the city's other gates. It was broad and majestic, built on 20 arches, and carried a road that had once been wide enough to permit wagons to pass freely in both directions. By Shakespeare's day, however, it was permanently clogged with traffic and people. The bridge had by that time come to be occupied by substantial houses built by "merchants of consequence," who would use the ground floor for their showrooms and have their apartments on the upper storeys. Right in the center was a huge Tudor building known as Nonsuch (because of its resemblance to the great royal palace of that name). Contemporary pictures show that there was a riot of improvised, parasitical construction, with structures sprouting from the solid houses, filling in the spaces, and making it almost impossible for the traveler to see the river beneath, where boats negotiated the narrow channels between the pillars. Along with the Tower, the bridge was a potent symbol of the city's uniqueness and its endurance.

As a spectacle, St. Paul's was equally extraordinary. It was a place where God and Mammon met on more or less equal terms, with the balance tilted somewhat toward the latter. In Shakespeare's day the cathedral church was still from a distance the most massive and splendid of all English cathedrals—although the wooden steeple (447 feet high) burnt down in 1561 after being struck by lightning. Travelers on the road in from the west could have seen its huge bulk from many miles away, as some contemporary drawings show.

Here, in the heart of the capital, great national occasions were staged: Sir Philip Sidney was laid to rest here in February 1587, and the service of thanksgiving for the victory over the Spanish Armada was held here on 24 November 1588. But a closer view, perhaps gained as the crowds gathered for a sermon at Paul's Cross in the churchyard, yielded a much less imposing image. The cathedral was falling apart. King James would eventually establish a Royal Commission (whose members included Francis Bacon, the duke of Buckingham, and Inigo Jones) to draw up a plan to remedy the structural damage and modernize the Gothic structure on neoclassical principles. But when Shakespeare arrived in London, he would have found the great edifice a faded, crumbling ruin outside and a scene of unique oddity inside.

Parts of the building still performed the normal functions of a cathedral; services were held in the usual way, lavish tombs were constructed for the nobility, and the choir sang as it always had. But the nave (variously known as "Paul's Walk" or "Duke Humfrey's Walk") was a riot of commercial life. If this temple was not full of moneylenders, it was because the moneylenders had lost the fight for breathing space with merchants, factors, tailors, lawyers, pickpockets, whores, and other dealers busily engaged in meeting clients, swapping information, selling services of all kinds, hiring workers who advertised their availability. The rood loft, tombs, and even the baptismal font were used as counters for paying out money, and beer, bread, fish, and fruit could be bought there.

In a limited attempt at reform, the mayor and council in 1554 had prohibited a few of the more egregious sacrileges—most notably the use of the church as a shortcut by delivery men and the practice of leading horses and pack mules through the building. But the cathedral was, and remained, a magnet for all sorts and conditions of Londoners. Gallants, wits, and other hustlers loitered there to try to sponge a meal or some other invitation (in Gabriel Harvey's phrase, a penniless gallant would be compelled to "seeke his dinner in Poules with Duke Humphrey") (Kay 1992, 77–78). Outside, in the churchyard, was the hub of the publishing trade. Stationers lived in the streets around the cathedral close, and set up stalls and shops to sell their wares in the shadow of the church.[8]

The city, as befitted the fortress of the descendants of the ancient Trojans, had a fierce pride in its independence and traditions. But although it was preeminent in commerce and industry, its neighbor, the city of Westminster, was the seat of the crown and of the government, as well as the main home of the court. Between the city walls and Westminster, between the Strand and the river, beyond the Temple Gardens, was a row of mansions, with gardens stretching to the water's edge. These were the residences of various court grandees—York House, Bedford House, Arundel House, the Savoy, Durham House, Somerset House, Essex House. The complex of palace buildings themselves stretched from Scotland Yard westward to Westminster Abbey: they were linked by a walled street to St. James's Park to the north.

Opposite was Lambeth, a village surrounded by treacherous marshes, and then the London palace of the Archbishop of Canterbury, which serves in the same capacity today. Contemporary maps indicate several ferry crossing points at this (relatively narrow) part of the river, notably those on the sites of the modern Westminster Bridge and Lambeth Bridge. The other part of the South Bank that sustained a population was the Southwark area around the southern end of London Bridge, and this was one of the suburban districts whose population grew most rapidly during Shakespeare's lifetime (Beier and Findlay, 43–45). He himself moved over there around the turn of the century, and it was there that the Globe theater would be built.

Let us imagine that the newly arrived Shakespeare has had his first sight of these great landmarks of the capital, that he has made his way from west to east, coming in through Newgate, then from north to south through the crowds, that he has crossed over the bridge to the South Bank, and that he turns to look back across the river toward the city. What he would have seen was a spectacular water frontage, stretching from the huge bulk of the Tower in the east, past Baynard's Castle and St. Paul's to Blackfrairs and the Temple, with the mansions of the Strand just out of his line of sight. He would have seen the spires and towers of a hundred churches within the city walls, the river teeming with small boats, the wharves alive with workers, the smoke belching from small factory chimneys and from domestic hearths. To the north, he might just have been able to see the wind-mills built on top of rubbish dumps in Finsbury fields: there were many similar structures on the higher ground, at Highbury and Hampstead. The city was both a collection of ancient monuments, embodying the nation's history, and an intensely modern development—a social phenomenon that nobody at the time was in a position to comprehend or manage.

The City's Recreations

Shakespeare's work was the city's play. But the theater was only one of the ways in which Londoners found recreation and amusement. To the north of the city, for example, in Finsbury fields, there were stakes set up with colored targets. In what seems to have been a hazardous cross between a modern golf course and driving range, citizens would stroll, dressed in fetching short cassocks, and fire arrows at these targets. Contemporary maps indicate that these fields were also used for musket practice and for grazing and milking cattle. And while the musket range was behind a wall, accidents with arrows were common. The diary of the London undertaker Henry Machyn records the death of a woman who was "slain going in Finsbury Field with her husband with an arrow shot in the neck"; Dame Alice Owen founded her school in Islington to thank God for a narrow escape when a stray arrow passed through her hat (Kay 1992, 81–82). The danger became a joke, too: at the end of Francis Beaumont's comedy *The Knight of the Burning Pestle* (1609), the grocer's son Rafe comes on stage with an arrow though his head, and tells the story of his accident:

> Then took I up my bow and shaft in hand,
> And walked into Moorfields to cool myself;
> But there grim cruel Death met me again,
> And shot this forked arrow through my head,
> And now I faint.

Rafe was a casual victim of "roving"—shooting over open ground at unknown distances. The other archery practices of the time—namely, "Prick" or "Clout" shooting (over measured distances of between 160 and 240 yards and designed to increase the length of shot) or "Butt" shooting (over distances between 110 and 140 yards and designed to foster accuracy)—were more obviously military in their application. When the musters were gathered to defend London from the Armada in 1588, between 20 and 50 percent were armed with bows, which indicates just how widespread was the practice of archery. In other parts of the city, and especially on the South Bank, quintains and other obstacles were set up to test equestrian skills.[9]

Many of the city's systems of communication were preliterate, visual rather than verbal. Public information was disseminated by proclamations; shops and inns were distinguished by signs; servants wore livery; different social ranks and professions were marked by their dress. Changes in public policy were often conveyed by pageants and processions, and records show how crowds would assemble to watch such sumptuous displays as the queen's journey from palaces at Westminster or Greenwich to the city.

The spectacle afforded by executions was enduringly popular as a public diversion. Huge crowds gathered at Tower Hill for beheadings, at Smithfield for the burning of heretics, or at Tyburn for the hanging, drawing, and quartering of convicted traitors—which, by Shakespeare's day, usually meant Jesuits. Such events were inescapably theatrical. The scaffold was a stage and the spectators an audience who could judge how well the convicted actors played their part. The officers were required to carry out their function with decency and solemnity, emptying themselves of personality to become mere instruments of justice. The victim would be expected not to shake, to show steadfastness, to make a ritual gift of earthly possessions, to utter some resolute or penitent words, expressing submission to the Almighty, and, perhaps, to make some final quip, some highly individual jest, as a finale to the performance of his life. The crowds became connoisseurs of these final scenes in the lives of famous men and women. As Montaigne said, "I have seen divers, by their death, give reputation to all their forepassed life."[10]

Just as modern politicians are well advised to have their resignation letter always at hand, Tudor and Stuart statesmen rehearsed their gallows performance and their last words. The parallel between the stage and political life was made explicitly in a famous poem by Sir Walter Ralegh, who spent much of his life under threat of execution:

> What is our life? A play of passion,
> Our mirth the music of division,
> Our mothers' wombs the tiring-houses be,
> Where we are dressed for this short comedy.
> Heav'n the judicious sharp spectator is,
> That sits and marks still who doth act amisse.
> Our graves, that hide us from the searching sun,
> Are like drawne curtains when the play is done.
> Thus march we, playing, to our latest rest—
> Only we die in earnest. That's no jest.[11]

Apart from official outdoor entertainment such as processions, sermons, and executions, Elizabethan London provided numerous diversions for those with time on their hands. But the civic authorities were usually anxious to exercise control over the leisure pursuits of the population. Specifically, they tried to ensure that certain kinds of merrymaking took place outside the city limits.[12]

On the South Bank, for example, citizens could disport themselves in brothels or at the bear-baiting stadium. Bear-baiting by dogs was a pastime in which the English took some considerable pride—a sport in which they regarded themselves as superior to their effete continental cousins. In 1506 Erasmus of Rotterdam commented on the great herds of bears maintained to supply the ring. From the reign of Henry VIII on, the office of master of the royal game was a significant court position. In 1526 a substantial amphitheater or circus (the classical titles were a deliberate attempt to dignify New Troy) was constructed in the Paris Garden on the bankside in Southwark. The building could hold about a thousand spectators, with admission later fixed at a penny for the cheap places and twice as much for the upper galleries. Both bulls and bears were baited by mastiffs in this building until 1570, when a second circus was constructed in an adjoining field and the bullfights were transferred there, leaving the bears in the older ring. And so they continued until suppressed by the Long Parliament in 1642, leaving behind a folk memory of the British bulldog as the embodiment of indomitable patriotism.

Queen Elizabeth herself seems to have been an enthusiast for animal contests. On 25 April 1559, for example, she entertained the French ambassador with bull- and bear-baiting by English dogs in Whitehall, and the ambassador followed this with a trip to Paris Garden for more of the same the next day. She put on a similar show for the Danish ambassador in Greenwich Park in 1586, and visited Paris Garden herself as late as 1599. King James organised a match between some champion dogs from the South Bank and one of the lions kept in the royal menagerie in the Tower. He wanted to see if the renowned English mastiffs deserved their reputation for bravery against the national beast of Scotland. The unsatisfactory contest ended in a draw with the lion perhaps winning on points. James then came up with the idea of a contest between a lion and a bear. Before a large crowd of dignitaries and the general public, the animals refused to fight each other, and the bear was led away in disgrace to be baited to death on a public stage some days later.

These royal combats were similar to the shows staged in the large stadia on the South Bank. At its peak, Paris Garden had a complement of some 70 mastiffs, 20 bears, and (for variety) three bulls. The bear would be tied to a stake in the middle of the ring. A group of some half-dozen mastiffs would be loosed on the bear; dogs slain or mutilated would be replaced by fresh dogs until they brought the bear down (at which point a new bear would be produced) or until none could be found to challenge him. Usually the wounded bear would be tended back to health: it was rare for the dogs to kill their prey outright. Sometimes there would be a novel touch, such as a blinded bear, or perhaps the day's festivities would conclude with the dogs set on a horse (running free) bearing an ape upon its back—a program might refer to "Pleasant sport with the horse and ape" as the comic conclusion of the day's entertainment.

We have some firsthand descriptions of bear- and bull-baiting from foreign travelers, who expressed amazement at what they witnessed. Paul Hentzner, for instance, was a dutiful tourist who "did" London in 1598, taking in all the famous public sights, such as St. Paul's, the Royal Exchange, and the Tower, and gaining access to the queen's presence chamber at Greenwich. A highlight of his trip was an excursion to the bankside, where he saw a venue "built in the form of a theatre," and described what he saw happen to the bears:

> they are fastened behind, and then worried by great English bull-dogs, but not without great risque to the dogs . . . it sometimes happens that they are killed on the spot. . . . To this entertainment, there often follows that of whipping a blinded bear, which is performed by five or six men, standing circularly with whips, which they exercise upon him without any mercy, as he cannot escape from them because of his chain; he defends himself with all his force and skill, throwing down all who come within his reach, and are not active enough to get out of it, and tearing the whips out of their hands, and breaking them.[13]

The shows on the Bankside attracted large numbers: when full, these stadia would have held about 1 percent of the entire population of London. Their operation was a major enterprise that involved the construction of substantial buildings, creation of facilities for the animals and the garden staff, as well as dealing with—assembling, feeding, diverting, dispersing, and controlling—considerable crowds.

The civic authorities were understandably anxious to exercise a measure of control over these businesses, but the results were mixed. In a note from the lord mayor to Lord Burghley in January 1583, the harassed official reports to the Privy Council on a disastrous collapse of part of the stadium, "a great mishap at Paris Garden, where by ruin of all the scaffold at once yesterday a great number of people are some presently slain, and some maimed and grievously hurt." As far as the Lord Mayor was concerned, the explanation for the event was obvious. It had taken place on a Sunday, and therefore, he went on, "giveth occasion to acknowledge the hand of God for such abuse of the Sabbath day, and moveth me in conscience to beseech your Lordship to give order for redress of such contempt of God's service." Burghley's smooth reply was that he would undertake to "treat with my Lords of the Council" and investigate the possibility of finding "some other day within the week meeter for bearbaitings and such like worldly pastimes" (Chambers 1923, 2: 462).

This exchange exemplifies the abiding hostility between the city and the thriving Elizabethan "entertainment industry" as well as its sponsors and supporters in the court. In addition, the vogue for bear-baiting opens a window onto a world in which the English were not, as later generations have been, renowned as animal lovers, where a regular holiday pastime was to visit the Bethlehem Hospital (known as Bedlam) for the insane and to laugh at the merry antics of the wretched inmates. And the story of these strange sports is wrapped up with the story of Shakespeare's career, and with the history of the London theaters. For when theaters came to be built on the South Bank, their size, design, and organization were strikingly similar to those of the bear gardens, so similar that at least one contemporary illustration mistakenly labeled the Globe as "The Bear Garden."[14] Such confusion of theatrical and animal-baiting enterprises is hardly surprising, given their many close connections.[15]

Shakespeare's London Residences

We do not know where Shakespeare lived when he first moved to London at some time in the late 1580s. The likelihood must be that he lived reasonably close to the playhouse known as the Theatre, and that he stayed either with other actors or with people he knew through his family and their acquaintances in Stratford.

By the mid-1590s the records show that Shakespeare had become a householder (Schoenbaum 1977, 220–23). All property was regularly assessed for the purpose of taxation. Thus, if the property was valued at

£10, and Parliament then voted a subsidy to the crown of 2 shillings on the pound, the taxpayer would be liable to pay 20 shillings—that is, £1. This was a tax that required a considerable effort to collect, and local officials had to render accounts at the end of the year. On 15 November 1597 the collectors of Bishopsgate ward made a list, parish by parish, of nonpayers. The list included people who had died, had left the district, or had hidden their assets, as well as those who had simply failed to pay. Under St. Helen's Parish we find that "William Shakespeare," assessed for £5, still owed the second installment of 5 shillings. What does this record tell us? It suggests that Shakespeare had paid the first installment and shows that he was not one of the powerful men in the district: 73 property owners are listed, starting with Sir John Spencer, whose mansion was valued at £300. Shakespeare's name is very low down on the list.

The parish of St. Helen's is near the present site of the Bank of England. It was then tucked inside the city wall, with Bishopsgate Street as the main northerly thoroughfare. The parish was quite prosperous and housed one mansion, Crosby Place, where Sir John Spencer lived. There were several water conduits provided by public-spirited merchants, as well as "divers fair and large built houses for merchants, and such like . . . many fair tenements, divers fair inns, large for receipt of travelers, and some houses for men of worship."[16] The center of the parish, of course, was the church, in which were handsome monuments to the wealthy parishioners, as well as a group of almshouses. The parish was part of the Bishopsgate ward, which was somewhat less exclusive than this comfortable enclave. As Shakespeare walked north out of the city gate toward the Theatre he would have seen less edifying sights, notably the squalor of the town ditch and the chained inmates of Bethlehem Hospital.

A further tax subsidy of late 1597 shows that Shakespeare was assessed for the whole amount of 13 shillings and 4 pence on a property valued at £5. The following year his name appears on a list of defaulters again, but this time the officials explain that he owns no property within the parish. The name appears in a document of 6 October, where Shakespeare is said to be living in Surrey. Then on 6 October 1600 the debt is again recorded, and this time referred to the Bishop of Winchester to pursue. The bishop, whose London palace was on the bankside near the Globe theater, was responsible for the territory known as the Liberty of the Clink in Southwark. We can then assume that

Shakespeare was a resident of this new suburb, and that he paid up what must have been a trivial sum to a man of his wealth: certainly his name disappears from lists of defaulters after this time. The records indicate, then, that Shakespeare lived in the mid-1590s within easy walking distance of his work in the two northern theaters. Then, at some point after the winter of 1596–97 and no later than the autumn of 1599, he moved across the river to the Liberty of the Clink, less than a five-minute walk from the newly constructed Globe.[17]

Two other London addresses are associated with Shakespeare. One gives us a chance to hear a little of his voice preserved in the documents of a lawsuit. Around 1604 he lived in rooms in a house owned by the Huguenot Christopher Mountjoy, at the corner of Silver and Monkswell streets in Cripplegate. We know this from the records of a court case brought in 1612, in which Mountjoy's son-in-law, Stephen Belott, sued the old man for failing to honor the terms of his marriage agreement. Shakespeare was asked to testify because he had played the role of go-between at the time of the wedding. He was present at a hearing on 11 May 1612 but missed the second hearing on 19 June—presumably because he was in Stratford.

Several witnesses recalled Shakespeare's involvement. Joan Johnson, a servant, stated, "As she remembereth, the defendant [Mountjoy] did send and persuade one Mr Shakespeare that lay in the house to persuade the plaintiff [Belott] to the same marriage." A family friend, Daniell Nicholas, reported a conversation with Shakespeare. The court noted, "Shakespeare told this deponent [Nicholas] that the defendant [Mountjoy] told him that if the plaintiff [Belott] would marry the said Mary . . . he would give him . . . a sum of money with her for a portion in marriage with her. . . . Shakespeare had told them that they should have a sum of money for a portion from the father, they were made sure by Mr Shakespeare by giving their consent, and agreed to marry."

"They were made sure by Mr Shakespeare"—but for how much? The young man expected £60 plus an inheritance of £200. Instead he got £10 and some household goods. For years the young man wrangled with his father-in-law, eventually moving out and leaving the old man to drunkenness and other excesses. When it was rumored he was going to cut the young couple out of his will, they brought him to court. Shakespeare's testimony was vital. The court report states that "he [Shakespeare] did know the complainant [Belott] when he was a servant with the defendant [Mountjoy] . . . during the time of his service,

[Belott] to this deponent's knowledge did well and honestly behave himself. . . . [T]his deponent sayeth that he verily thinketh that the . . . complainant was a very good and industrious servant in the said service."

On the central question of the marriage settlement Shakespeare could give only a partial answer: his memory seems to have failed him. The report says,

> This deponent saith that the defendant promised to give the said complainant a portion in marriage with Mary his daughter, but what certain portion he remembereth not, nor when to be paid, nor knoweth that the defendant promised the plaintiff two hundred pounds with his daughter mary at the time of his decease. But sayeth that the plaintiff was dwelling with the defendant at his house, and they had amongst themselves many conferences about their marriage which afterwards was consummated and solemnised. And more he cannot depose.

Most of the other witnesses had similarly imperfect recollections of the details of the settlement. The case was referred to authorities of the French church in London; Belott and Mountjoy were reprimanded, but they awarded a small sum of 20 nobles (a noble was worth 6 shillings and 8 pence—a third of a pound) to the younger man.[18]

A few months after the Belott/Mountjoy case, in March 1613, Shakespeare bought (from Henry Walker, "citizen and minstrel of London") a house in the Blackfriars complex, near to the Second Blackfriars theater and close to the pier at Puddle Wharf, from which he could cross the river to the bankside. It is not certain that he ever lived there, although he could hardly have chosen a more central or fashionable city address. The property included the former gatehouse of the pre-Reformation prior's lodgings. In Elizabeth's time, the area had been a nest of dissidents, mainly disaffected Catholics, who had made use of the maze of apartments and cellars to conceal themselves. Shakespeare bought the gatehouse, along with a patch of land enclosed on two sides by fences and the other by an old brick wall. It had been leased out for 25 years in 1604 to a haberdasher, William Ireland (Chambers 1930, 2: 154–69). Ireland's name is preserved in the present-day Ireland Yard, which must be just south of the site of Shakespeare's gatehouse.

Shakespeare had three partners in the deal: William Johnson, landlord of the Mermaid Tavern; John Jackson; and John Heminges, his colleague from the King's Men.[19] These friends were evidently to act as trustees for Shakespeare, who is described in the papers as living in

Stratford. He put up all the money—the total was to be £140, of which £80 would be paid in cash. On the following day the property was mortgaged back to Walker for £60, the remainder of the original price. This was a common arrangement at the time, and it gave the purchaser a fixed time to come up with the rest of the price—in this case until the following 29 September. After Ireland's lease was surrendered, a tenant, John Robinson, was installed. As we saw earlier, a consequence of this method of purchase and administration was that Anne Shakespeare was not entitled to the usual widow's portion in respect of this property on Shakespeare's death.

The experience of living and working in the metropolis is crucial to Shakespeare's writing. The very popularity and continued success of the public theater, which had no counterpart anywhere else in Europe and which nourished and sustained Shakespeare's art, was a social phenomenon intimately bound up with the nature of the city where he lived and worked.

Chapter Five

The Theater

Origins

Purpose-built theaters were a striking novelty in Renaissance England and were recognized as such at the time.[1] The decision to build such structures grew out of a complex set of circumstances. There had been a long tradition of staging plays and interludes in the halls of great houses or of schools and colleges, and for many years troupes of players—often bearing the badge of some noble or gentleman—had performed in the yards of inns and other improvised, temporary settings. This state of affairs was changed in 1572 by two acts of Parliament.

In the first, in January of that year, the queen referred to "the unlaw-ful retaining of multitudes of unordinary servants by liveries, badges, and other signs and tokens (contrary to the good and ancient statutes and laws of this realm)." The consequence of the existence of such groups of retainers, the Act argued, was "stirring up and nourishing of factions, riots, and unlawful assemblies (the mothers of rebellion) besides such other great inconveniences that already are seen and more likely daily to follow if speedy remedy be not provided" (Chambers 1923, 4: 268). Severe penalties were available to those charged with enforcing this law—a characteristic Tudor attempt to curb the power of local grandees and to bring the nation under more effective and cen-tralized control.

The second statute was of more immediate relevance to players and sought to deal with some of the consequences of disbanding the provin-cial households. Its effect on subsequent theater history was profound. The "Acte for the punishment of Vacabondes" was a measure that would quickly result in the disappearance of the strolling player and the even-tual creation of large, professional repertory companies based in purpose-built theaters, performing before audiences numbering in the thousands, and ultimately enjoying the personal support of the monarch. The 1572 act specified that every company of players had either to be under the patronage of one noble of the rank of baron or above or, alternatively, authorized by two senior justices of the peace of the county in which they wished to perform:

> All and every person and persons being whole and mighty in body and able to labour, having not land or master, nor using any lawful merchandize, craft or mystery [i.e. trade or profession] whereby he or she might get his or her living; & all fencers, bear-wards, common players in interludes, & minstrels, not belonging to any Baron of this realm or towards any other personage of greater degree; all jugglers, peddlers, tinkers, and petty chapmen; which said fencers, bear-wards, common players in interludes, minstrels, jugglers, peddlers, tinkers, and petty chapmen, shall wander abroad and not have licence of two Justices of the Peace, . . . shall be taken, adjudged, and deemed rogues, vagabonds, and sturdy beggars. (Chambers 1923, 4: 270)

Transgression carried severe penalties. Unless someone of good standing in the community came forward with an offer of a year's work for the vagabond, a "sturdy beggar" would be "grievously whipped" and then "burned through the gristle of the right ear with a hot iron of the compass of an inch about." A second conviction would lead to two years of enforced work in the household of some respectable individual; a third conviction condemned the vagabond to death as a felon, with consequent confiscation of lands and goods.

So an actor in 1572 faced a future that was, to say the least, uncertain. If he joined the household of a nobleman he might find himself penalized under the statute limiting numbers of retainers. If he tried to ply his trade as a freelance, outside the law, he would operate under constant threat of horrifying punishments. Nobles faced a problem, too. They had to be able to demonstrate that their large households represented no threat to the central authority; merely reclassifying their henchmen as servant-actors would fool nobody. If they claimed to be supporting a company of actors, it was now necessary to show that they could act (Kay 1992, 89–90).

From 1572 on the business of playing took place under the protective shield of noble patronage. Commercial considerations soon became significant. As the companies developed, they grew into quite substantial businesses. The usual organization involved a central group of shareholders (maybe a dozen, where traveling companies had had half that number) who determined policy; they were supported by a group of hired employees.[2] More crucially, they tended to work with a proprietor or impresario, who could furnish them with cash in advance in return for a share of the takings, and who could provide a venue. Companies who could find work in London fought to remain in business there. That was where the largest audiences could be found and where actors, technicians, and writers were in abundance. The building of permanent theaters along with the new legal developments created the theatrical environment Shakespeare met on his arrival in London.

To start with, the playing spaces in inn yards were developed into more permanent structures. From the 1560s on there are records of performances at such inns as the Bel Savage on Ludgate Hill, the Cross Keys and the Bell on Gracechurch Street, the Bull on Bishopsgate Street, and Red Lion and Boar's Head in Whitechapel. But it was only a matter of time before James Burbage conceived of a purpose-built theater. He brought with him a useful combination of talents and experience; a carpenter and joiner by trade, Burbage had become a player in the Earl of Leicester's troupe and had also developed an eye for business opportunities. As early as 1572 he wrote to Leicester to request patronage and protection. In the letter he reminds Leicester of the statute limiting numbers of retainers. Then he proceeds,

> We therefore, your humble servants and daily orators your players, for avoiding all inconvenience that may grow by reason of the said statute, are bold to trouble your Lordship with this our suit, humbly desiring your honour that (as you have always been our good Lord and Master) you will now vouchsafe to retain us at this present as your household servants and daily waiters, not that we mean to crave any further stipend or benefit at your Lordship's hands but our liveries as we have had, and also your honour's licence to certify that we are your household servants when we shall have occasion to travel amongst our friends as we do usually once a year, and as other noblemen's players do and have done in time past, whereby we may enjoy our faculty in your Lordship's name as we have done heretofore. (Chambers 1923, 2: 86; Gurr 1981, 30)

Burbage is not looking for money or work, but rather for the protection of Leicester's name—a kind of sponsorship, through which Leicester's status as a great lord will be enhanced by the magnificence and skill of these men who wear his livery. The commercial value of Leicester's endorsement was lessened two years later. In a patent of 10 May 1574, protection was granted from an even higher authority—the queen herself. She wrote,

Know ye that we of our especial grace, certain knowledge, and mere motion have licensed and authorised, and by these presents do license and authorise, our loving subjects, James Burbage, John Perkyn, John Lanham, William Johnson, and Robert Wilson, servants to our trusty and well-beloved cousin and counsellor the Earl of Leicester, to use, exercise, and occupy the art and faculty of playing comedies, tragedies, interludes, stage plays, and such other like as they have already used and studied, or hereafter shall use and study, as well for the recreation of our loving subjects, as for our solace and pleasure when we shall think good to see them, as also to use and occupy all such instruments as they have already practiced, or hereafter shall practice, for and during our pleasure. And the said comedies, tragedies, interludes, and stage plays, together with their music, to show, publish, exercise, and occupy to their best commodity during all the term aforesaid, as well within our City of London and liberties of the same, as also within the liberties and freedoms of any of our cities, towns, boroughs &c whatsoever as without the same, throughout our Realm of England. Willing and commanding you and every of you, as ye tender our pleasure, to permit and suffer them herein without any your lets, hindrance, or molestation during the term aforesaid, any act, statute, proclamation, or commandment heretofore made, or heareafter to be made, to the contrary notwithstanding. Provided that the said comedies, tragedies, interludes, and stage plays be by the Master of our Revels for the time being before seen & allowed, and that the same be not published or shown in the time of common prayer, or in the time of great and common plague in our said City of London. (Chambers 1923, 2: 87–88; Gurr 1981, 30–31)

The possession of this warrant was a valuable and powerful defense against the hostility with which playing was viewed by the authorities in many cities, most notably London. Its guarantees encouraged the company to seek a permanent home and made it appear attractive to potential investors. In Burbage's phrase, a permanent theater would give rise to "continual great profit." But now, with the patronage of the greatest nobleman of the kingdom, and the explicit protection of the monarch herself, the scale of the enterprise, and of the investment needed, were set to expand. Burbage borrowed from his brother-in-law John Brayne and took out a lease on a site in the Liberty of Halliwell (or Holywell), part of the parish of St. Leonard's, Shoreditch, in the fields just outside Bishopsgate. The land in this northern suburb—close to the modern Liverpool Street Station—had once formed part of a Benedictine priory. Its southern boundary was marked by the lane known to this day as Holywell Street. The former monastic buildings were not in good repair, and the eponymous Holy Well had come down in the world to serve as a source for a horse pond. The site Burbage leased for his building was probably just to the east of present-day Curtain Street. Construction work began after the lease was granted on Lady Day 1576.

Burbage's choice of a site outside the city walls is important: it connects play-acting with bear-baiting as an activity that could be tolerated only on the margins of the city. Civic authorities could console themselves that this godless pursuit with its popular support and aristocratic patronage could be confined to a licensed space given over to recreation and sport. But Burbage could be confident that spectators would come, even if they had to tramp across the open fields to get to the show. At least one contemporary referred to the "great press," a "concourse of unruly people," streaming out of the city to see the plays.[3]

The building, to which Burbage gave the grand classical name of The Theatre, was in all probability an amphitheater, constructed largely of wood, though with ironwork in some places. There was a tiring house for the players to dress in, and there were galleries, at least one of which offered the spectators the luxury of seats and privacy. Admission to the building cost a penny, with an extra penny or twopence payable for transfer to the galleries: these sums were collected by gatherers and placed in locked boxes that would be opened and the cash shared out after the performance. The players would have shared the entrance pennies among themselves, while the proprietors, Burbage and Brayne, took the gallery money.

The success of the Theatre is attested by the prompt appearance of a second playhouse just 200 yards closer to the city walls, on the other side of Holywell Lane. This building was called the Curtain, since it was in Curtain Close, and opened its doors to the paying public in the latter part of 1577, just a few months after the first performances at Burbage's house. The Curtain was built by Henry Lanman (or Laneham), who seems to have enjoyed a close business relationship with Burbage and his associates, with the Curtain serving as an "easer" for the Theatre and with profits being pooled between the two sets of proprietors: Laneham's house also staged nondramatic shows such as fencing exhibitions. The presence of these two thriving theaters at the very gates of the city was predictably distressing to puritan preachers: as early as November 1577 Thomas White urged his congregation to "behold the sumptuous theatre houses, a continual monument of London's prodigality and folly" (quoted in Chambers 1923, 4: 197; Schoenbaum 1977, 133).

These playhouses were facilities dedicated to the industrialization—even the mass production—of entertainment. Before their construction theatrical shows had been arranged on a one-time basis, made to order, whether in court or in some country town where the actors were obliged to carve out a space for themselves to perform in, passing the hat around for money. Although the new playhouses staged the same material as the earlier shows, every step in the process was suddenly better organized and coordinated: actors became more numerous, more competent, better dressed, and better rehearsed; the stages developed new resources, the potential for more elaborate effects.

The Public Playhouses

The public theaters were pulled down at the outset of the Civil War in 1642, and the playing spaces at the court and at Blackfriars were then long gone. In the absence of much hard evidence, there has been a great deal of speculation as to the physical qualities of the venues for which Shakespeare wrote. The sources for the debates include maps and panoramic views (notably those by Ralph Agas [ca. 1570], John Noorden [1600], C. J. Visscher [1616], and Wenceslas Hollar [1647]), builders' contracts for the Fortune (1600) and the Hope (1613), descriptions by travelers and references in legal and administrative documents, stage directions and references within individual scripts, and the famous sketch—originally by Johannes De Witt—of the interior of the Swan in about 1596.[4] The excavation of the site of the Rose theater in the late 1980s provided some important clues to the nature of that building and, more generally, to the qualities of the other public playhouses. De Witt, who visited London in 1596, categorized the four theaters he saw (Theatre, Curtain, Rose, Swan) as "*amphitheatra*" (Chambers 1923, 2: 362). To his eye, the finest was the Swan, although the Globe (1599) and the Fortune (1600) would shortly eclipse it in splendor. Both disapproving Puritans and awestruck tourists commented on the opulence and magnificence of the buildings.

The first public playhouses were built outside the jurisdiction of the city authorities. The first was the Red Lion, built in Stepney to the east of the city by John Brayne. The Red Lion had a large stage and galleries for the audience. As I have noted, Brayne and his brother-in-Law James Burbage then built the Theatre in 1576, followed by the Curtain (1577) to the north of the city walls. The fourth playhouse was built at

Newington, some distance south of the river, and the fifth was the Rose, which went up on the Bankside in 1587. As I have noted, there had been venues for bull- and bear-baiting on the bankside for a number of years. The Swan was built in that area in 1596. By that time, then, theatrical activity was concentrated in two areas: the bankside and the northern suburb of Shoreditch. The Bankside, like Shoreditch, was outside the city limits and closer to the majority of the population, as well as a recreational area reasonably well equipped to transport and amuse large crowds.

The amphitheater stages all seem to have been similar, although not identical. They were all large, many-sided structures, in which a stage platform was thrust out into an area partly exposed to the elements.[5] The stage itself had a roof, supported by a number of pillars. The building was mainly of wood, perhaps with some flint used in the walls. Some had thatched roofs, others tiled roofs. The design, which reminded some observers of the amphitheaters of the ancient world, were more prosaically developments of the inn-yard theaters and of animal-baiting venues. Several of the public theaters (the Swan and the Hope, for example) had stages that could be removed so that the whole arena could be used for nontheatrical entertainments.

Estimates of the number of spectators vary, but the larger buldings could probably accommodate between 2,000 and 3,000 people. The audience could stand in the arena close to the stage or pay extra for seating in the galleries. In some theaters there were "lords' rooms"—more exclusive and expensive private accommodation. It is also possible that elite spectators could be provided with seats on the stage itself. The facilities available for the audience were intially very basic, although there was an improvement with each new venue. The diary of theater investor Philip Henslowe records his attempts to make the galleries more comfortable (by plastering the walls) and to provide some more space for the actors by expanding the dressing room or "tiring-house."[6]

The interiors of the playhouses became progressively grander and more elaborate, especially the area of the stage. Judging by the famous drawing of the Swan, the supporting Corinthian pillars on the stage were expertly carved. The specifications for the design of the Fortune theater (reproduced in Gurr 1981, 126–29) call for the major beams in the structure to be carved to resemble classical orders of architecture and decorated with mythological creatures. As well as being splendid, the space was also invested with some symbolic significance. Thus the cover that projected over the stage was painted on its underside with stars, planets, the sun, the moon, and other heavenly bodies: it was known as "the heavens." The hollow space underneath the stage was jokingly referred to as "hell": it was from this zone, of course, that the ghost of Hamlet's father would call out, and where Malvolio would be imprisoned in *Twelfth Night* and complain that his lodging was as dark "as hell" (4.2.35). The physical dimensions of the stages have not been established.

Little is known for certain about the arrangements at the rear of the stage and about the dimensions and facilities in the tiring house. The Swan seems to have had two doors, which perhaps recalled the doors in the halls of colleges and the Inns of Court as well as private houses where plays were staged. The Globe and Fortune, however, had three doors set in a finely carved wall. The central door may only have given onto a small "discovery space" or inner room ("*Here Prospero discovers* Ferdinand *and* Miranda *playing at chess*" [*The Tempest*, 5.1.171]). Research indicates that at the polygonal Rose the inner wall constituted the rear of the stage.

The De Witt drawing suggests that the Swan had a gallery above the stage. If this was common practice, the location could have been used for both the most expensive private chambers and the musicians. Space there could also have been used to provide locations for some of the action. Numerous stage directions in Shakespeare's plays require actors to be "aloft" or "above." From the gallery, which overhung the stage, curtains could be suspended. It seems that tapestries were sometimes used, and that black hangings could be used for tragedies.[7] Actors could hide behind this material and could be revealed behind it. There has been much debate on the question of windows ("*Enter Romeo and Juliet at the window*" [*Romeo and Juliet*, 3.5]). If real rather than imaginary windows were specified, the obvious windows to use would be those of the tiring house that faced the center of the arena. On the other hand, the galleries at the rear of the stage were used to represent a variety of locations and could easily have been deemed windows.

It is important to remember that these theaters were open to the elements. Every new design seems to have decreased the degree of exposure (Foakes 1990, 23), but it was always necessary to make intelligent use of natural light (with the stages usually facing northeast). When the Globe was rebuilt in 1613 the roofed area was substantially expanded, and the structure overhanging the stage had two substantial gables.

Theatrical conventions underwent change throughout the period.[8] The older fashion for stations or "houses" on stage, used by John Lyly and George Peele, as well as by Shakespeare in *Henry VI* and *Richard III*, gave way to an apparently more free-flowing style, where the stage space could be held to represent any location and in which action could—as in, for example, *Antony and Cleopatra*—roam across the known world.

Some evidence attests to the splendor of the shows on these public stages. At the simple level of costume, the actors were often given castoffs from the fashionable wardrobes of courtiers. They also, of course, were trained to ape the speech and behavior, the styles in fencing and dancing, that were currently fashionable in the court. Thus the audience could see in their midst, close at hand, costume and manners from which they were normally kept distant. And the companies invested substantial quantities of their own money on costumes as well. *Henslowe's Diary* records regular payments for lavish costumes, and the overall impression must have been one of opulence, with garments in bright colors, trimmed with gold or silver. When John Alleyn sold off property belonging to his brother, the great actor Edward Alleyn, the inventory (dating from 1598–99) includes cloaks and doublets and hose in satin and velvet, trimmed in gold, silver, and fur.[9]

As far as properties are concerned, *Henslowe's Diary* provides the most famous illustration of what a proprietor would have in stock. At the Rose in March 1598 there were, for instance, a rock, a cage, a tomb, Hell's mouth, "the city of Rome," old Mahomet's head, one bay tree, a golden fleece, a stable, a Pope's mitre, a cauldron (for Marlowe's *The Jew of Malta*), a black dog, a lion skin, a bear skin, two steeples, and a beacon.[10]

Tapestries and painted cloths (Henslowe had "the cloth of the sun and moon") could be hung up at the back of the stage to set a scene, and black cloth, as previously noted, could be draped over the set to frame a tragedy. Beyond that, the relatively open stage could be defined by what the speakers were made to say. Thus Shakespeare has moments like "This is Illyria, lady," "I am a stranger here in Gloucestershire," and "Well, this is the forest of Arden."

Blackfriars

In 1596, at the height of a dispute with his landlord, Burbage acquired a potential theatrical venue in the Blackfriars complex, a range of former monastic buildings that, though physically within the city walls, was not subject to the city's jurisdiction. His attempt to develop the site was blocked, partly by local residents who complained about his proposal to a sympathetic Privy Council (Gurr 1981, 144). There had already been a successful theater at Blackfriars, and the plays of Lyly and Peele had been performed there. It was indoors, requiring artificial light, and quite small (a rectangular space of just 46 by 26 feet).[11] Plays were performed by boys' companies between 1577 and 1584 (Foakes 1990, 25).

The success of Paul's boys led Henry Evans to take a lease on Burbage's property in 1600, and his company was instantly established as a rival to the professional troupes. The theater in which he produced his plays—the so-called Second Blackfriars—was to be acquired by the King's Men in 1609 as a winter venue, when the Globe was unusable.

This new theater was twice the size of its predecessor, measuring 46 by 66 feet. There was accommodation, including two galleries of seats, for up to 500 spectators. The dimensions of the stage were less than those at the Globe, which had a stage 40 feet wide and thrust deep into the center of the arena. The Blackfriars stage may have occupied most of the short side, with the tiring house extending the width of the chamber. At stage level it was flanked by lord's rooms, and the space was much less deep. Gallants could sit on the stage—a practice that led to disputes, especially when the gallants wore fashionably large feathers in their hats and engaged in the conspicuous consumption of tobacco during the performance. Artificial light was used, usually in the form of candles (Gurr 1981, 26–31).

The Players

Before 1594

The early 1580s had seen the proliferation of dramatic companies (Gurr 1981, 30–34). Although Leicester's Men seems to have been the dominant group, and the one with a permanent home, settled membership and apparently secure patronage, it had plenty of rivals. The records speak of numerous other companies (Essex's, Oxford's, Sussex's, Warwick's). Their normal practice was to tour the provinces in the summer and to play in the capital at other times if they could be commissioned to do so. So the number and frequency of London performances increased, as did the vehemency of complaints from the city authorities. In time Sir Francis Walsingham intervened. He asked the master of the revels to cull out the best actors from the various troupes and form a company that would operate under the patronage of Queen Elizabeth herself. Thus did the Queen's Men come into being.

For the five years from 1583 to 1588 the Queen's Men were without dispute the leading company. And they dominated court performances at the holiday seasons for two more years until 1590–91. Their dominance was hardly surprising in view of their annexation of the leading talents of the day (at least three of the stars of Leicester's Men—Wilson, Laneham, and Johnson, for instance—were recruited) and in the light of the regulations by which they operated. Unlike the great troupes that would dominate theatrical activity in the 1590s, however, they were not a company of business partners, shareholders bound together by a common material interest. Nor did they have a permanent London base: they played at several different theaters.

Still, they had a very privileged position. Their names were registered with the authorities, and they had to undertake not to perform except as members of the queen's troupe. They alone were authorized to play within the confines of the city, in private houses or in other places where admission was not open to the public. They could put on public shows on any days, except on Sundays, and not before evening prayer on holy days (and their gates were to remain shut until evening prayer was ended). The times of performance (even on holy days) were to be so arranged that the entire audience could get home before nightfall. After an outbreak of plague they had to wait until the weekly death toll from the pestilence had been below 50 for three weeks. Apart from that—and apart from the threat that a single transgression was to be sufficient to annul the license—they were free agents.

The company's repertoire was distinctly contemporary, including the comedies of Robert Greene and George Peele, and a number of pieces treating the newly fashionable topic of English history. But their chief attraction was the archetypal Elizabethan clown, Richard Tarleton, the model for all other clowns, and probably the most famous theatrical performer of his day. His gifts included the ability to extemporize jokes, songs, and other diversions in response to promptings from the audience. One of his typical tricks was to deflate serious action on stage by poking his head out from behind a curtain or pillar. After his death in 1588 the fortunes of his company declined. He was meanwhile immortalized in a book called *Tarlton's Jests*, a compilation of anecdotes in which he—or at least his stage persona—is the leading actor.

Despite the preeminence of the Queen's Men, other companies continued to operate in the provinces and outside the walls of London, although their membership seems to have been fluid. Touring was a major factor in encouraging movement between companies—and at times in precipitating the breakup of particular troupes. Touring bands were inevitably much smaller than London companies and were also less well paid. In Henslowe's papers we can see that he paid hired men 5 shillings per week on tour as against 10 shillings per week in London (Gurr 1981, 39–40): any hired man offered London work while his fellows went on tour was likely to stay where the money was.

The company created by the amalgamation of the Admiral's Men with Lord Strange's Men lasted from about 1590 to 1594, when Lord Strange (Ferdinando Stanley, fifth earl of Derby) died. After that they became the Admiral's Men. In the early 1590s they were built on the talents of a single powerful actor, Edward Alleyn. Even after the merger Alleyn retained his personal position as the servant of the Lord Admiral. For a half-dozen years up to 1589, Alleyn had been one of Worcester's Men, at which point he went into the service of the Lord Admiral, whose players were suppressed in 1590 in the aftermath of the Marprelate controversy. Possibly some of Lord Strange's Men also suffered for allowing themselves to become involved in the same religio-political squabbles. In any event, the combined troupe began to perform at James Burbage's playhouse, the Theatre, in 1590–91.

From one of their earliest surviving "plots"—the single sheet listing entrances, exits, cues, properties, and sound effects—we know that one of the actors in the company was the young man who would challenge and eventually surpass Alleyn: Richard Burbage, the son of James Burbage. And there were several others in the troupe whose paths were to cross Shakespeare's (actors such as John Holland and John Sincler, whose names survive in Shakespeare's texts). Then, in May 1591, a quarrel broke out between the players and the elder Burbage. The proprietor was accused of withholding money taken at the gate of the playhouse. Alleyn and his band left the Theatre (Gurr 1981, 38). They soon found new venues on the South Bank (the Rose and the theater at Newington) under the aegis of the rival promoter Philip Henslowe. Alleyn married Henslowe's daughter in 1592, and he began to be increasingly involved in the business side of the operation.

During the 1590s Alleyn played Orlando in Greene's *Orlando Furioso* (his personal copy of the script survives to this day in Dulwich) and starred as Marlowe's Doctor Faustus, Tamburlaine, and Barabas in *The Jew of Malta*, as well as other heroic roles. The company also performed Thomas Kyd's *The Spanish Tragedy*, Greene's comedy *Friar Bacon and Friar Bungay*, and a host of other popular successes.

The short-lived company known as Pembroke's Men has attracted much speculation from scholars over the years because of its shadowy connection with Shakespeare. The group probably came into being in 1591–92, around the time the combined Admiral's–Lord Strange's Men decamped from the elder Burbage (although some evidence indicates a slightly later date for their formation, in the plague summer of 1592 [Chambers 1923, 2: 130–31]). The company performed in Leicester in 1592 and made its only recorded court appearances during the holiday season of 1592–93 on St. Stephen's Day and on the Epiphany. They toured the country during the plague months of the summer, performing at York, Rye, Ludlow, Shrewsbury, Coventry, Bath, and Ipswich. By the end of September, however, Henslowe wrote in a letter that the dispirited band had drifted back disconsolately to London some six weeks before: he reports that their gate receipts had not been sufficient to cover their costs, and that they had been obliged to sell off their costumes to pay their bills (*Henslowe's Diary*, 7). So their revels were ended, and other properties were put on the market—notably those most valuable assets: their scripts. The company's name appears on the title pages of four very distinguished plays that were published immediately after its dissolution.

These four plays are Marlowe's *Edward II* (entered in the Stationers' Register as early as 6 July 1593) and the so-called bad Quarto of *The Taming of a Shrew*, *3 Henry VI* (entitled *The True Tragedy of Richard Duke of York*), and *Titus Andronicus*. It is likely that the company had also performed *2 Henry VI*, published as *The First Part of the Contention . . .* in 1594. These books have been constantly scrutinized over the centuries, since they may contain clues that might help us to piece together the events of Shakespeare's early years in the theater, the chronology of his plays, and his plays' relation to the acting companies. The qualities of the volumes are held by some scholars to indicate that Pembroke's Men had reconstructed the scripts, essentially from memory, in order to sell them off. Examination suggests that these texts could have been performed by a small group of eleven men and four boys—by a touring troupe, in other words—and that such slimming down for traveling goes a long way toward accounting for the numerous discrepancies between these scripts and those later published officially. In other words, Pembroke's Men took on tour with them simplified and pared-down versions of plays that had been part of the repertoire of the larger London groups—groups with the human and material resources to stage them in their full splendor. A recently discovered will from an actor,

Simon Jewell, suggests that Pembroke's Men may have been a company set up specifically to tour when the catastrophic plague hit London in the summer of 1592 (Gurr 1981, 39).[12]

After 1594

After the plague and after the dispersal of the Queen's Men in May 1594, the theatrical business was streamlined. The relaunched Admiral's Men, under the leadership of Alleyn until his retirement, took up residence at the Rose, presided over by Philip Henslowe (Alleyn's father-in-law). The Chamberlain's Men, led by their chief tragic actor, Richard Burbage, and their star comedian, William Kempe (heir to Tarleton's crown), played a short season with the Admiral's Men at Henslowe's Newington Butts playhouse in the first half of June 1594 before moving north of the river to the elder Burbage's playhouse, the Theatre. Shakespeare was almost certainly a member of the troupe at the time. On 8 October the Lord Chamberlain asked the Lord Mayor of London to permit his newly formed company ("for the better exercise of their quality, and for the service of her Majesty if so need require") to rehearse and perform within the city precincts at the Cross Keys in Gracechuch Street. His letter goes on:

> These are to require and pray your Lordship (the time being such as, thanks be to God, there is now no danger of the sickness) to permit and suffer them so to do. The which I pray you the rather to do for that they have undertaken to me that, where heretofore they began not their plays till toward four o'clock, they will now begin at two, and have done between four and five, and will not use any drums or trumpets at all for the calling of the people together, and shall be contributories to the poor of the parish where they play, according to their abilities. (Chambers 1923, 4: 316)

Gracechurch Street would have given Shakespeare an even shorter walk to work from his house in St. Helen's than the Theatre had. The Cross Keys was an inn on the western side of Gracechurch Street: its yard had been adapted for theatrical use. There had been unauthorized performances there in the past, as in November 1589, when Lord Strange's Men were the subject of a complaint by the Lord Mayor to Burghley (Chambers 1930, 2: 305). In the same winter season the Chamberlain's Men performed at Court on 26 December and then had to adapt to yet another new venue—the Hall of Gray's Inn—for their contribution to the Christmas Revels on Holy Innocents' Day (28 December): Shakespeare's *Comedy of Errors*.

The following March the Chamberlain's Men performed for the queen at her Greenwich palace. The accounts of the royal household for 15 March record payments to "William Kempe William Shakespeare & Richarde Burbage seruantes to the Lord Chamberleyne" (Chambers 1930, 2: 319). Here at last Shakespeare can be linked to a particular performance with a known company, and his name appears sandwiched between two of the leading figures of the profession, which argues his own prominence. The other members of the company were veterans of the Admiral's–Lord Strange's merger.[13] Many of them (including, probably, Shakespeare, Henry Condell, Alexander Cooke, and Christopher Beeston) seem to have been in Pembroke's company after that, where they had been joined by men like John Holland, John Sinkler, and Nick Tooley.

Shakespeare was one of the "sharers" in the company—men who did not receive a wage but rather a share of the profits in return for putting up a share of the capital. By 1596, the Chamberlain's Men had eight sharers (Shakespeare, Burbage, Kempe, Bryan, Pope, Phillips, Sly, and Heminges). These men usually referred to each other as "Fellows": in his will Shakespeare would leave money to buy rings for "my Fellowes John Hemynge, Richard Burbage, & Henry Cundall." Bryan died in 1596 and Kempe in 1599, and Pope was terminally ill by 1603: their shares were taken over by Condell, Robert Armin, and Cowley. The number of sharers increased to 12 when the company became the King's Men in 1603.

In contrast with the fluidity of the theatrical world in the years leading up to the plague, the new circumstances were remarkably stable. With one or two notable exceptions, the following years were characterized by continuity, not least in the composition of the troupe.

Formation of the King's Men

Only 10 days after his arrival in London in 1603, King James instructed his principal secretary, Robert Cecil, to publish letters patent to appoint the Lord Chamberlain's Men the king's personal dramatic company. The document reads,

> Know ye that we of our Special grace, certain knowledge, and mere motion, have licensed and authorised . . . these our servants Lawrence Fletcher, William Shakespeare, Richard Burbage, Augustine Phillips,

John Hemings, Henry Condell, William Sly, Robert Armin, Richard
Cowley, and the rest of their Associates freely to use and exercise the art
and faculty of playing comedies, tragedies, histories, interludes, morals,
pastorals, stage-plays, and such others like as they have already studied or
heareafter shall use or study, as well for the recreation of our loving subjects, as for our solace and pleasure when we shall think good to see them,
during our pleasure. (Kay 1992, 290; Schoenbaum 1977, 250–51)[14]

The Lawrence Fletcher who heads the list of players is mysterious. He
disappears from the dramatic records of the company after 1605,
alhough he is known to have led a group of actors to Scotland at one
point: this has led to speculation that he might have been an intermedi-
ary between the troupe and the king (Chambers 1930, 2: 73–78). The
immediate consequences of the letter for Shakespeare and his fellows
were limited, since the theaters were closed owing to a severe outbreak
of plague. Nevertheless, the letters patent exhorted local authorities to
give a welcome to the company, and there are records of performances at
Bath, Coventry, Shrewsbury, and perhaps also at Oxford, Cambridge,
and Ipswich. In December they were summoned from their winter quar-
ters at Mortlake to play before the king and the Earl of Pembroke at
Wilton House. The announcement formally meant that Shakespeare and
his colleagues were members of the royal household, with the rank of
grooms of the chamber. Shakespeare's name appears at the head of a list
of players who received scarlet cloth from the royal wardrobe in order to
march, in the royal scarlet livery, in the king's processional entry into
London in May 1604 (Schoenbaum 1977, 250–52).

James's family was closely involved in dramatic patronage. The
Admiral's Men became Prince Henry's Men, and Worcester's Men
became Queen Anne's Men. But all the evidence attests to the supremacy of the King's Men. During the last years of Elizabeth's reign, they had
performed at court on an average of three occasions per year. After
James's accession, the picture changes markedly. In the first 10 years of
the king's reign (i.e., the final decade of Shakespeare's career) the troupe
played at court a dozen or more times every year—substantially more
than all the other companies put together. In Shakespeare's final two
seasons, 1611–12 and 1612–13, they gave some 20 court performances
(Chambers 1930, 2: 341–44). Shakespeare was now without question
the writer whose works were most frequently and regularly performed.
In 1604–1605, for instance, the King's Men appeared on eleven occasions, seven of them to perform plays by Shakespeare (*Love's Labour's
Lost, The Comedy of Errors, The Merry Wives of Windsor, The Merchant of*

Venice [twice], *Othello*, and *Measure for Measure*) (Chambers 1930, 2: 328–32). In the summer of 1604 they were attached to the household of the newly arrived Spanish ambassador, Velasco, for three weeks during the peace negotiations.

The implications of the stability that followed 1594—and that was confirmed and reinforced in 1603—are extremely important for Shakespeare's art.[15] Even as a freelance, of course, he would have been expected to tailor his writing to the preferences and acting styles of the companies who took on his scripts. But after 1594 and for the rest of his career he was in a position to write parts—perhaps to write all a play's parts—with specific actors in mind.[16]

The traditions from which they came encouraged versatility on the part of actors. Doubling was normal practice, especially on tour. John Sinkler played five parts in *The Seven Deadly Sins*, and no doubt his first years as a hired man for the Chamberlain's Men involved equally energetic work from him. From contemporary allusions, it appears that he was exceptionally thin, and writers (like John Webster in the Induction to *The Malcontent* [1604]) occasionally make jokes about his figure. Richard Cowley, Verges to Kempe's Dogberry in *Much Ado*, had played six parts in *The Seven Deadly Sins* and may have specialized in being a foil to clowns. Perhaps the most versatile member of the troupe was Augustine Phillips, judging by the array of musical instruments and costumes he left behind.

The most notable relationship was Shakespeare's with his chief actor, Richard Burbage, who was to achieve with Shakespeare's writing a status as tragic actor to equal Alleyn's. Of the two clowns for whom Shakespeare wrote, William Kempe was the more traditional: he saw himself as the heir of Tarleton, and like his master he was expert in the farcical "jig" with which shows often concluded. When he left the company early in 1599, it was to dance to Norwich, a stunt that made him the first "Nine-Days' Wonder." Yet he must also have been a considerable actor. His range included the conventional clowning of Peter in *Romeo and Juliet* and the more complex roles of Falstaff and Dogberry. His skills apparently developed in two different directions: one the impromptu exchange of repartee with an audience and a specialization in bogus, blustering authority figures. Robert Armin, who followed Kempe, was an author of note and evidently a more cerebral clown. He was to create Touchstone in *As You Like It*, Feste in *Twelfth Night*, and the Fool in *King Lear* (Kay 1992, 256–57).[17]

The evidence concerning acting styles is disappointingly slight.[18] The argument as to whether the actors in the boys' companies were men or marionettes continues.[19] It is, however, probably safe to assume they were necessarily "anti-mimetic," and that the audience was always aware of the fact that they were watching children imitate adults (Foakes 1990, 28–29). As far as the adult troupes are concerned, it is probably fair to speak of a movement from extreme formality of movement, speech, and gesture to a more "naturalistic" style—or at least a style that was praised for being lifelike, which is a very different thing. By the final years of the sixteenth century, a concept of "personation" had developed as an ideal of theatrical performance, and sophisticated critics of the time show signs of tiredness with a more "histrionic," broader style. In particular, the Lord Chamberlain's–King's Men acquired a special reputation for this more modern method. While a certain amount of swashbuckling was still in evidence at other theaters, the fare at the Globe was clearly of a different order. Burbage, in the role of Hamlet, instructed traveling players in the new style, telling them to avoid excess and to seek a "lively" truth in the performance. The anonymous author of an elegy on him wrote of his Hamlet (spelling modernized),

> oft have I seen him, play this part in jest,
> so lively, that Spectators, and the rest
> of his sad Crew, whilst he but seem'd to bleed,
> amazed, thought even then he died indeed.[20]

Censorship and Control

We have seen that the mainly Puritan civic authorities were generally opposed to the theater, and that the companies therefore had to perform outside the city's jurisdiction. They also had the benefit of support from leading courtiers. But this support was inseparable from ideas of service and control. In particular, the licensing function of the Revels Office (headed by the master of the revels) established the climate in which performances could occur and scripts could be published.[21]

The student of Shakespeare can see the Revels Office at work in an overt way in the case of *Thomas More*, a script in which Shakespeare may have had a hand.[22] Censorship and control tended to be erratic and unpredictable, and perhaps it was all the more effective for that.[23] Even after gaining approval from the Revels Office, a play could still fall foul of the higher authority of the Privy Council. Thus Jonson was interrogated about *Eastward Ho!*, *Sejanus*, and *The Magnetic Lady*; Daniel about *Philotas*; Middleton about *A Game at Chess*; and Shakespeare's company about *Richard II*. While plenty about the day-to-day operation of censorship remains obscure, most scholars have tended to agree with G. E. Bentley's observation: "The inhibitions which such knowledge provided are not difficult to imagine. They affected what the professional dramatist wrote for the companies; they affected what the managers and sharing members were willing to accept; and they affected what the book-keeper did to the MS as he worked on the prompt-copy."[24]

In recent years there has been considerable interest in these matters.[25] At the heart of the interest has been the question, Did the theater tend to reinforce established authority or to subvert it?[26] A way of expressing this is to consider a form such as tragedy. If an audience paid money to watch the humiliation and slaying of a monarch in a play, did that make them able, even if only subconsciously, to conceive of such an event actually happening?[27] Or did it, on the contrary, act as a safety valve, through which such events were safely contained in the unreal, recreational play space of the theater? The fact that prologues and epilogues of plays often make the latter point is relevant to this argument. But so is the elaborate machinery of censorship and control that was maintained throughout the period. And so too, of course, is the trial and execution of Charles I, referred to by Andrew Marvell in 1649 as the "Royall Actor."[28]

The Plague

As I have noted, London's theaters were regularly closed down as a public health measure in times of plague.[29] Major outbreaks occurred in 1593, 1603, 1610, 1625, 1630, and 1636–37, and theaters could be closed for many months (13 months in 1603–1604, for example). In his 1603 pamphlet *The Wonderful Year* Thomas Dekker describes the various remarkable events surrounding the death of Queen Elizabeth and the accession of King James. But then he turns to a matter more grievous and more urgent—the plague that was then raging in London: "A stiff and freezing horror sucks up the rivers of my blood. My hair stands on end with the panting of my brains. Mine eye-balls are ready to start out, being beaten with the billows of my tears. Out of my weeping pen does the ink mournfully and more bitterly than gall drop on the pale-faced paper even when I do but think how the bowels of my sick country have been torn out."[30]

Shakespeare's life, as I have noted, had begun under the shadow of the plague. In the summer of 1564 the borough authorities at Stratford-upon-Avon had done their best to alleviate suffering, to collect for the relief of the bereaved. They had taken rudimentary precautions, such as holding meetings of the council out of doors in order to reduce the risk of infection. But still the plague had numbered its victims in the hundreds. In London, throughout Shakespeare's life, the visitations of the plague were regular and on a scale that must have been almost beyond comprehension. Many weeks saw death tolls in excess of the total population of Stratford (more than 1,200 people). Even more devastating was the Great Plague of 1665, wherein on a single September day in a single part of London—Stepney—no fewer than 11,154 plague victims had to be buried.

The plague was a fact of life, and of death, in Renaissance London, as it was from the time of the Black Death in 1348 to the Great Plague in 1665–66. Thanks to the industry and assiduity of Tudor bureaucrats, sufficient evidence has survived, at least from the outbreak of 1563 on, to chart its impact on the city and the suburbs. It looks as though, with the exception of only a few brief periods (perhaps in the 1550s, or from 1616 to 1624 or 1650 to 1664) when there were hardly any deaths from the disease, its impact took one of two shapes. Either it struck in the form of a major epidemic, to be followed by a year of relatively few deaths (1563, 1593, 1603, 1625), or else it was restricted to a point where the normal mortality rate was increased by up to 20 percent.

Gradually a series of public health measures was formulated by the authorities to try to contain the spread of disease. These included isolation, quarantine, the establishment of plague hosptials ("pesthouses") and specialized medical teams (a plan realized in the 1630s), and the formation of groups of officials to monitor the regulations. From the point of view of the dramatic companies, the most significant restriction was that on public assembly. It was recognized—even if not adequately understood—that bubonic plague was highly contagious and spread when people were gathered together. So the theaters were shut down, along with most forms of public entertainment. Other assemblies were harder to control: funeral processions, for example, or congregations praying beside plague pits. What is more, plague victims and those fatally trapped with them in quarantine did not always go quietly. Pepys would later record that some such unfortunates in Westminster would lean out of their windows to "breathe in the faces of well people going by."

There were regulations limiting attendance at funerals to the immediate family, but some poor mothers with babes in arms would make a point of following the procession and standing by the open pit to show they did not fear the plague. And some preachers were determined to carry on with funerals despite official disapproval: they furnished a necessary and wholly understandable outlet for the city's grief—an opportunity for public mourning, for social and communal intercourse, while all around was suspicion, incarceration, silence, and death.

The plague that struck in 1592–93 was severe, although not quite as catastrophic as 1563 or 1603. By the time it ran its course it had claimed almost 11,000 lives out of a total population of some 125,000. It was also the first to establish a new pattern by being most severe in the poorest and most crowded areas—notably in the northeastern city parishes of St. Botolph, Aldgate, and St. Botolph, Bishopsgate, which Shakespeare would have known well since he seems to have lived in that part of the city for much of the 1590s.

Restraints against playing were published on 23 June 1592, when plays were suspended until Michaelmas because of the danger of plague, and also because of a fear of civil unrest—a fear stimulated by an affray of apprentices ("a great disorder & tumult") in Southwark a few days before (Chambers 1923, 4: 267). In such documents, especially those written by the city authorities (mostly reproduced in Chambers 1923, vol. 2), the language used blurs the distinctions between the two threats to the city: large assemblies are held to have spread the "contagion" of unruly behavior, or they are charged with having brought down the plague as a divine punishment (Gurr 1981, 76–77). In 1584, after all, the corporation of London had fired off a letter to the Privy Council attacking plays and players, in which they asserted, "To play in plaguetime is to increase the plague by infection: to play out of plague-time is to draw the plague by offendings of God upon occasion of such plays." Another preacher argued that "the cause of plagues is sin, if you look to it well; and the cause of sin are plays; therefore the cause of plagues are plays."[31] This time the prohibition stretched on and on. Michaelmas Term was deferred twice, and then transferred to Hertford. In January 1593 a new and stronger prohibition was published, forbidding "all manner of concourse and public meetings of the people at plays, bear-baitings, bowlings and other like assemblies for sports," and instructing local authorities to make sure "by special watch and observance" that no such gatherings ("preaching and divine service at churches excepted") took place within a seven-mile radius of the city.

The impact of these events on London was powerful. Those who could escape the pestilent city did so: shops, markets, water supplies—the whole structure of metropolitan life—provided endless opportunities for infection. And though the steps taken to deal with the plague were increasingly practical and disciplined, the conditions obtaining in the city's most densely populated neighborhoods made survival random. Thomas Dekker compared the silent watches of the plague nights in London to the experience of being locked in an infinite charnel house, with decomposing bodies at every turn:

> For he that durst in the dead hour of gloomy midnight have been so valiant as to have walked through the still and melancholy streets—what think you then should have been his music? Surely the loud groans of raving sick men, the struggling pangs of souls departing; in every house grief striking up an alarum—servants crying out for masters, wives for husbands, parents for children, children for their mothers. Here, he should have met some frantically running to knock up sextons; there, others fearfully sweating with coffins to steal forth dead bodies lest the fatal handwriting of Death should seal up their doors. And to make this dismal concert more full, round about him bells heavily tolling in one place or ringing out in another. The dreadfulness of such an hour is unutterable. (Wilson 1925, 27–28)

Audiences

Who was at risk at these playhouses? The composition and temper of the theater audience has been much debated over the years. Some scholars have held that the audiences were predominantly wealthy; others argue that they contained a substantial representation of the lower orders. After 1600 there is increasing evidence of sophisticated disdain on the part of elite theatergoers for the more old-fashioned public theaters such as the Red Bull. But we should recall that the King's Men performed at a range of venues, including exclusive court spaces and the Globe.

An attraction of the public theaters was the way the actors and audience shared the same conditions and place. According to R. A. Foakes, "One reason these theatres stayed in business was that they provided an especially close relationship between actors and audience, with no visual barrier between them, allowing the actor to identify himself as intimately as he pleased with the spectators, or to distance himself within the action" (1990, 24). In other words, the aside and the soliloquy were flexible devices for instantly transforming relationships on stage and between the stage and the audience.

The evidence relating to the experience of playgoing and the composition of the audience is sketchy, but there have been attempts to examine the social composition of the crowds since the 1930s.[32] Alfred Harbage, in *Shakespeare's Audience* (1941) and then in *Shakespeare and the Rival Traditions* (1952), developed an opposition between a "coterie" drama in the "private" theaters, with an audience in the region of 600–700, and a more truly national theater at the Globe with a mixed audience of about 2,500. Anne Jennalie Cook, in a controversial assault on the post-Harbage orthodoxy, argued in her *The Privileged Playgoer in Shakespeare's London, 1576–1642* (1981) that the theater was a relatively expensive pursuit. Only the elite, in her view, had the time or resources to attend—although she also claimed that the "elite" constituted a surprisingly large proportion of the London population: "London's large and lively privileged set ruled the playgoing world quite as firmly as they ruled the political world, the mercantile world, and the rest of the cultural world."[33]

Cook's analysis was forcefully challenged by Martin Butler in *Theatre and Crisis, 1632–1642* (1984). More recently Andrew Gurr has gathered together almost every scrap of surviving evidence in his *Playgoing in Shakespeare's London* (1987). He points out that the total audience for the public playhouses from the 1560s to the 1640s runs to well over 50 million. His book includes description and analysis, as well as two remarkable appendices—one a list of every person (162 of them) who is known to have attended playhouse performances, the other a chronological list of evidence concerning audiences. Gurr studies the rise of the term "spectator" to challenge and in some cases replace the term "auditor" in characterizing the dominant activity of those attending a play. It appears that "spectator" was a term introduced by Sidney and Spenser, and it was soon taken up by Shakespeare. According to Gurr, "From 1600 onwards, Shakespeare abandoned the idea of the auditory in favour of spectators"; he cites passages such as that of time in *The Winter's Tale* ("imagine me, / Gentle spectators, that I now may be / In fair Bohemia" [93]). For Jonson and others who saw themselves as poets, however, the rise of the "spectator" was of a piece with the primacy of visual display and the demotion of words and solid learning. Jonson saw "spectators" and "hearers" as two different kinds of playgoers, and he left no doubt as to which enjoyed his approval.[34] It seems that dramatists and their customers came to distinguish between hearing and seeing as two distinct modes of engagement between playgoer and performance, and the terms were used with increasing precision.

The Crisis of the Late 1590s and the Move to the Globe

The Chamberlain's Men were often in dispute with their landlord Giles Allen. Allen and James Burbage had signed a lease for 21 years back in 1576, and both parties had explored possible future arrangements for the site for some time. Burbage wished to negotiate a new lease, in accordance with the provisions of the old one, but Allen held back. In 1585 and then in 1591 Burbage brought in expert craftsmen to draw up plans of the site and to support his claim that he had spent in excess of £200 on the property. As the lease drew to a close, Burbage was happy to settle for an increased rent (from £14 per annum to £24). But Allen wanted to include a clause that would enable him to take possession of the site after five years in order to convert the buildings to some other use. Negotiations came to a standstill.

Burbage, perhaps expecting support from court allies, decided to try to move into the city. For the substantial sum of £600 he acquired part of the large complex of buildings of the former Blackfriars monastery—where, as it happened, the Lord Chamberlain was living. One attraction was that the site was not within the jurisdiction of the city authorities. He put more money into creating a theatrical space there, but opposition to the conversion from the influential residents meant that the Privy Council stalled Burbage's ambitious plans (Chambers 1923, 4: 320). It would be 10 years before Shakespeare and his fellows would stage plays there.

So Burbage was faced with serious problems, having sunk money into a site that might not be available for a long time and having reached an impasse with his landlord. He was not to live to resolve the crisis. When he died at the end of January 1597 his business was carried on by his son Cuthbert, but no new lease was signed, and the antitheatrical forces were growing stronger by the day. On 28 July 1598 the Privy Council received the annual letter of complaint from the Lord Mayor and the Court of Aldermen, in which the council was, as usual, alerted to the depravity, disorder, and scurrility of public theaters and urged to close them down. The mayor and the alderman probably expected the usual bland, official brushoff, as the Privy Council had already been angered by what it saw as the unpatriotic failure of the city to raise troops for the current action against the Spanish. So the brief meeting between the citizens and the Privy Council ended, and since the city's representatives did not expect a reply, they adjourned for a month.

But for once they found a receptive audience—indeed, the Privy Council had already acted savagely. On the same day—presumably before the council had considered the Lord Mayor's letter—it expressed a hitherto unprecedented hostility to the stage. A prohibition in the summer to reduce the risk of plague was one thing, but now, in 1598, the council ordered the playhouses to be "plucked down" because of the "lewd matters that are handled on the stages" and the "very great disorders" resulting from the "resort and confluence of bad people." Their proclamation went into some detail, naming the playhouses so to be "plucked" and urging how, when, and by whom the "plucking" was to be done.

Richard Topcliffe, the government's most assiduous pursuer and interrogator of Jesuits and a man with a well-earned reputation as a torturer, joined in the open season that seemed to have been declared on the theaters. Just a few days after the council's decree, he reported to Robert Cecil that information had come his way of "a lewd play that was played in one of the playhouses on the Bankside, containing very seditious and slanderous matter." As a result, several members of the company were imprisoned, "whereof one of them was not only an actor but a maker of a part of the said play." That individual was Ben Jonson. His co-author, Thomas Nashe, had wisely fled the city. So Cecil instructed Topcliffe to round up as many of the company as he could and interrogate them systematically and also to conduct a minute inspection of papers that had been found in Nashe's lodgings.[35]

The play that became the subject of the inquiry is now—hardly surprisingly—lost. Faced with the prospect of a conversation with Topcliffe, the players were doubtless anxious to destroy any scraps of text that might be twisted against them. The piece that caused all this fuss was a satire called *The Isle of Dogs*. The title suggests that it was an anticourt satire. Just across the river from the royal palace of Greenwich, the Isle of Dogs and was used to house the royal household's hounds. No doubt parallels were suggested between the queen's animal subjects and her human courtiers, alternately cooling their heels and dancing attendance on Gloriana. But not even Topcliffe could make the charge of sedition stick effectively, and the next we hear is that early in October Jonson was released, as were the two actors originally apprehended, Gabriel Spencer and Robert Shaw. The playhouses were not "plucked down." The two great companies continued to provide entertainment for the great court festivals in the winter of 1598–99.

The main victims of this peculiar episode were the newly formed company calling themselves Pembroke's Men and Francis Langley, the proprietor of the Swan. The Privy Council had earlier been suspicious of Langley's business dealings and were probably anxious to restrict the number of theatrical enterprises to two. Conceivably, the council's vehement words of July were really directed to those ends, and it was expedient to be able to show that the company was under arrest for performing a seditious play. Once the company folded and its men drifted back to the other groups (mainly to the Admiral's Men), the immediate danger to the public theaters subsided (Foakes 1990, 7).

These events can hardly have encouraged the Lord Chamberlain's Men. Their patron had signed the document of 28 July, and their landlord must have been gratified at the prospect that the vogue for public playhouses was at an end. At Allen's request, the Chamberlain's Men moved out of the Theatre after a short season and set up operations at the Curtain. The deserted amphitheater became a byword for solitary desolation ("One like the deserted Theatre / Walks in dark silence, and vast solitude," wrote the satirist Edward Guilpin in his *Skialetheia* of 1598), and Burbage's company now had to face the future without a permanent home. Late in 1598 Burbage reluctantly acceded to new terms, which he regarded as excessive and exorbitant, but he felt there was no alternative if the company was to continue on its previous footing. He named his actor brother Richard—already a considerable celebrity—as security.

Allen announced that he refused to accept Richard Burbage as security and that, having exhausted his patience with the players, he now resolved to demolish the Theatre and "convert the wood and timber thereof to some better use" (Schoenbaum 1977, 207). He then left town on business. News of his decision galvanized the Burbages and their friends to take action of the most drastic kind. Under the watchful eye of their mother, the Burbage brothers assembled a party (including the master carpenter, Peter Street, with a dozen workmen and the Burbages' business partner, William Smith) to take advantage of a covenant in the original lease, under which the tenants were entitled, under certain conditions, to dismantle the amphitheater. The group gathered during the Christmas season of 1598, on 28 December.

A vivid account of the ensuing events was delivered by Allen himself, two years later, when he sued Burbage for £800 (£700 representing his valuation of the Theatre). In his words, the brothers, their mother, their carpenter, their banker, and their laborers riotously assembled themselves

> and then and there armed themselves with divers and many unlawful and offensive weapons, as, namely, swords, daggers, bills, axes, and such like, and so armed did then repair unto the said Theatre. And then and there, armed as aforesaid, in very riotous, outrageous, and forcible manner, and contrary to the laws of your Highness' realm, attempted to pull down the said Theatre, whereupon divers of your subjects, servants, and farmers, then going about in peaceable manner to procure them to desist from that their unlawful enterprise, they (the said riotous persons aforesaid) notwithstanding procured then therein with great violence, not only then and there forcibly and riotously resisting your subjects, servants, and farmers, but also then and there pulling, breaking, and throwing down the said Theatre in very outrageous, violent, and riotous sort, to the great disturbance and terrifying not only of your subjects, said servants, and farmers, but of divers others of your Majesty's loving subjects there near inhabiting. (Schoenbaum 1977, 208)[36]

The timbers were unlikely to have been treated as roughly as the complaint suggests. They were a valuable asset and were carried carefully through the city's wintry streets, ferried across the river, and brought to a plot of vacant land in the shadow of St. Mary Overy in Southwark. There they were used in the construction of the most famous of all English theaters, the Globe.

The structure grew rapidly, to the amazement of some and the dismay of others. By May of 1599 it was referred to as "newly built" and was said to be "in the possession of William Shakespeare and others."[37] The site was about halfway between Henslowe's house and his theater, the Rose; he was alert to the threat to his business. The Rose had not been well maintained; it was built on wet land and was going to look very unappealing once Burbage's operation got under way. The records of takings in *Henslowe's Diary* in the spring of 1599 show that, despite some better days, the Rose had lost a substantial part of its audience to the Chamberlain's Men within a very short time of their transfer.

Alleyn and Henslowe acted rapidly to improve the situation: they leased land in Finsbury—higher, drier, in another area to which Londoners were accustomed to resort for recreation; like the Theatre and the Curtain, half a mile to the east, it was outside the city's jurisdiction. They built a theater called the Fortune between Golden Lane and Whitecross Street (there is still a Fortune Lane on the site) and opened it to paying customers in the later months of 1600. Burbage's carpenter, Peter Smith, worked to specifications that have survived to this day, constituting a valuable guide to the archaeology of the London stage in its greatest days (Gurr 1981, 126–30). Meanwhile, the Rose was to fall from prominence, being shut for long periods, and not very profitable when it reopened.

Half of the lease of the new Globe theater belonged to the Burbages; the other half was split between five sharers in the company—William Kempe, Augustine Phillips, Thomas Pope, John Heminges, and Shakespeare. Each of these men had a 10 percent stake in the business, and they took steps now to make sure their families and heirs could profit from the new enterprise. The partnership was changed from a "joint tenancy" (in which a departing shareholder left his share to be divided among those remaining, until in time only one remained) into a "tenancy in common" (whereby a tenant could pass on his tenancy to his heirs).

With the building of the Globe, the Lord Chamberlain's Men had finally moved from crisis to an unarguable preeminence. They now became established as both a leading troupe on the public stages and as a major court attraction. They performed at court during the Christmas seasons of 1598–99 (the same time they were moving the timbers of the Theatre across the river!), 1599–1600, 1600–1601, and 1601–1602.

This new industry was the business in which the young Shakespeare chose to make his fortune. Whereas his father seems to have had a sponsor or mentor to direct him and guide his first steps in the commercial life of Stratford, William Shakespeare can have had no such established assistance. Yet even if he came south knowing of the theater only what he had encountered in Stratford in his formative years, he would have seen ample evidence to suggest that the business of providing entertainment for the swelling population of the metropolis was moving from a random, ad hoc, disorganized phase into something altogether more substantial and commercially promising.[38] He may have come to London with a dawning awareness of his acting and writing talent, or he may have come with some modest capital, salvaged from his father's decline, to invest in a developing new business. Perhaps it was a combination of these factors that led him to tie his fortune to the public theater.

Chapter Six
Elizabethan

In 1619 Ben Jonson visited the Scottish poet William Drummond at his home in Hawthornden, and his host made notes of their conversation. Jonson aimed a series of lusty blows at the reputations of some celebrated Elizabethans, roundly debunking and demythologizing them. Of the queen he is reported to have said,

> Queen Elizabeth never saw her self after she became old in a true Glass. they painted her & sometymes would vermilion her nose, she had allwayes about Christmas evens set dice, that threw sixes or five, & she knew not they were other, to make her win & esteame her self fortunate . . . she had a Membrana on her which made her uncapable of man, though for her delight she tryed many. . . . King Philip had intention by dispensation of the Pope to have maried her.[1]

Others had different recollections. In 1598 Paul Hentzner observed of the queen (then age 64) that "her bosom was uncovered, as all the English ladies have it till they marry." In the previous year two audiences with the French ambassador evidently made a striking impression on the amazed diplomat, who reported that at the first meeting the queen "kept the front of her dress open, and one could see the whole of her bosom, and passing low, and often she would open the front of this robe with her hands as if she was too hot. . . . Her bosom is somewhat wrinkled . . . but lower down her flesh is exceeding white and delicate, as far as one could see. As for her face, it is and appears to be very aged." Then, at the second audience: "She had a petticoat of white damask, girdled, and open in front, as was also her chemise, in such manner that she often opened this dress and one could see all her belly, and even to her navel. . . . When she raises her head, she has a trick of putting both hands on her gown and opening it insomuch that all her belly can be seen."[2]

Jonson's sourness is a rarity. All the evidence suggests that Elizabeth I managed her reputation astutely. Since her death in 1603 she has generally been as well served by historians as she was by her chief courtiers. That in itself is a notable achievement, especially since her preparation for government had been so unstable. She had seen her mother, Anne

Boleyn, beheaded. She herself had been declared a bastard and imprisoned as a potential traitor. As a young woman she had been a pawn in the political intrigues at her brother's court. Throughout her sister's reign she had been under close watch, and her religious affiliations and personal associations were matters of intense scrutiny.

When Elizabeth became queen she found herself pressured from all sides, notably from zealous Protestants who wanted a return to the reforming energy of Edward's reign, and from all her advisers who wanted her to decide on a suitable husband as soon as possible. She satisfied neither group, and when she died 45 years later she had maintained her enigmatic reserve about her own religious preferences; she had resisted advice to name a successor; and, of course, she was unmarried.

Literary students are no longer routinely invited to view Elizabethan literature as a reflection of a system of ideas and values identified by E. M. W. Tillyard as "The Elizabethan World Picture." Political and social historians always claimed that Tillyard's work was oversimplified; for a variety of reasons, literary scholars in recent times have developed similar and other critiques of monolithic systems of interpreting and classifying history. According to Arthur Kinney, "There has been in Renaissance literary criticism of the past two decades . . . a marked shift from a reliance on such fixed, stabilizing nouns as *order, degree, hierarchy, integration*, and *equilibrium* to a reliance on more, unstabilizing (if often specialized) verbs as *appropriate, situate, inscribe*, and *subvert*."[3]

Tillyard's view was that Elizabethan England was essentially an ordered society—a culture marked by stability and by the striving for stability. Men and women inhabited a mental world in which those who threatened cosmic order (such as Macbeth and Richard III) were to be condemned, while those who strove for it (such as Henry V) were to be praised.[4]

Elizabeth's realm was not like that. She may have wanted it to be, but that is another matter. Undoubtedly it is possible to find writings from her time that eloquently advocate order and stability. Their very prevalence, however, should alert us to the contested and problematic nature of the Elizabethan compromises.[5]

When Elizabeth succeeded to the throne the doubts cast on her legitimacy did not vanish overnight. Then in 1570, after the defeat of the rebellion of the northern earls, she was excommunicated and "deposed" by the Pope. Elizabeth's strategy for dealing with these threats included the use of the pulpit to reinforce her authority. The Elizabethan Prayer Book contains a series of homilies (*Certain Sermons*) that were to be read out "distinctly and plainly" to instruct the congregation, for "the better understanding of the simple people" (see Schoenbaum 1977, 57). The early editions of the Prayer Book contain a sermon in three parts called "An Exhortation to Obedience." After 1570 the instructions were prolonged: a six-part sermon was added, entitled "An Homily against Disobedience and Wilful Rebellion." Thus, for an unbroken sequence of nine services (including Sundays and holy days), the congregation was exhorted to order and obedience. Attendance at church was both a spiritual duty and a token of loyalty and was carefully monitored.[6]

Countless bureaucratic measures—including the creation of records of baptisms, marriages, and funerals—all testify to the efforts made by the rulers of Elizabethan England to construct a centralized and powerful state, exercising forceful control over the bodies and minds of the population. These measures were never completely successful, however, and they had to be repeated time and again throughout the queen's 45 years on the throne.

Some of the most characteristic features of Elizabeth's reign were established very early, though they were not generally recognized. For the first part of her reign she had to deal with competing claims for her hand in marriage. Her advisers were in a quandary; as sixteenth-century men, they could hardly conceive of a woman ruling alone. They were also anxious to secure the succession. On the other hand, they recognized that any choice the queen made would risk disturbing the political and religious situation. A Catholic suitor—especially such a one as her former brother-in-law, Philip II of Spain—would bring back the difficulties of Mary's reign. A committed Protestant would please the bishops but perhaps alienate the population and risk involvement in war with the European Catholic powers. They assumed, being men of their time, that the queen would be subject to a husband. This would pose one sort of problem if the husband were already a king, and quite another sort if he were merely a member of her own court. To elevate one of the great lords would risk the disruption of the power relations within her council and within the country more generally.[7]

Such questions were also intimately connected to international politics and to the great religious disputes of the time. Where did England stand? Where did the queen's own preferences lie? There was intense speculation about her private devotions. An unequivocal answer would define England's relations with the European powers at a time when brutal religious war was ravaging the Continent.

What began as a cautious balancing act by the new queen turned into a conscious policy. As the years went by, Elizabeth transformed indecision into a political art—a means of exercising control by refusing firm decisions. To some of her advisers, she was inconsistent and unreliable, a person capable of saying one thing and doing the reverse. From her point of view, she presented herself to her nation as unchanging—her motto was *Semper Eadem*, "Always the Same"—although her image underwent several transformations during her reign. In the words of Thomas Dekker, "some call her *Pandora*: some *Gloriana*, some *Cynthia*: some *Belphoebe*, some *Astraea*: all by severall names to express severall loves: Yet all those names make but one celestiall body, as all those loves meete to create but one soule."[8]

Elizabeth lived a very public life.[9] She can hardly ever have been truly alone. Her dictum, "We princes are set on stages, in the sight and view of all the world duly observed," reminds us that her career involved an unbroken series of performances, played out before audiences primed to decode their every nuance.[10] Many Elizabethans subscribed to the doctrine of the queen's "two bodies," in which there was held to be a clear distinction between the public body—the embodiment of everlasting authority and power—and the private body—the human and mortal individual.[11] In the letter to Sir Walter Ralegh prefaced to *The Faerie Queene*, Spenser claimed that the queen "beareth two persons," and that he had praised her as both "a most royall Queene or Empresse" and as "a most vertuous and beautiful Lady." In the Proem to the third book of his epic, Spenser advises the queen that she has been represented in what follows in two complimentary guises:

> Ne let . . . fairest *Cynthia* refuse,
> In mirrors more then one her selfe to see,
> But either *Gloriana* let her chuse,
>   Or in *Belphoebe* fashioned to bee:
> In th'one her rule, in th'other her rare chastitee.

Nevertheless, the separation was more theoretical than actual. The queen's most private attributes (most obviously her virginity) were invoked as part of political discourse, and her public, ritual function was developed in accordance with the intimate particulars of her life and personality.

The queen's official iconography began in a severely biblical mode. When she came to the throne, she presented herself to the people as a new Judith, a new Esther or Deborah—a woman inspired with godly zeal, filled with moral and spiritual courage. Judith's defeat of Holofernes could be read as a prediction of Elizabeth's triumph over hostile Catholic forces. The image of Deborah, who had rescued the Israelites from the worship of idols, was especially congenial to the returned Marian exiles.[12]

In her private person, Elizabeth was praised in the traditional queenly role as the bride of the kingdom, or the bride of Christ. Such images drew on the Solomonic traditions of the Song of Songs and the story of the Queen of Sheba. Unlike most predecessors, however, Elizabeth was not a consort but a ruler in her own right. Therefore she also echoed Solomon and David in her public person. In fact, celebration of the queen often involved blurring traditional categories, including that of gender.[13] She herself stressed her "masculine" aspects: "I know I have the body of a weak and feeble woman, but I have the heart and stomach of a king, and of a king of England too."[14] If we remember that David and Solomon were poets, the praise also involves seeing Elizabeth as both author and subject.[15] George Puttenham stresses that the queen was herself a poet: "Your self being already, of any that I know in our time, the most excellent Poet."[16]

There are places in Elizabethan literature when the Queen is represented in a fairly straightforward way, although usually such treatment serves as a foil for more elusive and ambiguous material. There are two especially striking examples that draw on the well-established official imagery. Queen Elizabeth's colors were black and white, as may be seen in the *Ermine* and *Seive* portraits. The qualities designated by the colors were purity and steadfastness, as Abraham Fraunce explained in his *Insignium* (1588).[17] So, at the very outset of *The Faerie Queene*, Spenser's Una is first seen riding a white ass, while she is dressed all in white but covered with a black stole. And there can have been little doubt in the minds of the *Arcadia*'s first readers about who was represented by Sidney when Queen Helen of Corinth appears: "They met with a coach drawn with four milk-white horses furnished all in black, with a blackamoor boy upon every horse—they all apparelled in white, the coach itself very richly furnished in black and white."[18]

The most extensive praise of Helen occurs in the prelude to the account of the jousts held to celebrate the wedding anniversary of the

Queen of Iberia, and it clearly alludes to Elizabeth's strategies of rule. Pyrocles reports,

> As her beauty hath won the prize from all women that stand in degree of comparison . . . , so hath her government been such as hath been no less beautiful to men's judgements than her beauty to the eyesight; for being brought by right of birth (a woman—a young woman—a fair woman) to govern a people in nature mutinously proud, and always before so used to hard governors as they knew not how to obey without the sword were drawn, yet could she for some years so carry herself among them that they found cause, in the delicacy of her sex, of admiration, not of contempt. (253)

When moving on to praise her government, Pyrocles invokes the familiar oxymoronic and antithetical mode of the Elizabethan cult:

> She using so strange and yet so well-succeeding temper that she made her people (by peace) warlike, her courtiers (by sports) learned, her ladies (by love) chaste; for, by continual martial exercises without blood, she made them perfect in that bloody art; her sports were such as carried riches of knowledge upon the stream of delight; and such the behaviour both of herself and her ladies as builded their chastity, not upon waywardness, but by choice of worthiness: so as, it seemed that court to have been the marriage place of love and virtue, and that herself was a Diana apparelled in the garments of Venus. (283)

Puttenham had similarly praised Elizabeth for "by your princely purse, favours, and countenance, making in manner what ye list, the poor man rich, the lewd well learned, the coward couragious, and vile both noble and valiant" (*Arte*, 4–5).

Like any ideal Petrarchan mistress, the queen was held to be both infinitely describable and utterly mysterious. Poets and painters strove to construct representations of her, but part of their performance was always the acknowledgment of failure. One of the most remarkable contributions to the literature of Elizabeth's cult was John Lyly's prose fiction *Euphues and His England* (1580). This was the sequel to his immensely popular *Euphues* (1578). In it the two young scholars, Euphues and Philautus, whom readers had previously followed on their jaunts around the Mediterranean, decide to come to England, drawn by reports of the wonderful queen who lives there. As they travel north from the coast, they encounter a wise old hermit called Fidus, whom they ask about the queen. With no warning, the old man becomes extra-ordinarily agitated: "Gentlemen . . . if because I entertain you, you seek to undermine me, you offer me great discourtesy: you must needs think me very simple, or your selves very subtle, if upon so small acquaintance I should answer to such demands, as are neither for me to utter being a subject, nor for you to know being strangers. I keep hives for bees, not houses for busybodies."[19]

Seeking to reassure Fidus, the young men argue that they mean to glorify the queen, not to diminish her. The old man refuses to comply and proposes as a rule of life the following: "So ought we, Euphues, to frame our selves in all our actions and devices, as though the King stood over us to behold us, and not to look what the King doth behind us" (2: 42). Then the narrative, having started with the blocking of the heroes' desires, ultimately fragments, faced with its inability to deal with Elizabeth. In the appended letter, "Euphues Glass for Europe," however, an account of England concludes with a lengthy and eloquent praise of the Queen. The narrator reiterates the impossibility of the task he has taken on:

> Touching her Magnanimity, her Estate Royal, there was neither Alexander, nor Galba the Emperor, nor any that might be compared with her. . . . But whether I do wade . . . , as one forgetting him self, thinking to sound the depth of her virtues with a few fathoms, when there is no bottom: for I know not how it commeth to pass, that being in this Labyrinth, I may sooner lose my self, than find the end. . . . Behold Ladies in this Glass a Queen, a woman, a Virgin, in all gifts of the body, in all graces of the mind, in all perfection of either. (2: 215–16)

The anxiety exhibited by Fidus may be paralleled in many texts. Spenser reiterates and explores the relation of *The Faerie Queene* to the queen: "the matter of my song" (3.4.3). The reference in the Proem to book 2, to "fruitfullest *Virginia*," which connects colonial expansion to the queen—a figure in whom an impossibility, or what is in its language a contradiction or paradox—is, like the other wonders of the New World, "now found trew."[20]

It was one of the purposes of censorship and repression to encourage the self-discipline exemplified by Lyly's Fidus. Statistically there were few instances of savage censorship, but the potential power of censorship was great. John Stubbes lost his hand for writing his *Gaping Gulfe* against the queen's proposed marriage to the French Duke of Alençon in 1579. One of Spenser's versions of Elizabeth,

Mercilla in book 5 of *The Faerie Queene*, deals a fierce form of justice to a slanderous poet:

> There as they entred at the Scriene, they saw
>> Some one, whose tongue was for his trespasse vyle
>> Nayled to a post, adiudged so by law:
>> For that therewith he falsely did teuyle,
>> And foule blaspheme that Queene for forged guyle,
>> Both with bold speaches, which he blazed had,
>> And with lewd poems, which he did compyle;
>> For the bold title of a Poet bad
> He on himselfe had ta'en, and rayling rymes had sprad.
>
> Thus there he stood, whylest high ouer his head,
>> There written was the purport of his sin,
>> In cyphers strange, that few could rightly read,
>> BON FONT: but *bon* that once had written bin,
>> Was raced out, and *Mal* was now put in.
> So now *Malfont* was plainely to be red. (9.25–26)

The predicament of artists was similar to that of politicians: they were driven to use allegory, obliquity, ambiguity, and indirection. George Puttenham observed of the courtier that "in any matter of importance his words and meaning very seldom meet." For him *Allegoria* was "the Courtly figure . . . when we speak one thing, and thinke another, and . . . our words and our meanings meet not" (*Arte*, 299–300, 186).[21]

Elizabeth was fortunate in her chief ministers, many of whom provided continuity, experience, and advice in the court and council for much of her reign. William Cecil (later Lord Burghley), Robert Dudley (later the earl of Leicester), Sir Christopher Hatton, Sir Francis Walsingham, Sir Nicholas Bacon, and Sir Francis Bacon were all men of considerable ability. Many of them stayed too long in power, however, and a younger generation grew up only to find its prospects for office and promotion were limited. These men had been trained in the optimistic spirit of Renaissance humanism to expect that their talents would find some useful outlet. When they encountered the gerontocracy that ran the country, many were disillusioned. Some would be drawn to foreign wars and adventures and ultimately to open rebellion in the support of Essex. Others set off to found colonies, search for El Dorado, or trade with Muscovy and Persia. For many, the cult of melancholy—so vividly expressed in Hamlet, Orsino, Donne, John Dowland, and Essex him-self—provided a code through which to articulate a sense of exclusion.

The conflict of age and youth is everywhere to be seen in Elizabethan literature: much of its forms are those calculated to appeal to the irrev-erent, marginalized, student mentality of the Inns of Court and the uni-versities. Satire, city comedy, spoofs of tragedy, erotic verse that specifically set out to debunk the idealism of Petrarchan images, innova-tive prose fiction: all this abounded in the London in which Shakespeare made his way. This was the audience of *The Comedy of Errors*, of *Twelfth Night*, perhaps of *Love's Labour's Lost* and *The Taming of the Shrew*, as well as the narrative poems, *Troilus and Cressida*, and *Hamlet*. Central to Elizabethan fiction is the idea of the prodigal, of the rebellious young man whose wisdom is bought in the harsh market of profligacy and alienation.[22]

Perhaps the greatest single instance of this widespread cultural phe-nomenon was the failure to find any real outlet for the exceptional tal-ents of Sir Philip Sidney. It was only when he was about to set sail for the New World with Drake that the queen brought him back and posted him to the wars in the Netherlands. But Sidney had to be careful about expressing his frustration. When he wrote in a letter, "My only service is speeche and that is stopped," he seemed to refer to his own political impotence. And yet the rest of the letter makes it clear that Sidney, as well as being denied the queen's favor, was, quite unmetaphorically, suf-fering from a head cold. He describes himself as "so full of the colde as one can not heere me speake," and goes on, "I hope within 3 or 4 daies this colde will be paste, for now truly I weare a very unpleasante compa-ny keeper."[23] Sidney's letter could therefore be defended against any accusation of disloyalty: to any inquisitor who asked, he could demon-strate that he was complaining about his ill health. It is a textbook case of what Puttenham understood as courtly speech.

Ambiguity, fluidity, and instability were endemic in Elizabethan cul-ture. It was noted earlier that celebration of the queen often involved blurring of traditional categories, including gender categories. The prevalence in plays and stories of cross-dressing, for instance, speaks to the uncertain boundaries of gender at the time, and it is an uncertainty exploited on the stage, where the use of boy actors to play female roles inevitably drew attention to such matters. But cross-dressing is a feature of other genres, such as prose fiction, where no such obvious social prac-tice accounts for its prominence. Its prevalence under Elizabeth is an important illustration of a significant quality of her cult.[24]

Elizabeth's reign also saw two distinct periods when marriage—what it is, what it is for, what its obligations are—was the subject of popular debate: one period, unsurprisingly, was at the beginning of the reign; the other was in the early 1590s, when there was widespread anxiety about the lack of an obvious heir. These debates are crucially related to the queen. A third area of fluidity was in the patriarchal structure itself. It arose from the phenomenon of the so-called masterless women—women (often young widows) who had the means and abilities to run their own lives and businesses, without reference to the wishes and prejudices of men. Such economic and social independence was perceived as a threat both to individual men and to the social fabric. We can assume that it would have been treated very differently under a male ruler.[25]

Elizabeth's presence on the throne also coincided, however, with many representations of a demonized opposite of the qualities she was held to embody, in the shape of monstrous women, whores, and witches (such as Shakespeare's Margaret of Anjou and Joan La Pucelle).[26] Just as the queen might define herself against her sister Mary and against Mary Queen of Scots, so her surrogates in *The Faerie Queene* are frequently defined by their opposites. Thus Una in book 1 functions as an emblem of national oneness, of the integrity of the nation, expressing an important facet of Elizabeth's cult. Una is a veiled virgin: her enclosed, whole body, like Elizabeth's, is, in Bakhtinian terms, classical. As such it is starkly opposed to the doubleness of her evil parody, Duessa, whose lack of control over her person is expressed as much in the outpourings of words, and her pouring out of her self, as in the excrescent dung that decorates her grotesque appendage, the fox's tail.[27]

It became conventional to talk about the queen as essentially paradoxical, as the embodiment of diversities, of opposites. But this fruitful virginity, this youthful age, this permanent instability, had a cost. Panegyric and humiliation, celebration and degradation often went hand in hand. The queen displayed and secured her own hegemony, affirmed and reinforced her power, through the medium of an establishment that was, in Stephen Greenblatt's phrase, "institutionally committed to the arousal of anxiety" (1988, 137).[28]

In the later part of her reign, and certainly from her final break with the Pope and Catholic Europe in 1570, the most significant element in Elizabeth's iconography was her appropriation of many of the components of the cult of the Virgin Mary. Elizabeth had always drawn on aspects of the cult: from the beginning of her reign "the queen was praised variously as the Virgin giving birth to the gospel and as the Virgin Mother of the English people."[29] After 1570 Marian images became more common, and there are several references to the idea that she had somehow supplanted the Virgin. In Sidney's *Lady of May* the Puritan Earl of Leicester is described as "a huge *catholicam*" devotedly "telling his beads." In his entertainment for the queen at Ditchley in 1592, Elizabeth's former champion, Sir Henry Lee, appeared as a hermit and claimed that in retirement he had exchanged "Vivat Eliza for an Ave Mary."

This Marian cult blended with Petrarchism. The vogue for Petrarchism had been spasmodic in England before Elizabeth: there is a Petrarchan passage in Chaucer's *Troilus and Criseyde*, and there are translations and adaptations from the 1530s by Wyatt and Surrey. But it was under Elizabeth that Petrarchism became the most characteristic form of court poetry, in which dejected poet-lovers lamented the unyielding resistance of their would-be mistresses. It is easy to suppose the vogue is linked to the queen. Certainly she was often praised in terms that could have come straight out of one of the sonnet sequences: see, for example, the remarkable *blason* or inventory of the qualities of the queen's fictional alter ego, Belphoebe, in *The Faerie Queene* (2.3.21–31). More remarkably, the predicament of the Petrarchan lover—dejected, frustrated, self-divided, lamenting—provided a parallel to the predicament of the Elizabethan courtier.

This phenomenon was strengthened by a remarkable semantic shift that occurred about this time. In earlier periods, the verb "to court" simply meant "to be [or reside] at court." During the second half of the sixteenth century in England, the word developed a second, amorous, sense—namely, "to woo." It would be convenient to suppose this was a "result" of Elizabeth's rule, but the fact that the phenomenon occurs all over Europe at roughly the same time reduces the correspondence to a mere coincidence. It was, however, a coincidence that was vigorously exploited by the queen and her court. Being at court now meant wooing—and the Petrarchan quest for grace or relief from the beloved gained a crucial political dimension. Speeches and proposals directed at the queen had to be couched in terms of wooing: policy was advanced through ritualized seductions.[30]

Marie Axton has demonstrated, for example, that the Earl of Leicester orchestrated a series of pageants and displays for the queen that deployed the rhetoric of wooing (after all, he was for a time her acknowledged suitor) in order to try to persuade her of the value of certain options in policy. When Leicester courted the queen a series of roles was being played by all who were party to the exercise. His behavior represented elements of personal desire, political and religious persuasion, as well as, in narrowly literary terms, the stereotypical relation of courtly lover and lady.[31]

If politics was eroticized and couched in the language of love, so too the language of love was inescapably made political. When an Elizabethan courtier described himself in the standard situation as the Petrarchan lover—that is, frustrated, thwarted, and melancholic in the face of an unyielding and distantly beautiful beloved—there was an obvious parallel to his political predicament.[32]

But changes did occur over time. Courtship became more allegorical, more controlled. For example, Lyly's Endimion (*Endimion* [1591]) loves the moon goddess and intends to possess her: "Sweet Cynthia," he asks, "how wouldst thou be pleased, how possessed? . . . Desirest thou the passions of loue . . . ?" (2.1.4). The play unfolds by teaching him the lesson that his desire can never be achieved: eventually Cynthia may kiss the sleeping Endimion, in a gesture that would have been recognized as chaste—indeed, as a token of the absence of sexual desire. When Endimion wakes up, his address to the queen typifies the officially sanctioned, morally defensible, pose of the abject courtier: "Such a difference hath the Gods sette betweene our states, that all must be dutie, loyalitie, and reuerence; nothing . . . be termed loue. My vnspotted thoughts, my languishing bodie, my discontented life, let them obtaine by princelie fauour impossibilities; with imagination of which, I will spend my spirits, and to my selfe that no creature may heare, softlie call it loue. And if any vrge to vtter what I whisper, then will I name it honour" (5.3.170–75).

Lyly thus stages a miniature version of the training Elizabeth provided for her courtiers, teaching them the limits and obligations of their courtiership (Bates, 83–88). When he came to look back at Elizabeth's reign, Bacon addressed the question of propriety raised by the eroticization of political discourse at her court. He observed that although the queen had "allowed herself to be wooed and courted, and even to have love made to her," nevertheless, such "dalliances detracted but little from her fame and nothing at all from her majesty."[33]

If the queen presided over fluidity and uncertainty, she also ruled over a number of individuals who were striving to arrive at new definitions of some important spheres of thought, knowledge, and belief. While some of the younger Elizabethans were understandably disaffected, there was a group of brilliant young men who threw themselves into redefining such spheres of learning as history, law, and language.[34] Such enterprises may be related to the ideas of expansion and empire that Elizabeth eventually promoted. The comparative failure of overseas enterprises—whether in Ireland, the Netherlands, or the New World—was less important culturally than their extraordinary confidence. Britain was an empire, the queen and empress descended from Trojan royalty. Her cult gave nourishment to those who sought to give concrete actuality to these national myths.[35]

Jonson observed that "they painted her, and sometimes would vermilion her nose." It seems clear from these words that Elizabeth came to be transformed from the subject of painters to an object on which paint would be applied.[36] The images through which she had secured her iconography, which made her likeness current and permanent, were now painted onto her as a grotesque emblem of the operation of time. In this process lie the seeds of the images used in Catholic attacks on the queen's reputation—the claim that her body exploded in its coffin, that it was her first sight of a mirror for 20 years that precipitated her death.[37] It would take only a year or so for the author of *The Revenger's Tragedy* to feel free to invest the fatally attractive painted skull with the name "Gloriana."[38]

Chapter Seven

Jacobean

What are the qualities connoted by the term *Jacobean*? If *Elizabethan* is a term commonly associated with forms such as the madrigal, the lyric, and the sonnet, *Jacobean* is usually associated with domestic furniture and bloody tragedy. The change from Elizabeth to James has often been seen as a movement from light to darkness, from the expansive optimism of her glittering court to the sinister intrigues and murders of a more suspicious and corrupt age. In fact, as we have seen, Elizabeth's reign was rarely untroubled. From the 1590s on there had been a powerful sense that an era was drawing to a close and that the future was uncertain and potentially alarming.

So when James arrived there was a palpable surge of optimism. The new king was an experienced and learned ruler. His very presence on the throne meant that Scotland was no longer a military threat or a potential ally of England's enemies. Above all, perhaps, he brought with him a wife and children. In *The Trew Law of Free Monarchies* (1598) he had written that "for all other well ruled Common-wealths, the stile of *Pater patriae* was ever, and is commonly used to Kings." For the first time since the death of Henry VIII in 1547, the succession seemed secure and unquestioned.

One of the great triumphs of Elizabeth's administration was that it was able to organize a relatively smooth transition to the new reign. The Queen steadfastly refused to name a successor, but her chief ministers prepared the ground carefully for the accession of James. There was to be no repetition of the Lady Jane Grey episode, no new Perkin Warbeck or Lambert Simnel.

As the queen faded, strenuous efforts went into maintaining public order. Contemporary accounts of her passing on 24 March 1603 stress the quietness of the city and the sobriety of the mourning:

> This morning at about 3 o'clock her Majesty departed this life, mildly like a lamb, easily like a ripe apple from a tree. . . . About 10 o'clock the Council and divers noblemen, having been a while in consultation, proclaimed James the 6, King of Scots, the King of England, France, and Ireland. . . .

The proclamation was heard with . . . silent joy, no great shouting. I
think sorrow for her Majesty's departure was so deep in many hearts they
could not so suddenly show any great joy, though it could not be less
than exceeding great for the succession of so worthy a King. And at night
they showed it by bonfires. . . .

No tumult, no contradiction, no disorder in the city; every man went
about his business, as readily, as peaceably, as securely, as though there
had been no change, nor any news ever heard of competitors. God be
thanked, our King hath his right.[1]

Meanwhile, a substantial group of aristocrats began an undignified
scramble northwards to be the first to meet the new monarch as he
crossed the border into England. James was greeted by them at Berwick-
on-Tweed on 6 April, and the great gathering moved south, arriving in
London early in May, just as a severe outbreak of plague was beginning.
The epidemic was so serious that public assemblies could not take place
for almost a year. Theaters were closed, for the coronation in July there
was no procession and the public was kept away, and the king's tri-
umphal entry pageant in the city of London took place on 15 March
1604, almost a year after the accession.

In the ceremonies and displays of the early part of his reign, James
took considerable pains to construct a public image that was distinctive.
Whereas Elizabeth had started by presenting herself as as a biblical hero-
ine, James appeared before his subjects as the new Solomon—king,
judge, and poet—as the builder of the temple, the fount of wisdom. He
was also praised as the new Augustus, the founder of an empire and
maker of peace between nations. He took to himself the sobriquet *Rex
Pacificus*, "Peacemaker King." Where Elizabeth had cultivated an image
of changelessness, James proposed a guarantee of the future. He wanted
to be seen as the founder of a dynasty, as the father of the nation.[2]

From the start James tried to emphasize the new beginning he was
offering. Whereas Elizabeth expressed herself in allegories and presided
over a government where policy was often debated indirectly, James
explicitly repudiated this strategy in speaking to Parliament in 1604.
The speech was published so that Europe would know where England's
new king stood:

It becometh a King, in my opinion, to use no other eloquence than plainness and sincerity. By plainness I mean, that his speeches should be so
clear and void of all ambiguity, that he may not be thrown, nor rent
asunder in contrary senses like the old oracles of the pagan gods. And by

sincerity, I understand that uprightness and honesty which ought to be in a King's whole speeches and actions; that as far as a King is in honour erected above any of his subjects, so far should he strive in sincerity to be above them all, and that his tongue should be ever the true messenger of his heart.[3] And this sort of eloquence may you ever assuredly look for at my hands.[4]

There is no doubt that this advocacy of plain-speaking was part of James's personality. It was in this persona that he summoned the Hampton Court Conference, which would eventually lead to the Authorized Version of the Bible—the so-called King James Bible—one of the great monuments of James's reign. Henry VIII and his advisers had objected to a hundred specific points in the translation of the "Great Bible" in the 1540s. James, a much more expert scholar than his predecessor, was concerned that the word of God should be, as far as possible, rendered in unambiguous English, in language that could not be "thrown, nor rent asunder in contrary senses like the old oracles of the pagan gods."

On the other hand, from the moment he arrived in England James showed himself just as capable as his predecessor of behaving and speaking in allegorical and theatrical ways. On his journey from Berwick to London his displays of the theatricality of power could have been learned from Shakespeare's Henry V. At Newark, for example, he gave two exemplary displays of retribution and clemency. Arriving in the town the British Solomon caused general astonishment when he was presented with a pickpocket who had been caught stealing in the crowd. The man was ordered to be instantly hanged. Then, as James was leaving the town, he suddenly ordered all prisoners in the town jail to be released to celebrate his visit.[5]

James seems to have delighted in such contradictory and perplexing behavior. What Stephen Greenblatt has termed the "manipulation of anxiety" proved an effective means of securing control, of keeping his subjects at all levels of society on their toes. There are countless examples. Sir Walter Ralegh, for instance, lived in the Tower of London under sentence of death from 1603 to 1616, and he was regularly threatened with the imminent execution of his sentence. As Ralegh's patron, Henry Prince of Wales, observed, "Who but my father would keep such a bird in a cage." Ralegh was released in order to sail to South America in a renewed quest for El Dorado but was specifically forbidden to engage with any Spanish forces. In the course of a disastrous expedition, a skirmish with a Spanish ambush left Ralegh's son Walter dead, and Ralegh had to sail dejectedly home in the full knowledge of the fate that awaited him. James, who had received a formal complaint from the Spanish ambassador to London, Count Gondomar, ordered that the death sentence, suspended since 1603, should be carried out. It was.

The senior participants in the so-called Bye plot had to watch as one by one their associates were publicly tortured and executed. They were then led onto the scaffold themselves, only to be told they had been granted a two-hour reprieve. The confused prisoners were then asked if they believed that the sentences imposed on them were just. When they agreed that they were, and that they deserved to die, the sheriff announced that the king had spared their lives. An observer, Dudley Carleton, who described the scene in a letter, wrote that the three men stood in amazement "together on the stage as use is at the end of the play" (quoted in Mullaney 1988, 106–107).

Such behavior is perhaps echoed in *Measure for Measure* (1604), where the duke arouses anxiety in a similar fashion by allowing Isabella to believe that her brother has been executed and then watching as she pleads for the life of Angelo, her brother's judge. It operated on a more intimate level, too. Several reports suggest that James relished the comic possibilities of absolute rule: one commentator said of the king, "He was very witty, and had as many ready witty jests as any man living, at which he would not smile himself, but deliver them in a grave and serious manner" (Ashton, 14).

Descriptions of James are generally less flattering than those of Elizabeth. Sir Anthony Weldon, later to be a committed supporter of Parliament in the Civil War, wrote the following celebrated account of the king, whom he characterizes as being "naturally of a timorous disposition," wearing thick padded doublet and hose to deflect the assassin's knife:

> His beard was very thin: his tongue too long for his mouth, which ever made him to speak full in the mouth, and made him drink very uncomely, as if eating his drink, which came out into the cup on each side of his mouth . . . his legs were very weak, having had (as was thought) some foul play in his youth, or rather before he was born, that he was not able to stand at seven years, that weakness made him ever leaning on other mens' shoulders; his walk was ever circular, his fingers ever in that walk fiddling with his cod-piece. (Ashton, 12)

As soon as the accession was proclaimed, the king's writings were published in London, and his subjects had a chance to size up the new monarch. He had already published volumes of poetry and had let his hostility to "harshe verses after the English fashion" become known. But it was his treatise on kingship, *Basilikon Doron* (dedicated to his son Prince Henry), that aroused most curiosity in England. Several editions appeared within the first months of the new reign. Readers would have been struck by the lofty claims made for the royal authority—primarily that the king was ordained by God and was answerable only to Him. They would probably not have recognized that the forcefulnesss of the king's pronouncements reflected the situation he found in Scotland, where the more extreme Presbyterians argued that church and state constituted "Two Kingdoms" and held that the state had no power to interfere with the affairs of the church. More sophisticated readers might have understood that James's writings appeared to represent the rejection of the way he had been brought up. James had been trained by the great humanist scholar George Buchanan, who advocated a Calvinist political theory of elective monarchy in which the ruler was answerable in some way to the people. Indeed, the compulsory abdication of James's Catholic mother, Mary Queen of Scots, in 1567 had been justified in such terms. But James developed his ideas in different directions as he grew older and as the challenges he faced became more intractably complex.

Readers of *Basilikon Doron* would also have found in the king's advice to his son plenty of wholly practical advice. In the section dealing with government, James appears not as the theorist of kingship but as someone who has learned lessons in the hard and bloody school of Scottish politics. He advises that it is the king's duty to "root out" factionalism and feuding among the nobility, and he condemns those lords who "bang it out bravely, he and all his kin, against him and all his." He advises his son to make use of the great lords ("delight to be served with men of the noblest blood that may be had"), because "virtue followeth oftest noble blood," and it therefore made sense to "garnish" the court with them, who would be "your arms and the executors of your laws."

Such passages would have encouraged the English nobility as they struggled north to meet the king. The traditions of courtly behavior in Elizabethan England were very different from those James had been used to. He would find himself flattered in novel and lavish ways and praised extravagantly by courtiers trained by Elizabeth. As time went by the king made much of his desire to see through the veils of flattery, to search out hidden motives and read the hearts of his subjects.

Thanks to his writings, a great deal could be known about the king by his new subjects.[6] The contrast with Elizabeth was considerable. Elizabeth had been sparing in her public appearances and pronouncements. She had allowed her image to become current, to be reproduced and circulated. But she had not attempted to become an author in her own right. James, on the other hand, strove to extend his authority through authorship, but he failed in the attempt. By entering the literary marketplace, by becoming a writer, James in effect debased the currency of his power. His *Works* were published in 1614, setting an example that was followed in Ben Jonson's *Works* of 1616 and the Shakespeare Folio of 1623. Where Elizabeth had been celebrated by Edmund Spenser in *The Faerie Queene* as the "matter of my song," James diluted his royal magic by participating in the print culture.

Such an unintentionally self-defeating act was characteristic of James, whose quirky, contradictory nature was summed up by one commentator as being that of the "wisest fool in Christendom."[7] What is more, from the standpoint of the student of Shakespeare and drama, it is clear that the king's personality, writings, and reputation were vitally implicated in the literary culture of the age.[8]

In 1604 Samuel Daniel's *The Vision of the Twelve Goddesses* was staged at Hampton Court, with Queen Anne herself performing. In the following year the partnership between the great architect and designer Inigo Jones and the would-be laureate poet Ben Jonson created *The Masque of Blackness*, which effectively established the genre. From that point on James and his family used the masque—which grew into a form of increasingly spectacular conspicuous consumption—as a vehicle for displaying royal power and authority in a very arresting way, as well as a means of articulating—and sometimes debating—policy.

The masque grew out of the court displays and chivalric pageants of Elizabeth's court and initially employed similar dramatic techniques. Few scripts of Elizabethan entertainments survive, although there are many descriptions of the displays. In James's court the involvement of Daniel and, especially, Jonson, altered the balance of the relationship between words and spectacle. Jonson's famous quarrel with Inigo Jones was based on his belief in the primacy of words: for him, the spectacle was "momentary, and merely taking," an ephemeral trick affecting only the animal senses of the audience. Words, on the other hand, were to be savored and interpreted and used to direct the audience to understand the "more removed mysteries" that were the real substance of the masque.[9]

Daniel made less grandiose claims for his scripts: indeed, he recognized that in masques "the only life consists in show."[10] In Jonson's early masques, words and spectacle were generally directed toward the single, unequivocal end of celebrating royal authority. Often the celebration is heightened by the representation of the effortless triumph of kingly power over some grotesque or ignorant force. In Jonson's hands the "antemasque"—the prelude to the show proper—became the "antimasque," a display of the alien or disreputable forces that would be vanquished once the forces of truth, order, or union made their appearance. It was in the presence or participation of the king that diverse elements could be reconciled, concord drawn out of discord.

This fiction was given concrete expression—much to Jonson's distaste—by Inigo Jones's stage designs, which could make the King's throne the focus of all attention. Because the sets were designed with the king in mind as the ideal spectator—compared to whom everybody else would have only a partial or incomplete view—they could represent James's primacy silently but with immense power.[11]

Jonson's later masques, such as *Pleasure Reconciled to Virtue* (1618), are more complex and display a certain amount of dramatic conflict, which may in part reflect the declining fortunes of the ideology of absolutism. Perhaps the most interesting masques are those associated with Prince Henry, where there appears to have been a return to the Elizabethan fashion for conducting policy debate through the medium of court shows. The Arthurian masques Jonson wrote for the prince—*Prince Henry's Barriers* (1610) and *Oberon, the Fairy Prince* (1611)—use the Spenserian and Arthurian mythology that was associated with the prince's militant Protestantism. Jonson attempts to reconcile dramatically the king's persona as *Rex Pacificus* with the prince's stance as the new Alexander or Arthur: the challenge he faced was as much generic as political, and it caused him to revise his concept of the form.

There was a return to spectacular absolutism in the heyday of Charles I during the 1630s. From 1610 until then, however, masques became more varied in their focus and less unequivocal in their message. In the words of a recent commentator, "masques could be used to talk back to the King in his own language."[12] The King's Men were involved in a number of the court shows, and Shakespeare's later plays reflect this. There are many specific links between Shakespeare's plays and the masque. The morris dance in act 3 of *The Two Noble Kinsmen* is taken from Francis Beaumont's *Masque of the Inner Temple and Gray's Inn* (performed on 20 February 1613). Before that Shakespeare had included in *Pericles* a chivalric pageant on the Sidneyan model that includes the "matachine dance" performed by men in armor. The dance of the 12 rustics in act 4 of *The Winter's Tale* may well be the same dance performed by 12 satyrs to celebrate Oberon in Jonson's masque for Prince Henry. The prophetic pageants in *Cymbeline* and *Macbeth* have obvious analogies with the masque, as does the show of Juno and Ceres that Prospero conjures up in *The Tempest*. And it was during the masque in *Henry VIII* that a cannon ignited the thatched roof of the Globe, leading to the total destruction of the playhouse.

From the last years of Shakespeare's life there is a record of his involvement in a court pageant. For a show to be held on 24 March 1613 the designer of the mottos and *imprese* (decorated shields) for a production of *Pericles* was commissioned by Francis Manners, sixth earl of Rutland, to design a decoration for his shield, which was to be carried in a tilt. The multitalented Burbage was to paint the design. The two men were paid 24 shillings each a week later. The pageant seems to have involved an especially cryptic set of designs. Sir Henry Wotton commented that "some were so dark [obscure], that their meaning is not yet understood, unless perchance that were their meaning, not to be understood" (Kay 1992, 384–85; Schoenbaum 1977, 372).

Courtly entertainments were not always so elevated in their conception and execution. James was known to be an impatient spectator, on occasion urging the masquers to get on with the dance and drop the philosophical verses. There is a hilarious account of a masque presented for the King of Denmark in 1604, in which Sir John Harington describes the progressive effects of a tidal wave of drunkenness affecting both audience and participants. Harington concludes his account with a nostalgic look back to Queen Elizabeth and a wish to be back in the countryside. Such sentiments were common among courtiers, especially those who felt excluded by the new regime (Ashton, 244).

Thus the culture that grew up around James was as paradoxical as he. Whereas James promoted patriarchal values to the extent that the ideal of the aristocratic family was reflected in a new genre of court portraiture—the family group—he himself was far from the bourgeois ideal of fatherhood. His relations with his wife were not good, and he seems to have been very uneasy in the company of his children. Charles, and possibly Henry too, exhibited many symptoms of emotional disturbance, including marked nervousness in speech.

James was also homosexual and was throughout his life drawn to the company of brilliant and handsome young men (Ashton, 114). As with Elizabeth's suitors and favorites, the most significant consequence was a widespread anxiety that the monarch might fall under the influence of some unsuitable or ambitious individual, and that such a development would distort the power relations within the council. James's chief favorites were Robert Carr and George Villiers. Villiers acquired influence to rival that of Leicester in Elizabeth's court. As Duke of Buckingham he grew into perhaps the most powerful politician of his day and was the most trusted adviser of the young Charles after he succeeded to the throne. Like James, both Carr and Villiers married and sired children. The animus directed against them was generally of the standard kind that any royal favorite might expect: James was mocked more for making a fool of himself than for unorthodox sexual orientation.[13]

We can never know for sure if personal behavior was very different in James's court from what it had been in Elizabeth's. Disaffected survivors of Elizabeth's reign looked back to a golden age of sobriety and good taste. Of course the court of Elizabeth, as we have seen, had its eloquent detractors, but there can be little doubt about the reputation of James's court. Webster's Antonio pleads, "Let my son fly the courts of princes" (*The Duchess of Malfi*); his perception of the court as a place of corruption, intrigue, and immorality was very common. Such a view would have been reinforced by the celebrated court scandals—the most lurid of which was the murder of Sir Thomas Overbury and the subsequent trial. Frances Howard, the niece of the powerful Earl of Northampton, was married to the Earl of Essex. Perhaps through the intrigues of Northampton himself, Lady Essex became involved with King James's current favorite, the dashing Robert Carr, then Viscount Rochester, and sought a divorce from Essex. The only ground for divorce that was possible was nonconsummation, and so a council of eminent bishops was convened in order to establish that Lady Essex was still a virgin. Her testimony could have been challenged by Sir Thomas Overbury, who was Carr's secretary. He was duly imprisoned in the Tower of London, where she caused him to be poisoned. It was only after the divorce and subsequent remarriage that details began to emerge. There was a murder trial, in which Lady Essex (she was still a teenager) saw her sexual conduct subjected to salacious scrutiny. She and Carr were found guilty but suffered only exile from court. Their accomplices, however, including the governor of the Tower of London, paid for their parts in this intrigue with their lives (some documents reproduced in Ashton, 108–18).

A work from the center of this court culture is the romance *Urania*, written by Lady Mary Wroth. Wroth incurred the hostility of those who saw themselves and their interests represented in the text, and the massive second part of this remarkable work was never published. According to Barbara Lewalski, "The work only occasionally behaves like a true *roman à clef*, but it points insistently to Jacobean England and its ethos."[14]

James presented himself to his people as a theorist of power and kingship. He based some of his ideas on his experiences as a ruler since childhood, but he also engaged with religious and philosophical writers on political theory. He was convinced that his conclusions were correct, and that the king was anointed to be God's deputy on earth. He was sufficiently confident of the arguments in favor of this and related propositions that he evidently enjoyed argument and debate on the subject.

James also took an immediate interest in the patronage of the arts, especially drama. As in so many other spheres, the contrast with his predecessor was striking. Where Elizabeth had engaged in very little direct patronage and had been famously cautious in spending money or dispensing honours and titles, James took a very different line. He massively increased the number of knighthoods: in particular, he sold titles, especially baronetcies, as a way of raising revenue. In 1617 he financed a trip to Scotland to revisit the land of his birth (he compared himself to a salmon) by the sale of two earldoms. He and the other members of the royal family took on personal clients in a way Elizabeth never had. She had given a royal pension to only two writers, the poets Thomas Churchyard and Edmund Spenser. James, by contrast, lavishly patronized the arts. He, Queen Anne, and Prince Henry each took over the patronage of a dramatic troupe. James, as befitted his status, decided on the leading company, the Lord Chamberlain's Men.

Shakespeare and his fellows were the immediate beneficiaries, as we have seen. Only 10 days after arriving in London, James instructed Cecil to publish letters patent announcing what the king had done:

> Know ye that we of our Special grace, certain knowledge, and mere motion, have licensed and authorised . . . these our servants Lawrence Fletcher, William Shakespeare, Richard Burbage, Augustine Phillips, John Hemings, Henry Condell, William Sly, Robert Armin, Richard Cowley, and the rest of their Associates freely to use and exercise the art and faculty of playing comedies, tragedies, histories, interludes, morals, pastorals, stage plays, and such others like as they have already studied or

shall hereafter use or study, as well for the recreation of our loving subjects, as for our solace and pleasure when we shall think good to see them,
during our pleasure. (Chambers 1930, 2: 72)

After 1603 many dramatists wrote about kingship in new ways. At
first, the King's Men seem to have taken the king at his word and
sought to please him with a play based on an incident in his own life.
During 1604 they performed at court a play called the *Tragedy of Gowrie*,
presumably based on the events of August 1600, when King James
claimed that he had been miraculously rescued from the hands of two
would-be assassins, the Earl of Gowrie and his brother. James had
ordered a pamphlet to be printed giving his version of the extraordinary
episode. On his accession he had caused the Church of England to follow
the Scots example and make 5 August a holy day, establishing an order
of service to celebrate the king's miraculous rescue from evil hands. So
the players might have been justified in thinking the subject was in the
public domain and a fit theme for a play. John Chamberlain wrote a letter on 18 December 1604 in these terms: "The Tragedy of *Gowrie*, with
all the Action and Actors hath been twice represented by the King's
Players, with exceeding concourse of all sorts of People. But whether the
matter be not well handled, or that it be thought unfit that Princes
should be played on the Stage in their Life-time, I hear that some great
Councillors are much displased with it, and so 'tis thought shall be forbidden." It was indeed forbidden, and it has vanished without trace.[15]
Jonson's *Sejanus* (performed 1603; published 1605) provoked similarly
fierce responses from "great Councillors" and the author had to answer
to charges of treason.[16]
Such cases are a useful caution against the excessive literalism that
sometimes occurs in interpreting plays from this period. Obviously, not
all rulers are versions of King James, not all corrupt courts are mirrors of
Whitehall. But many plays unquestionably participate in the specifically
Jacobean discourses of politics and rule. The representation of male
rulers in fiction, and especially drama, in the years after 1603 is often
closely related to James's writings and actions. Sometimes the image is
positive, sometimes equivocal, occasionally critical. Another play from
the first year of the king's reign, Shakespeare's *Measure for Measure*, shows
a paradoxical or condradictory ruler, a kind of walking oxymoron—the
undercover uncoverer. The duke is at once permissive (presiding over a
collapse in moral standards in Vienna, for example) and forcefully
authoritarian (most obviously in the final scene).

A great variety of rulers was depicted on the Jacobean stage. There is rarely a one-to-one correspondence with James; often authors supply defensive prologues and epilogues to discourage such interpretations. It is easy to see why. *Eastward Ho!* (1605), by Jonson and George Chapman, features a man with a heavy Scottish accent who observes, "I ken the man weel, hee's one of my thirty pound knights": one of the knights referred to, Sir David Murray, drew the play to the attention of the king and the two dramatists were duly imprisoned and threatened with the mutilation of their ears and noses.[17]

The variety of stage rulers included the virtuous and the wicked, the decisive and the vacillating, the legitimate and the usurper, those addicted to flattery and those immune to it. The very range testifies to the age's fascination with the nature of rule and of rulers—a fascination encouraged by the king himself. An illuminating subgenre opened up the possibility of seeing legitimate rulers who, for one reason or another, are out of office. These are the "disguised duke" plays, such as Middleton's *The Phoenix*, Marston's *The Malcontent* and *The Fawn*, and Shakespeare's *Measure for Measure*, all from the first year of James's reign.

There are few stage rulers who wield absolute power throughout. If they are figured as virtuous, they achieve authority or are restored to it at the end of the drama (Shakespeare's Prospero is an obvious example). If they are figured as despotic or deluded, their power is generally removed or limited as the play proceeds (the Tyrant in the anonymous *Second Maiden's Tragedy* typifies this model). In the vast majority of cases the moral status and personality of the ruler resists such polarities. At the same time, considerations of legitimacy, the limits of authority, and the relationship between the ruler's public and private selves are continually brought to the audience's attention.[18]

A characteristic dramatic form of the early years of King James was the so-called closet drama—plays written to be read privately, perhaps to be declaimed, but emphatically not for the public stage. Although the vogue for such plays predates 1603 by a a few years, its peak was in the years immediately after that date. The authors of the "closet" plays were generally men and women from the highest ranks of society such as the Countess of Pembroke, Fulke Greville, Lady Elizabeth Cary, and the king's closest literary collaborator, Sir William Alexander. These writers constructed dramas, usually on classical models (often based on French Senecan originals), which took as their subjects topics from classical history (such as the Countess of Pembroke's *Tragedie of Antonie*; Alexander's plays on Alexander the Great, Caesar, and Darius; and Cary's biblical *Tragedy of Mariam*). The plays commonly include essaylike passages that comment on general questions raised by the stories about authority, history, virtue, or human nature.

The generalizing tendency of the closet plays—the impulse to relate individual people and events to ideas and principles of moral or political philosophy—was paralleled on the public stage. The tragedies of George Chapman, for instance, have sometimes been seen as the dramatic equivalent of the king's *Basilikon Doron*. Their author seems to have conceived of them as essays in political thought directed to the heir to the throne as a part of his education in kingship.

So it is the sheer variety of stage rulers and the tendency of the plays to raise and explore questions of political theory that is especially "Jacobean." Dramatists of the period consider the questions the king had brought up for examination. From Duke Vincentio and the king in *All's Well That Ends Well* to Duke Theseus in *The Two Noble Kinsmen*—by way of Lear, Macbeth, Octavius, Antony, Cymbeline, Leontes, and Prospero—Shakespeare presents an anthology of rulers, with their vices and virtues held up for detached inspection and engaged sympathy. They participate, though often in an ambiguous way, in James's cult of the philosopher-king.

Let me clarify what I mean by "ambiguous." At the simplest level, it is difficult to know what to make of the very fact of tragic drama on the public stage in the context of an authoritarian monarchy. As I have noted, some critics argue that the repeated staging of the deaths of rulers, the habitual castigation of courtiers and politicians (and often churchmen) as corrupt, must have had an impact on the audience's sense of values. It has been argued that the consequence was to make it easier for the English to resist and ultimately to remove their king from office. Others draw an opposite conclusion. They argue that the public stages operated as a kind of safety valve, where ritual displays of revolution, rebellion, king slaying, and the rest took place in clearly demarcated areas and at specified and limited times. Similar arguments exist in relation to other forms, especially comedy.[19]

A second point about political life and tragic drama is that the impact of the Earl of Essex's fall continued to resonate for at least a decade after the event. The Essex story, after all, could be understood as a conflict between the will of a man of honor and a centralizing, absolutist state hungry for power and control. The conflict was restaged often in

Shakespeare, frequently by investing contrasting individuals with competing values, as in the pairing of Coriolanus with Aufidius and Mark Antony with Brutus.

This is one of the ways in which we can understand the political implications of literary genre in the period. Revenge tragedy and historical tragedy come to be based on conflicts that are more than merely personal, in which the issues raised are more general and, potentially, more urgently contemporary. Related to the conflict between nostalgic honor and ruthless, unheroic pragmatism is the common opinion that heroism and chivalry had become anachronistic in the modern world. The Homeric hero of Chapman's tragedies is left like a beached whale, gasping for breath in a hostile environment. He may be admirable, but he is doomed. Cervantes's *Don Quixote*, which first appeared in translation in 1609, is the most extraordinary examination of a life lived by the standards of a bygone age.

Jacobean comedy is a more heterogeneous phenomenon than the tragedy of the period. Shakespeare's "problem plays" were originally so-called precisely because they were not assimilable to conventional generic categories. Other contemporary writers similarly exploited a sense of the instability of genres. Perhaps the most remarkable surviving example is Marston's *The Malcontent*, which has been described as a "revenge comedy." Leaving aside such experiments, however, the two chief kinds were urban comedies and romance comedies. Either kind could accommodate satire, driven into the theaters by the late Elizabethan prohibitions.

As with tragedy, it has been recognized that Jacobean comic drama is related closely to the political and social concerns of the time, especially in terms of family structures, sexual relations, and identity and the social order. Whether its approach is subversive or conservative is no less clear, however. Ben Jonson's urban comedy *Bartholomew Fair* (1614), for example, seems to embody the spirit of the carnival, the alternative order of values that power structures cannot contain.[20] And yet the piece has two endings. The speakers on stage resolve to go off and get drunk, to "drown the memory of this enormity in our biggest bowl at home." The play's Epilogue, however, then addresses remarks to the king himself, who is imagined to be present. He says, "Your Majesty hath seen the play, and you / Can best allow it from your place and view." One ending prolongs the spirit of the fair and extends it beyond the play itself; the other closes it off and acknowledges that its very existence has depended on the king's permission.

Although Shakespeare did not write urban comedy in the style of Jonson or Chapman, he did make use of elements of the form, with its focus on trickery, cuckoldry of older husbands, and the temporary absence of controlling authority. Traces of the genre may be found in several of his Jacobean plays, such as *Measure for Measure, Othello, Cymbeline,* and *The Winter's Tale.* He also performed in such plays, notably in Jonson's *Every Man in His Humour*—an important source for his own *Othello.* A record survives of a double bill by the King's Men at Oxford in September 1610, where *Othello* was twinned with Jonson's *The Alchemist* (Kay 1992, 361; *Riverside Shakespeare,* 1852).

The inseparability of politics and aesthetics in Stuart culture has long been recognized.[21] "In a King," wrote George Chapman, "all places are contained."[22] The phrase sums up the ideal of the centralizing, absolutist monarch, the fount of power, honor, justice, authority, and form. The neoclassical drama of seventeenth-century France may be seen as expressions of the culture of *Le Roi Soleil,* the king who was the sun at the center of the known universe—the very embodiment of the state. The culture of Jacobean England, in contrast, was characterized by hybrid forms. Even the court masque expanded to include the antimasque and was often used, as on a smaller scale under Elizabeth, as an oblique form of political persuasion and argument.

James's cult was patriarchal: one of its most important features was its stress on a a newly established dynasty. This meant that the image of the young Prince Henry was assiduously promoted. Henry died at age 18 in 1612, but in the four or five years before that time he became an important figure in political discourse. James had taken pains over Henry's education, and the boy had turned out to be a solemn and learned young man who had developed a hatred of Catholics and enthusiasm for martial sports, fierce sermons, and colonial expansion. He was made Prince of Wales in 1608 (the first for a century) and then established his own court, where he was surrounded by men who were drawn by conviction or ambition or a combination of the two.[23]

From that point on, until Henry's death four years later, the idea of authority and power in Jacobean England had to be modified. Henry's court was different from the king's in several ways, but although Henry's views on some issues were different from his father's, it is too crude to think of this second court as a center of opposition. James intended Henry's household to be "a courtly college, or a collegiate court," and one element of the exchanges between father and son was educational—

Henry was being trained in statecraft. Another element was generational: James was passing on ideas and experience to his successor.

Nobody in the period could have been prepared for the implications of this phenomenon. Few rulers in those turbulent days had the self-assurance and confidence to establish their acknowledged successor with a court in the midst of the state's capital. From that moment on, the understanding of power and authority underwent changes to accommodate this new situation. And just as absolutism had its artistic forms, so in time did this novel variant.

We need look no further than the later plays of Shakespeare to understand this. At the most basic level, most of the late plays deal very directly with interactions between generations, with the transfer of power from the older to the younger generation. Sometimes (as in *Cymbeline* and *Antony and Cleopatra*) that transfer is connected with the shift from a pagan to a Christian era, with the fulfillment of prophecies and the operation of Providence. No less obvious is the vogue for the mixed form of tragicomedy. And the ruling aesthetic principle we can identify in these pieces is not "unity" in the classical, Aristotelian sense but rather something less intellectual, less formal.

Shakespeare's last play, *The Two Noble Kinsmen*, performed in honor of the wedding of Prince Henry's sister Elizabeth, just three months after Henry died, ends with the injunction from Duke Theseus: "Let's go off, and bear us like the time." He stands before us as an absolute ruler, faced (like King James in 1613) with two contrasting outcomes to the story: a death and a marriage. To bear oneself "like the time" must mean to try to comprehend both, not to set one up as superior to the other. Shakespeare gave us a model of such doubleness in the gentleman's description of Paulina in *The Winter's Tale*: "But O, the noble combat that 'twixt joy and sorrow was fought in Paulina! She had one eye declin'd for the loss of her husband, another elevated that the oracle was fulfill'd" (5.2.72–76).

We have already seen that the court masque had generally been structured around the narrative of a quest, of a journey toward truth. That truth was a political truth, a discovery of the reality of power. As in Jonson's *Bartholomew Fair*, the great vision or revelation at the end was normally of the king himself, and his appearance reasserted the social hierarchy. Similarly, at the end of *Measure for Measure* the duke doles out information while retaining control of it: "we'll show / What's yet behind, that's meet you all should know."

Shakespeare's late plays tend to present truth in a much less hierarchical, much less circumscribed way.[24] Thus the subtitle (perhaps its actual title) of *Henry VIII* is "All Is True," and the show's Prologue invites the audience to "think ye see / The very persons of our noble story as they were living." In so doing the Globe spectators will be "sad, as we would make ye." The play presents a period of English history that continued to arouse fiercely partisan feelings, and yet it includes sympathetic portraits of, for example, Wolsey and Cromwell, Catherine of Aragon and the infant Elizabeth. Successive events, which might in a political or historical sense qualify or contradict each other, are presented in a strange, evaluative limbo. There is no attempt to provide a central focus. The king himself is a manipulator and impresario, but the limits of his authority are as noticeable as its strength.

If anything, *Henry VIII*, like *The Tempest*, places its audience in the position the king took in a royal masque: it is for them to draw together all the disparate strands of the story. And yet at that moment Shakespeare puts into the mouth of Archbishop Cranmer a prophecy of the reign of King James that will follow the death of the child he holds in his arms. The king will be one

> Who from the sacred ashes of her honour
> Shall star-like rise, as great in fame as she was,
> And so stand fixed. Peace, plenty, love, truth, terror,
> That were the servants to this chosen infant,
> Shall then be his, and like a vine grow to him;
> Wherever the bright star of heaven shall shine,
> His honour and the greatness of his name
> Shall be, and make new nations. He shall flourish,
> And like a mountain cedar, reach his branches
> To all the plains about him: our children's children
> Shall see this, and bless heaven. (5.4.45–54)

As James's reign proceeded, the separation between elite and popular forms, especially in drama, became increasingly marked. Tragicomedy and romance in particular became more refined, more aristocratic in their appeal. Members of the upper classes began to write plays for performance on some of the public stages, and professional playwrights displayed elaborate and at times brilliant art. A recent commentator has observed of John Fletcher that "he developed a comic eclecticism so refined it gives the impression of homogeneity."[25]

The last year of the king's reign was marked with controversy, however, as an elite play once again touched a nerve with the wider public. Middleton's allegorical play *A Game at Chess* addressed highly contentious political issues—notably, the plan to marry Prince Charles to a Catholic princess. The allegorical chess game shows white Protestant souls under threat from the black Jesuit pieces, and there are recognizable portraits of Jacobean politicians in the course of an elaborate and vigorous satirical attack on the threat posed by Catholicism to the church and state. The King's Men, who staged the piece, were banned for a time, and the author was obliged to make himself scarce. But this was not before the play had been by far the biggest box office success of its generation, playing to upwards of 2,000 spectators on each of nine successive days.

The controversy about *A Game at Chess* is an appropriate incident with which to conclude this brief survey of the contradictory qualities of Jacobean culture and their relation to the drama. It eloquently shows that, however powerful the central authority, however effective its censorship, the drama could communicate outside its controls—even if only briefly—and could articulate contrary viewpoints.[26]

For the student of Shakespeare, there are some more specifically "Jacobean" elements in some of his plays that should be borne in mind. The political situation in his Vienna, for example, has been related both to the peace negotiations with Spain that took place in the summer of 1603 and to contemporary arguments about the nature and constitution of elective government in and around London. Critics have recognized for many years that the corn riots that swept across England in 1607—some of them in Hampton-on-Arden, not far from Stratford—are alluded to in *Coriolanus*. They have argued about the significance for the interpretation of the play but not about the fact that the riots (if that is what they were—historians disagree about this) are part of the play's context. When King Lear says, "They cannot touch me for coining. I am the King himself," his words would have had a special resonance in view of a dispute about who was entitled to mint coins in James's realm. And when the foolish king divides his kingdom the audience can hardly have failed to pick up a reference to the lively political debate then raging about King James's wish to unify under one crown all the kingdoms of Britain. The Cedar, which is Cymbeline's emblem, was James's emblem also. And of course James believed he was descended from Banquo.

It would be possible to list numerous correspondences of this kind. It is perhaps more relevant to stress that Shakespeare was the leading dramatist of the king's own troupe of actors, that he was an immensely successful practitioner of an art that was both politically sensitive and hugely popular. His success, in matching his art to the forms and pressures of the time, was rivaled by none of his contemporaries.

Chapter Eight
Shakespeare's Career

Like Caesar's Gaul, Shakespeare's career may be divided chronologically into three parts, covering first the years up to 1593; then his work with the Lord Chamberlain's Men, from 1594 to 1603; and then with the King's Men, from 1603 to 1613.

Up to 1593

By 1592 Shakespeare was established as an important figure in the London theatrical world—important enough to be the subject of an attack by the leading playwright Robert Greene in his pamphlet *Groatsworth of Wit*. Yet all that is known for certain about Shakespeare before 1592 is that he was baptized, that he took out a marriage license in 1582, and that his three children were baptised in 1583 and 1585. It is also universally assumed that he attended school in Stratford until about 1579. What is clear is that he must have been conspicuously active in the theater in order to have attracted Greene's perhaps envious hostility. Whether that implies he had written 12 plays or half that number by 1592 is a matter about which scholars continue to argue (the almost Swiftian debate between the "early start" school and their "late start" opponents has the great scholarly virtue of being unresolvable, short of a miraculous discovery).

How did Shakespeare spend the "lost years" between 1579 and the late 1580s? Theories abound.[1] One or more of the following (in any combination) has been suggested at some stage: he may have traveled; worked as a schoolmaster, a lawyer, or a soldier; trained as an actor; embraced (or left) the Roman Catholic Church; poached deer; or indulged in heroic bouts of heavy drinking. Many of these suggestions—free as most of them are of documentation—tell us more about the developing reputation of the national Bard than about the life of the historical William Shakespeare.[2]

An exception may be the possibility of Shakespeare's teaching in the country. The source is the seventeenth-century diarist John Aubrey, who claimed in his *Brief Lives* that his informant was the actor William

Beeston (d. 1682). Beeston was the son of Christopher Beeston, a colleague of Shakespeare's in the Lord Chamberlain's Men (his name appears with Shakespeare's in the cast list for Ben Jonson's comedy *Every Man in His Humour* [1598]). Aubrey reports that Shakespeare "understood Latin pretty well, for he had been in his younger years a schoolmaster in the country." This probably means that he acted as an assistant to a better qualified master, since it would have been unusual (though not completely unprecedented) for someone of Shakespeare's youth, with only a grammar school training, to set up independently as a schoolmaster.

There may be some more evidence to support this idea. In 1581 the master of Lea Hall near Preston in Lancashire, Alexander Houghton, drew up his will. He made provision for numerous retainers, including one "William Shakeshafte," and enjoined his heir, Thomas Houghton, to "be friendly unto" Shakeshafte and either find work for him or help him to another position. Was Shakeshafte William Shakespeare? The name is hardly a problem—the Stratford Shakespeares are sometimes called Shakestaffe or Shakeshaft, and at the height of his fame William appears in records as "Shaxberd." One of the Stratford schoolmasters may provide a link to the Houghtons. When Richard Jenkins gave up the post in 1579 he recommended to the town a scholar from Brasenose College, John Cottom. Cottom resigned in 1581, about the time his younger brother, a Jesuit priest, was arrested with Edmund Campion. John Cottom retreated to his native Lancashire, where he lived openly as a Catholic, paying the stipulated fines. Cottom's father was a tenant of the Houghtons. If William Shakespeare is "Shakeshafte," then at sometime between 1579 and 1581 he was moved from Protestant Stratford to Catholic Lancashire and rapidly achieved a prominent position in a large household.[3]

This story implies a closer conjunction between Shakespeare and Catholicism than would be consistent either with the nationalistic Protestantism of the Shakespeare myth or with the strong anti-Catholic sentiments articulated from time to time in William Shakespeare's plays. And there were other Shakeshaftes in Lancashire. Nevertheless, the Lancashire story offers one explanation of Shakespeare's route to London. Houghton's players probably went into the sevice of the Hesketh family, and thence into the service of Ferdinando Strange, the earl of Derby. When Lord Strange died, his players were assimilated into the Lord Chamberlain's Men, and it is as a member of that company that William Shakespeare is first recognizable as a figure in the documentary history of the London theater companies.

As I have discussed, it is not known when Shakespeare came to London or how his association with the professional theater began and developed. There are suggestions, for instance, that he was recruited in Stratford by the Queen's Men who lost an actor (the aptly named William Knell), slain in a tavern brawl at Thame in Oxfordshire in June 1587 (Schoenbaum 1977, 116–17). Such uncertainty is partly a function of the London theatrical milieu in the years before the severe plague of 1593.

The dominant company between 1583 and 1588 was the Queen's Men, a company that had assimilated survivors of the previous leading troupe, Leicester's Men. This group played at several different venues but enjoyed the inestimable benefit of royal support, which meant they could perform with somewhat greater license than their competitors. The company's repertoire was distinctly modern: it put on plays by Greene and Peele and staged several history plays. Their main attraction was the celebrated clown Richard Tarleton. After Tarleton's death in 1588 their fortunes declined, and by 1591 they were no longer preeminent in court performances. Shakespeare's involvement is suggested, though not proved, by the fact that three of his plays, written at different points of his career—*Henry V, King John*, and *King Lear*—are based on plays that had formed part of the Queen's Men's repertoire.

Another important troupe was formed by the combination of Lord Strange's Men with the Admiral's Men between 1590 and Lord Strange's death in 1594.[4] The company's chief asset was the leading actor, Edward Alleyn, formerly one of Worcester's Men. They began to perform at James Burbage's playhouse, the Theatre, in 1590. One of the actors in the company was Richard Burbage, and there were several other men who would eventually work with Shakespeare, as we have seen. After a dispute with James Burbage, the troupe began to perform at Henslowe's Rose on the South Bank. They performed Marlowe (*The Jew of Malta* and *Doctor Faustus*), Greene (*Orlando Furioso* and *Friar Bacon and Friar Bungay*), Kyd (*The Spanish Tragedy*), and the work of many other popular playwrights.

The obscure history of Pembroke's Men begins either in 1591, in the aftermath of the Admiral's–Lord Strange's dispute with Burbage, or in the following year. The group performed at court and went on tour. It lost a great deal of money and was disbanded; the disposal of its assets included the publication of its scripts. They included Marlowe's *Edward II, 3 Henry VI* (entitled *The True Tragedy of Richard Duke of York*), *Titus Andronicus*, and the enigmatic *The Taming of a Shrew*.[5] The versions of the plays are consistent with the idea that Pembroke's Men were formed essentially as a touring company, and that they took with them pared-down versions of London successes, designed for performance by smaller groups with less elaborate resources.

The evidence, fragmentary as it is, suggests that Shakespeare started out with the Queen's Men, perhaps simply as a player, although he might have begun to revise scripts for the company. He then became involved with the Admiral's–Lord Strange's Men conglomerate. This large group certainly would have possessed the resources and skill to stage pieces like *Richard III* and *Titus Andronicus* (Schoenbaum 1977, 165–67). Then followed the short-lived operation of Pembroke's Men, and after that the plague struck again and the theaters were closed.

The theatrical profession was thrown into confusion by the length and severity of the plague. When the theaters reopened, as we have seen, only two companies were to flourish, the Admiral's Men and the newly formed Lord Chamberlain's Men, of which Shakespeare was to be a partner, a "sharer." The significance of his place in that troupe suggests that he brought with him assets beyond simple acting ability. On the evidence of later publication, it looks as though he brought with him the most valuable commodity of all: scripts that had proved their worth on the stage. They would have been at least *The Comedy of Errors, The Taming of the Shrew, The Two Gentlemen of Verona, 1, 2, 3 Henry VI, Richard III, Titus Andronicus*, and perhaps some other plays as well. In a theatrical milieu that had lost Greene and Marlowe and would look in vain for new work by Lyly, Peele, and Lodge, Shakespeare had become almost overnight a significant figure.

Of course if Shakespeare had begun to entertain lofty notions of himself as something more than a mere scriptwriter, his ambition could not at that time have been realized on the stage. No playwright of the generation would have considered himself an author, a maker. In the early 1590s the medium was held to be too ephemeral, too modern, and unstable.[6]

The young man from Stratford rapidly established himself as an actor and scriptwriter, probably on a freelance basis, working for several of the theatrical troupes of the time. It is also possible that he had become involved in the financial side of the business as a partner in one (or more) of the companies. By 1592 he was sufficiently well known to be the subject of the attack by Greene (see Schoenbaum 1977, 147–58; Kay 1992, 162–66). Greene would be able to pour scorn on the upstart for being a jack of all trades ("an absolute *Iohannes fac totum*") who had too high an opinion of himself ("in his own conceit the only Shake-scene in a country"). How much did he need to have achieved to warrant this attack? If we accept the "early start" view, Shakespeare might have written more than 10 plays by 1592. If the "late start" is believed, then maybe only three or four.

If Shakespeare worked for the Queen's Men, he would have encountered Greene, formerly of St. John's, Cambridge (B.A. in 1580), who was one of a generation of university-educated men trying to make a living as writers. In a letter appended to Greene's *Groatsworth of Wit*, the speaker, "R.G.," addresses three "University" writers, conventionally identified as Marlowe, Nashe, and George Peele, before proceeding:

> Base minded men all three of you, if by my misery you be not warned. For unto none of you (like me) sought those burrs to cleave—those puppets (I mean) that spake from our mouths, those antics garnished in our colours. Is it not strange that I, to whom they all have been beholding: is it not like that you, to whom they have all been beholding, shall (were ye in that case as I am now) be both at once of them forsaken? Yes trust them not: for there is an upstart Crow, beautified with our feathers, that with his *Tiger's heart wrapped in a Player's hide*, supposes he is as well able to bombast out a blank verse as the best of you: and being an absolute *Johannes fac totum*, is in his own conceit the only Shake-scene in a country. O that I might entreat your rare wits to be employed in more profitable course, and let those Apes imitate your past excellence, and never more acquaint them with your admired inventions. I know the best husband of you all will never prove an Usurer, and the kindest of them all will never prove a kind nurse. . . . Trust not then (I beseech ye) to such weak stays: for they are as changeable in mind as in many attires. (*Riverside Shakespeare*, 1835)

Greene signals the chief target of his attack by punning on Shakespeare's name, and by parodying York's description of Queen Margaret in *3 Henry VI* as a "tiger's heart wrapped in a woman's hide." But Shakespeare is cited as typical of a class of usurpers—of puppets, antics, dissemblers (i.e., actors rather than university graduates)—who, having mouthed others' words, now presume to write for themselves, stealing the finery provided for them by their betters. Greene, a professional writer, protests that his specialized province has been invaded by untrained actors, whose scripts are shallow, derivative, and annoyingly popular.

Professor Honigmann has pointed out that Greene's volume does not end with the much-quoted letter. Instead we are presented with an allegory—a fable of the ant and the grasshopper, in which Greene's dazzling, brilliant grasshopper is denied hospitality and support by the killjoy plodding ant. When winter comes, the prodigal grasshopper is dismissed by the insect embodiment of the work ethic ("Thou scorndst to toil, and now thou feelst the storm"). Does the fable paint a picture of the profligate genius (Greene) as the victim of the selfish heartlessness of the bourgeois, antlike thrifty husbandman (Shakespeare)? Had the improvident Greene turned to Shakespeare for financial help and been refused? For him Shakespeare was not just a "puppet" who had had the nerve to usurp the puppeteer's role. Worse than that, he deemed himself their artistic superior ("in his own conceit the only Shake-scene in a country"), and gave himself unwarranted airs, capriciously exercising powers of patronage without the breeding or education of a lord.[7]

Very soon an apology, almost a recantation, of Greene's attack appeared. The author was Henry Chettle, whom some believed to be behind the earlier book. In the epistle dedicatory to his *Kind-Hart's Dream* he wrote,

About three months since died M. Robert Greene, leaving many papers in sundry book sellers' hands, among other his *Groatsworth of Wit*, in which a letter written to divers play-makers, is offensively by one or two of them taken; and because on the dead they cannot be avenged, they wilfully forge in their conceits a living author: and after tossing it too and fro, no remedy, but it must light on me. How I have all the time of my conversing in printing hindered the bitter inveighing against schollers, it hath been very well known; and how in that I dealt, I can sufficiently prove. With neither of them that take offence was I acquainted, and with one of them I care not if I never be. The other, whom at that time I did not so much spare, as since I wish I had, for that as I have moderated the heat of living writers, and might have used my own discretion (especially in such a case) the author being dead, that I did not, I am as sorry as if the original fault had been my fault, because my self have seen his demeanour no less civil than he excellent in the quality he professes. Besides, divers of worship have reported his uprightness of dealing, which argues his honesty, and his facetious grace in writing, that approves his art. (*Riverside Shakespeare*, 1835–36)

Chettle's book was entered in the Stationers' Register on 8 December 1592 and probably appeared not long after, in the early months of 1593.

The author protests (too much?) that he was not the author of the *Groatsworth*—"it was all Greene's, not mine." To Schoenbaum (1977, 154), Chettle's apology provides "the first glimpse we get of [Shakespeare] as a man." Chettle vouches for Shakespeare's character quite fulsomely and on the basis of personal acquaintance—"my self have seen his demeanour no less civil than he excellent in the quality he professes." He concedes the good opinion held of Shakespeare by "divers of worship" (in the elaborately stratified language of address in Elizabethan England, this must mean gentlemen rather than nobles—aristocrats would have been referred to as "divers of honour"). The earlier attack clearly caused influential men to rally around Shakespeare and praise his "uprightness of dealing" and "honesty" (in writing and in business, presumably) as well as his "facetious grace" and "art" in composition. The pamphlet testifies to the force of Shakespeare's personality among his friends and colleagues.

The plague ended a period of rapid expansion in the number of actors and companies. From then on they were to be more tightly organized, more stable, and increasingly run by theatrical professionals with a stake in the business. The ascendancy of the so-called University Wits ended with the deaths of Greene (1592) and Marlowe (1593). The dominant voice was to be that of the "upstart crow."

1593–1603: The Poems and the Lord Chamberlain's Men

While the theaters were closed, Shakespeare embarked on a more conventional literary career with his poems. Through these texts he became known outside the theatrical world. They were his first official publications, the first of his writings to appear with his name on the title page. It was a further five years before he put his name to the printed script of a play. After the successful publication of the poems, Shakespeare's reputation was high and must have drawn more spectators to his plays. Yet he seems not to have traded on the name for some time, and the implication must be that he did not need to do so.[8]

Shakespeare's first publication, *Venus and Adonis*, was dedicated to the 18-year-old Henry Wriothesley, third earl of Southampton. The dedication reveals a frank appeal for patronage, couched in the normal terms of such requests, perhaps slightly less servile than most. In it the poet offers his work as a nobleman's recreation to read, as it had been his own recreation to write it "in all idle hours"; he promises to follow up with something more substantial, something "graver." The text runs thus:

> Right Honourable, I know not how I shall offend in dedicating my unpolished lines to your Lordship, nor how the world will censure me for choosing so strong a prop to support so weak a burden. Only if your Honour seem but pleased, I account myself highly praised, and vow to take advantage of all idle hours, till I have honoured you with some graver labour. But if the first heir of my invention prove deformed, I shall be sorry it had so noble a godfather, and never after ear so barren a land, for fear it yield me still so bad a harvest. I leave it to your honourable survey, and your Honour to your heart's content, which I wish may always answer your own wish, and the world's hopeful expectation.
>
> Your Honour's in all duty,
William Shakespeare

Much about this passage is, as critics have pointed out, highly conventional. The image of the text as offspring, for instance, is standard Elizabethan usage (Sidney presented his *Arcadia* as "this child I am loth to father"), as is the element of nonchalant self-deprecation or *sprezzatura*. The tone is relatively formal, arguing no intimacy: it was quite common for such dedications to be essentially speculative.[9]

Richard Field, Shakespeare's printer was both professionally accomplished and a Stratford neighbor (Eccles, 59–60). Field was born in Stratford-upon-Avon in November 1561. His father, Henry Field, worked as a tanner on Bridge Street, less than five minutes' walk from John Shakespeare's Henley Street house. The two fathers, in similar lines of business, were acquainted: when the elder Field died in 1592 John Shakespeare helped to value his estate. Both men had seen their sons make their way in the new industries of the metropolis. Field's boy was apprenticed to Thomas Vautrollier, whose printing shop was in the Blackfriars complex. When Vautrollier died in 1587, his widow married Richard, then 27 and only recently out of his apprenticeship. The firm had specialized in high-quality, often technically difficult work, including such books as Richard Mulcaster's *Elementarie* and North's *Plutarch*. *Venus and Adonis* is recognizably of a piece with their normal output. In 1591 they had printed the massive translation of Ariosto's epic romance *Orlando Furioso*, by Sir John Harington, and in 1598 they would produce the handsome folio *Arcadia*, along with other collected works by Sidney. Field himself had begun to issue books under his own imprint as early as

1589, and his output included George Puttenham's *The Arte of English Poesie*, the 1596 edition of *The Faerie Queene*, and Spenser's *Daphnaida* and *Four Hymns*.

The subject of Shakespeare's next publication indicates that *Venus and Adonis* had been well received. The tone of the dedication to *Lucrece* is markedly warmer than that of its predecessor. It looks as though Shakespeare has come to know Southampton as more than a remote potential benefactor:

> The love I dedicate to your Lordship is without end: whereof this Pamphlet without beginning is but a superfluous moiety. The warrant I have of your honourable disposition, not the worth of my untutored lines, makes it assured of acceptance. What I have done is yours; what I have to do is yours; being part in all I have, devoted yours. Were my worth greater, my duty would show greater; meantime, as it is, it is bound to your Lordship, to whom I wish long life still lengthened with all happiness.
>
> Your Lordship's in all duty,
William Shakespeare

Like its predecessor, *Lucrece* was instantly popular. Gabriel Harvey observed that Shakespeare's "Lucrece, & his tragedy of Hamlet, Prince of Denmark, have it in them, to please the wiser sort" (*Riverside Shakespeare*, 1840). The poem went through eight editions before 1640.

The structure and organization of the Lord Chamberlain's Men has already been described, with some indication of their repertoire and styles. Shakespeare's involvement with them was very substantial—as actor, scriptwriter, and "sharer." His work can be seen to develop with the company (Kay 1992, 173–286). At a basic level, the company's human resources and its fluctuating political fortunes dictated what he could not—and sometimes what he could—write. As far as his status as a writer is concerned, the two most significant developments during the period were the publication of scripts with his name on the title page and the company's momentous move to the Globe.

It was Ben Jonson who first sought in 1597–98 to exercise control over the publication of his scripts and to claim a higher literary status for dramatic texts than they usually enjoyed. His efforts coincided with a period of conflict between the theatrical troupes and the censoring authorities, culminating in the order of 28 July 1598 that the theaters should be "pluckt down." At about the same time Francis Meres published his *Palladis Tamia*, a work that includes a famous passage praising

Shakespeare's achievement as the equal of great writers of the ancient world. Shakespeare had published two poems and perhaps as many as eight plays when Meres composed an extended praise of his writing:

> As the soul of Euphorbus was thought to live in Pythagoras: so the sweet witty soul of Ovid lives in mellifluous and honey-tongued Shakespeare, witness his *Venus* and *Adonis*, his *Lucrece*, his sugared Sonnets among his private friends, etc.
>
> As Plautus and Seneca are accounted the best for Comedy and Tragedy among the Latins: so Shakespeare among the English is the most excellent in both kinds for the stage; for Comedy, witness his *Gentlemen of Verona*, his *Errors*, his *Loves Labours Lost*, his *Loves Labours Won*, his *Midsummer Night's Dream*, and his *Merchant of Venice*: for Tragedy his *Richard the 2*, *Richard the 3*, *Henry the 4*, *King John*, *Titus Andronicus* and his *Romeo and Juliet*.
>
> As Epius Stolo said, that the Muses would speak with Plautus tongue if they would speak Latin: so I say that the Muses would speak with Shakespeare's fine filed phrase, if they would speak English. (*Riverside Shakespeare*, 1844)

The example of Jonson, the status implicit in the praise of Meres, and the new threat to the economic viability of the theaters are part of the context in which Shakespeare declared himself to the public as an author of dramatic texts. In 1598 appeared *Love's Labour's Lost* and new editions of *Richard III* and *Richard II* above Shakespeare's name. This was a significant moment in his professional career. It also signaled that it was now possible for a writer to claim the lofty status of an author through the publication of plays. The title page of *Love's Labour's Lost* declares itself to be both a literary work "newly corrected and augmented by W. Shakespere" and the record of an elite, courtly event, "As it was presented before her Highnes this last Christmas." This last case is a reminder that the Lord Chamberlain's Men performed regularly at court—an obligation that brought with it challenges as well as lucrative opportunities.

Shakespeare's arrangement with the troupe seems to have been for two plays per year—one comic, one "serious" (a tragedy or history). The height of his achievement in the years before 1598 had been the so-called lyrical plays—namely, the comedies *Love's Labour's Lost* and *A Midsummer Night's Dream* and the tragedies *Richard II* and *Romeo and Juliet*. Such plays clearly indicate the broadening scope of Shakespeare's literary and social aspirations. The move to the Globe promised a new security to the company, and the building itself, as we have seen, encouraged a new ambition in its actors and writers by embodying in its very architecture the idea that "all the world's a stage." The first "Globe" plays—*Julius Caesar, As You Like It, Twelfth Night, Troilus and Cressida, Hamlet*, and *All's Well That Ends Well*—take these ambitions further. These plays were also written in the context of the renewed success of the "little eyases" of the boys' companies and the vogue for sophisticated metropolitan satire north of the river. The very scale of Shakespeare's pieces, and the demands they made on their talented adult actors, were powerful counters to any potential challengers to the theatrical primacy of the Lord Chamberlain's Men.

This period of artistic triumph brought the company closest to the dangerous world of power politics. Supporters of the Earl of Essex paid the Lord Chamberlain's Men to perform *Richard II* on the day before Essex's uprising. The queen was only too aware of the historical parallels that might be drawn between her and the deposed ruler: she remarked, "I am Richard II, know ye not that?" The Earl of Southampton, to whom Shakespeare had addressed his narrative poems, was one of the leading plotters and was instantly arrested. Yet, though some of the company were questioned, they suffered no penalty for the use made of their play and their services. Indeed, they were engaged to perform for the queen at court on the night before Essex was beheaded.[10]

1603–1613: The King's Men

I have already described the composition, organization, and repertoire of the King's Men. With the exception of *Measure for Measure*, Shakespeare's first productions as a member of the troupe were the tragedies *Othello, King Lear, Macbeth, Antony and Cleopatra*, and *Coriolanus*. All of these plays connect in some way with the king's policies and image, or with contemporary political events and arguments. As we have seen, the company was regularly in demand for performances at court, and some of the plays—notably *King Lear*—seem to have been shaped with such a performance in mind. The court records remind us that the king's taste extended beyond tragedy. In the first court season, for example, he asked for *The Merchant of Venice* to be repeated on 12 February, having seen it already on the 10th. He also saw revivals of *Love's Labour's Lost, Henry V, The Merry Wives of Windsor*, and *The Comedy of Errors*, as well as the new plays *Othello* and *Measure for Measure* (Chambers 1930, 2: 329–45). A recent commentator has summed up the King's Men as having "one foot in court life and another in the commercial world of the theatre" (Dutton 1989, 138). This often meant that, as with Lyly's plays, scripts were adapted for presentation at different venues: the two versions of *King Lear*—one for the court, the other for the Globe—illustrate this well.[11]

Shakespeare had always been expected to write plays that could be staged at public playhouses, at court, and on tour. In 1608, as we have seen, he and his "Fellows" at long last acquired the Blackfriars theater (they started to perform there after the plague relented, in late 1609). *Pericles* predates this move and was certainly performed at the Globe, as were *The Winter's Tale* and *Henry VIII*, as well as (probably) *Cymbeline*. Thus, although the new venue must have had an impact on Shakespeare's imagination, his plays continued to be performed in a wide variety of settings, including on board ship off the coast of Sierra Leone.[12] On the other hand, the exceptional popularity of *The Winter's Tale* at court—there were at least seven revivals of the play—testifies to the extent to which the late romances participate in court culture.[13]

As I have noted, Shakespeare began to spend increasing amounts of time in Stratford from about 1610. His semi-retirement coincides with a period of extraordinary artistic experiment. It also coincides with his beginning a literary partnership with John Fletcher, who would in due course succeed him as the chief scriptwriter of their company. It is only in recent years that critics have begun to explore the aesthetics and politics of such collaboration and to relate it to such phenomena as the vogue for hybrid forms such as tragicomedy and romance on the stage. We are beginning to see that Shakespeare's career ended as it began, with works that were artistically innovative and experimental at the same time as they were social and collaborative. In any case, it might be argued that all of his plays were collaborative at some level: to two of his recent editors, the theater itself was Shakespeare's most regular and important collaborator.[14]

When Shakespeare began his career the status of scriptwriters for the public stage was low. By the end of his career the situation had changed utterly. Ben Jonson's handsome Folio *Works* in 1616 presented the dramatist as an author fit to rank with those of the ancient world; he was the literary counterpart of his monarch. King James's *Works* had been published in 1614, and Jonson's book emulates the style and display of the king's (Marcus 1988, chap. 1, 108–109, 143–44). Shakespeare's earliest publications had appeared under the aegis of the companies that had staged them.[15] It was only when he published his poems that his name appeared on the title page. The visual appearance of these works conforms to the conventions of their time: the aspiration to the status of author involves emulation of the classics and an attempt to secure aristocratic patronage through the use of dedications.

Yet two things need to be borne in mind about Shakespeare as a theatrical professional. First, he did not need patronage in the way his rivals did. His London income derived from the theater as a business, from his position as shareholder and actor, more than from his pen. Second, he had achieved real financial independence before the end of the sixteenth century. The coat of arms in 1596 and the purchase of New Place in 1597 both testify to the restoration of his family's fortunes in Stratford, and from that time on he clearly devoted more energy to the preservation and augmentation of his estate than to the preservation and publication of his plays. With the exception of *King Lear*, the immensely popular *Pericles*, and perhaps the *Sonnets* (although it is not known if Shakespeare intended their publication) Shakespeare published none of his Jacobean plays: indeed, he hardly published anything new after the move to the Globe. There were sound economic reasons for this in many cases: the value of a play like *The Winter's Tale* to the company was its popularity for lucrative court performances. Publication would have signaled the end of its appeal.

None of Shakespeare's personal books and papers have survived—no drafts, no letters from eminent admirers, no inscribed or annotated volumes. It is thanks to the diligence of his partners and colleagues that we have the collection of his works that was published in 1623 as the *Folio*. In their Preface the compilers remind us that what they are doing is an act of translation. They are presiding over the transformation of Shakespeare's plays from theatrical scripts to literary documents: the stress they place on the act of reading by those who buy the Folio confirms this. As they put it, "It is not our province, who only gather his works, and give them to you, to praise him. It is yours that read him" (*Riverside Shakespeare*, 63).

Shakespeare the man seems to have attracted very few negative comments, apart from those attributed to Robert Greene. As an artist, too, he was widely praised. Even Ben Jonson's jibes at the "mouldy tale" of *Pericles* or his fastidious reaction in conversation with Drummond to the (manifestly untrue) report that the mellifluous Shakespeare never blotted a line ("would he had blotted a thousand") need to be set alongside Jonson's own celebration of Shakespeare, prefaced to the First Folio, as "Not of an age, but for all time."

Jonson's words are part of the act of translation that takes place in the Folio. They proclaim Shakespeare's scripts to be transformed into literature: something to read, study, remember, and value. They do not, as some have suggested, make a claim for Shakespeare's status as a transcendent genius, as the supreme artist. That is a much later development. There is not space here to do more than report on the numerous recent studies of the development of the Shakespeare myth.[16] What is particularly significant is that the image of Shakespeare promoted from the late seventeenth century was not that of a universal poet but rather that of the embodiment of robust Protestant Englishness. He was celebrated for his iconoclasm, his drinking and poaching, and for his scorn of affectation. To a nation seeking to construct a political settlement after the "Glorious Revolution" in 1688, and faced with Catholic Jacobite uprisings in 1715 and 1745, the bluff, no-nonsense Shakespeare was held up as a national ideal. The image he was given is similiar to that which Henry Fielding promoted for himself. This was also the period in which Malone, Rowe, Pope, and others "canonized" Shakespeare by producing lavish and scholarly editions that established his works as worthy of serious study, as English equivalents of the classics. With these monumental editions Shakespeare was achieving the status of a national treasure. One editor, Edward Capell, claimed that the plays were

> a part of the kingdom's riches. They are her estate in fame, that fame which letters confer upon her; the worth and value of which either sinks or raises her in the opinion of other nations, and she takes her rank among them according to the esteem which these are held in. It is then an object of national concern that they should be sent into the world with all the advantage that they are in their own nature capable of receiving.[17]

The concept of the universal genius came later, and is well illustrated by David Garrick's extraordinary celebrations of the Shakespeare Jubilee in 1769. Garrick's ode, with its refrain "We shall not look upon his like again," still exercises its influence, as does his symbol of Shakespeare—a rainbow sash that represented the universality of his brilliance.[18] After that time it becomes clear that the Shakespeare cult is both a facet of the Romantic movement and a central feature of the British colonial project.[19] Henry Morton Stanley was not the only explorer to carry the Bible and Shakespeare with him to dignify his attempts to open up Africa for trade.[20] Arguments and debates continue to rage. In some parts of the world it is claimed that Shakespeare has been appropriated by successive regimes as an instrument of suppression and control; in others the fall of repressive regimes has been celebrated by the performance of Shakespeare's plays. Subversive or conservative? Liberating or repressive? Of an age or for all time? Every age has its own answer or answers. I will simply end by recalling the words of the editors of the First Folio: "It is not our province, who only gather his works, and give them to you, to praise him. It is yours that read him. And there we hope, to your divers capacities, you will find enough, both to draw, and hold you: for his wit can no more lie hid, than it could be lost. Read him, therefore; and again, and again."

Notes and References

Chapter One

1. The works referred to regularly throughout this chapter are S. Schoenbaum, *Shakespeare: A Compact Documentary Life* (Oxford: Oxford University Press, 1977), E. K. Chambers, *William Shakespeare: A Study of Facts and Problems*, 2 vols. (Oxford: Oxford University Press, 1930), and Mark Eccles, *Shakespeare in Warwickshire* (Madison: University of Wisconsin Press, 1961). Almost all the documents considered in this chapter and most of the biographical documents cited later are reproduced in facsimile in S. Schoenbaum, *William Shakespeare: A Documentary Life* (Oxford: Oxford University Press, 1975): see also his *William Shakespeare: Records and Images* (Oxford: Oxford University Press, 1981). Of older biographies, especially informative is E. I. Fripp, *Shakespeare, Man and Artist*, 2 vols. (Oxford: Oxford University Press, 1938). Two more recent studies cited from time to time are Richard Dutton, *William Shakespeare: A Literary Life* (London: Macmillan, 1989), and my *Shakespeare: His Life, Works and Era* (New York: Morrow, 1992).

2. Leslie Hotson, "Three Shakespeares," in *Shakespeare's Sonnets Dated and Other Essays* (London: Rupert Hart-Davis, 1949), 231.

3. Most of the detail is drawn from D. L. Thomas and N. E. Evans, "John Shakespeare in the Exchequer," *Shakespeare Quarterly* 35 (1984): 315–18.

4. The "Annals" section of the *Riverside Shakespeare* (ed. G. B. Evans [Boston: Houghton Mifflin, 1974]) lists records of the visits of dramatic companies to Stratford.

5. On the economic recession, see D. Hamer's review of S. Schoenbaum's *Shakespeare's Lives*, *RES* n.s. 32 (1971): 483–84.

6. The tradition associating the house with the Ardens can be traced to John Jordan, writing in 1794 (Schoenbaum 1977, 20). Yet the house preserves many characteristic features of a farmhouse of Mary Arden's time: the Birthplace Trustees have also assembled a fine collection of farming and domestic artefacts of the sixteenth century.

7. The records kept at the Church of the Holy Trinity in Stratford-upon-Avon run only from the beginning of Elizabeth's reign in March 1558. Baptisms, marriages, and burials of townspeople are recorded in a great leather-bound volume decorated with the Tudor rose. The book bears the date "1600" on the cover of the first volume, because of the instruction from the Archbishop of Canterbury obliging parish priests to make their records more durable by transferring all the records compiled since 1558 from paper to parchment. The task would have fallen on Richard Byfield, who became vicar of Stratford-upon-

Avon in 1597, and so the records that survive of the major events in the lives of the Shakespeare family and their neighbors during Elizabeth's reign are almost certainly in his hand. Elizabeth I required every parish priest to swear, "I shall keepe the register booke according to the Queenes Majesties injunction." In addition, the vicar and churchwardens had to examine and certify each page that was copied into the new book (Kay 1992, 17–18). Schoenbaum (1975), Chambers (1930), and the Riverside edition of the plays conveniently display details from the Stratford records.

      8.   Joan could have bought out his interest in the farm for £40 (Eccles, 68–69).

      9.   Shortly thereafter, during one of the official attempts to regulate private stores of corn, barley, and malt during the sequence of bad harvests, Shakespeare was recorded in February 1598 as having a store of 10 quarters of malt—one of the larger hoards in the town but far from the largest.

     10.   In 1616 Richard Quiney's son Thomas married Shakespeare's younger daughter, Judith.

     11.   An important study is E. R. C. Brinkworth, *Shakespeare and the Bawdy Court of Stratford* (London and Chichester: Phillimore Press, 1972).

     12.   The only evidence dates from the English Civil War. In July 1643 Queen Henrietta Maria, leading her army across country, stayed at New Place for two nights. Susanna Hall gave a book to Richard Grace, a colonel in the queen's forces and the Duke of York's chamberlain. The book, Henri Estienne's *Marvellous Discourse upon the Life, Deeds and Behaviours of Katherine de Medicis*, bears the inscription *"Liber R: Gracei ex dono amicae D. Susanne Hall."* It could well have formed part of her father's library, and it is now in the Library of the Shakespeare Birthplace Trust.

     13.   There were three such occasions in the council's year: the Hamlet Smith at Easter, the Perrott at Whitsuntide, and the Oken in September, on the day of council elections. From 1614, thanks to John Combe's will (from which Shakespeare was himself to benefit), an additional sermon was endowed (see Schoenbaum 1977, 280–81).

     14.   Thomas Beard told his readers in 1597 that "a whole town hath been twice burned, for the breach of the Sabbath" by its inhabitants. Lewis Bayly, preaching at Evesham in 1611, said the town had been burned "chiefly for prophaning the Lord's Sabbath" (see Fripp, 1: 402–3, 419; Schoenbaum 1977, 43; Eccles, 135–36).

     15.   The name of one of the administrators, Richard Tyler, was deleted at a late stage from Shakespeare's will, perhaps as a result of some wrongdoing (Kay 1992, 398).

     16.   For documents and narrative, see Chambers 1930, 2: 141–52; Eccles, 136–38; Schoenbaum 1977, 281–85; Kay 1992, 398–402. Documents are reproduced in Schoenbaum 1975, 230–34.

     17.   He advised them that they had "by stirring in this business got—he

would not say the greatest, but *almost* the greatest men of England, to be their enemies" (Eccles, 137).

18.   C. M. Ingleby, *Shakespeare and the Enclosure of Common Fields at Welcome* (Birmingham: privately printed for the editor, 1885), 16–18, 12.

19.   Schoenbaum 1977, 272–75. Matthew Morris had formerly been in the service of John Hall's father, William, and John Greene was the brother of Shakespeare's former house guest Thomas and had many ties with the family. In this conveyance he was acting for Susanna Hall.

20.   Their misdemeanour had been slight and commonplace: probably they had merely been unlucky to fall victim to an unscrupulous summoner—in this case one Walter Nixon, who was later tried for falsifying evidence in similar proceedings.

21.   Hugh A. Hanley, "Shakespeare's Family in the Stratford records," *TLS* 21 May 1964, 441; Brinkworth, 80–83. See also Schoenbaum 1977, 292–97; Kay 1992, 403–4.

22.   The text of the will is in the Riverside edition, Appendix B.5, and in Chambers 1930, 2: 169–80. There is a full-size reproduction in Schoenbaum 1975, 243–45. See also Schoenbaum 1977, 297–306.

23.   Underneath the final signature is a note in Latin to the effect that the will had been proved by Hall on 22 June 1616 and that an inventory follows. The inventory has not survived.

24.   See Frank Marcham, *William Shakespeare and His Daughter Susanna* (London: Grafton, 1931), 66–71; Schoenbaum 1977, 305.

25.   See the reproduction of the Shakespeare monument and that of John Stow (also by Janssen) in Schoenbaum 1975, 253–54, and the discussion of the two in Kay 1992, 409–10.

Chapter Two

1.   As a lawyer he acted for Shakespeare's cousin Robert Webbe and lived until at least 1582 in Chapel Street; he witnessed deeds with John Shakespeare in 1573.

2.   See Chapter 8, and E. A. J. Honigmann, *Shakespeare: The "Lost Years"* (Manchester: Manchester University Press, 1985), for suggestions on the role Cottom might have played in shaping Shakespeare's career.

3.   In 1594 Aspinall, long a widower, married the widow Anne Shaw (one of whose sons would eventually witness William Shakespeare's will). Sir Francis Fane of Bulbeck (1611–80) recorded in his commonplace book a "posy" allegedly given by Aspinall to Mrs. Shaw with a present of a pair of gloves. Fane attributed the lines to "Shaxpaire." The posy runs: "The gift is small; / The will is all; / Asheyander Asbenall" (see Schoenbaum 1977, 66–67, and Eccles, 57–58).

4.   The standard authority is still T. W. Baldwin, who covered the early

years in *William Shakspere's Petty School* (Urbana: University of Illinois Press, 1943), and the rest of the curriculum in his *William Shakspere's Small Latine & Lesse Greeke*, 2 vols. (Urbana: University of Illinois Press, 1944). See also M. H. Curtis, "Education and Apprenticeship," *Shakespeare Survey* 17 (1964): 53–72.

5. Two writers of this sort mentioned in the plays are Palingenius (*As You Like It* [2.7.139]) and Mantuan (*Love's Labour's Lost* [4.2.94–98]).

6. For a recent study of Shakespeare's use of Ovidian material, see Jonathan Bate, *Shakespeare's Ovid* (Oxford: Oxford University Press, 1992).

7. Wiliam Smith, who was a pupil at Winchester College and studied at Exeter College, Oxford, from 1583, was the only one out of 26 males baptized in Stratford in 1564 to go to university. He became a schoolmaster in Essex (Eccles, 57–58; Schoenbaum 1977, 71).

8. According to T. W. Baldwin, "No miracles are required to account for such knowledge and techniques from the classics as he exhibits. Stratford grammar school will furnish all that is required" (1944, 2: 663).

9. For a fine study of the relationship between this educational system and dramatic composition, see Joel B. Altman, *The Tudor Play of Mind* (Berkeley: University of California Press, 1978). See also Arthur F. Kinney, *Humanist Poetics: Thought, Rhetoric, and Fiction in Sixteenth-Century England* (Amherst: University of Massachusetts Press, 1986).

10. Richard Mulcaster, *The First Parte of the Elementarie* (1582), 254.

11. The "Annals" section of the *Riverside Shakespeare* conveniently provides brief records of the visits of traveling acting troupes to Stratford.

12. [Richard Laneham], *A Letter whearin Part of the Entertainment vntoo the Queenz maiesty at Killingwoorth Castil . . . iz Signified* (?1575), 43.

13. Cited in A. H. Nelson, *The Medieval English Stage* (Chicago: University of Chicago Press, 1974), 138–39.

14. The standard account is still R. Noble, *Shakespeare's Biblical Knowledge and Use of the Book of Common Prayer as Exemplified in the Plays of the First Folio* (London: S.P.C.K., 1935).

15. The most powerful recent articulation of the arguments for Shakespeare's Catholicism is Peter Milward, *Shakespeare's Religious Background* (London: Scolar Press, 1973).

16. See David Cressy, *Literacy and the Social Order* (Cambridge: Cambridge University Press, 1980).

17. Shakespeare provides a parody of this method in *Henry V*, where Fluellen makes parallels between Henry and Alexander the Great (4.7). This scene may suggest that Shakespeare had been reading the Alexander/Caesar section in preparation for writing *Julius Caesar*.

18. Shakespeare's literary career, and his sense of the worth of his own writing, are discussed in Chapter 8. For a study of Sidney's reputation, see my "Sidney: A Critical Heritage," in *Sir Philip Sidney: An Anthology of Modern Criticism*, ed. D. Kay (Oxford: Oxford University Press, 1987), 1–41.

19. See Emrys Jones, *The Origins of Shakespeare* (Oxford: Oxford

University Press, 1977); David M. Bevington, *From "Mankind" to Marlowe* (Cambridge, Mass.: Harvard University Press, 1962); and Altman 1978.

20. See Emrys Jones, *Scenic Form in Shakespeare* (Oxford: Oxford University Press, 1970).

Chapter Three

1. See David Underdown, *Revel, Riot, and Rebellion: Popular Politics and Culture in England, 1603–1660* (Oxford: Oxford University Press, 1985), and Penry Williams, *The Tudor Regime* (Oxford: Oxford University Press, 1977).

2. Louis Adrian Montrose, "The Elizabethan Subject and the Spenserian Text," in *Literary Theory/Renaissance Texts*, ed. Patricia Parker and David Quint (Baltimore: Johns Hopkins University Press, 1986), 305. For a thoughtful survey of the "new historicist" movement, see Jean E. Howard, "The New Historicism in Renaissance Studies," in *Renaissance Historicism: Selections from "English Literary Renaissance,"* ed. Arthur F. Kinney and Dan S. Collins (Amherst: University of Massachusetts Press, 1987), 3–33. Space permits the citation of only a few especially significant works, including Stephen Greenblatt, *Renaissance Self-Fashioning from More to Shakespeare* (Chicago: University of Chicago Press, 1980); John N. King, *English Reformation Literature: The Tudor Origins of the Protestant Tradition* (Princeton: Princeton University Press, 1982); David Norbrook, *Poetry and Politics in the English Renaissance* (London: Routledge, 1984); Marjorie Garber, ed., *Cannibals, Witches, and Divorce: Estranging the Renaissance* (Baltimore: Johns Hopkins University Press, 1987); Heather Dubrow and Richard Strier, eds., *The Historical Renaissance* (Chicago: University of Chicago Press, 1988); Stephen Greenblatt, ed., *Representing the English Renaissance* (Berkeley: University of California Press, 1988); Stephen Greenblatt, *Shakespearean Negotiations: The Circulation of Social Energy in Renaissance England* (Berkeley: University of California Press, 1988); Annabel Patterson, *Shakespeare and the Popular Voice* (Oxford: Basil Blackwell, 1989); Phyllis Rackin, *Stages of History: Shakespeare's English Chronicles* (Ithaca, N.Y.: Cornell University Press, 1990); Jeffrey Knapp, *An Empire Nowhere: England, America, and Literature from "Utopia" to "The Tempest"* (Berkeley: University of California Press, 1992); and Richard Helgerson, *Forms of Nationhood: The Elizabethan Writing of England* (Chicago: University of Chicago Press, 1992).

3. For the historical narrative that follows, I have mainly used J. Guy, *Tudor England* (Oxford: Oxford University Press, 1988); J. S. Morrill, *Seventeenth-Century Britain* (London: Longmans, 1980); and Conrad Russell, *The Crisis of Parliaments: English History, 1509-1660* (Oxford: Oxford University Press, 1971).

4. The Lancastrian emblem is the red rose, the Yorkist the white.

5. Guy 1988, 78. See E. Eisenstein, *The Printing Press as an Agent of Social Change* (Cambridge: Cambridge University Press, 1979).

6. See John Stevens, *Music and Poetry in the Early Tudor Court* (Cambridge: Cambridge University Press, 1961).

7. The remains have been preserved in Portsmouth; they constitute a remarkable "time capsule" of Tudor life and show a microcosm of Tudor society.

8. See Patrick Collinson, *The Religion of Protestants* (Oxford: Oxford University Press, 1984).

9. *Minutes and Accounts of the Corporation of Stratford-upon-Avon*, ed. R. Savage and E. I. Fripp (Oxford and London: Dugdale Society, 1921–30), 1: 138, 2: 47–54.

10. See, for example, John Bossy, *Giordano Bruno and the Embassy Affair* (New York: New York University Press, 1991).

11. For studies of the place of riot in Elizabethan and Jacobean culture, see Underdown (1985) and Peter Stallybrass, "'Drunk with the cup of liberty': Robin Hood, the Carnivalesque, and the Rhetoric of Violence in Early Modern England," *Semiotica* 54 (1985): 113–45.

12. See Mervyn James, *Society, Politics, and Culture* (Cambridge: Cambridge University Press, 1986), 416–65.

13. Important and influential studies of the transformations in culture include Lawrence Stone, *The Crisis of the Aristocracy, 1558–1641* (Oxford: Oxford University Press, 1965), and his *The Family, Sex, and Marriage, 1500–1800* (New York: Oxford University Press, 1977), and Keith Thomas, *Religion and the Decline of Magic* (New York: Scribners, 1971). An intellectual framework was suggested by Christopher Hill in *Intellectual Origins of the English Revolution* (Oxford: Oxford University Press, 1965).

14. The population of England and Wales before the Great Famine (1315–17) and Black Death (1348–49) may have been as high as 5.5 to 6 million. The lowest point was about 1450, when the population stabilized at about 2 milion. There were about 2.5 million people in England and Wales in 1500 and about 4.5 million in 1603. See Guy (1988).

15. See Roger Findlay, *Population and Metropolis: The Demography of London, 1580–1650* (Cambridge: Cambridge University Press, 1981).

16. Peter Clark and Paul Slack, *English Towns in Transition, 1500–1700* (Oxford: Oxford University Press, 1976).

17. The eight children died at the following ages: Joan as an infant; Margaret, 1; William, 53; Gilbert, 45; Joan, 77; Anne, 7; Richard, 38; Edmund, 27.

18. See Keith Wrightson, *English Society, 1580–1680* (London: Hutchinson, 1982), 13.

19. The definitions derive from Sir Thomas Smith's *De Republica Anglorum* (1583); William Harrison's "A Description of England" in the 1577 edition of Holinshed's *Chronicles*; and Thomas Wilson, "The State of England" (1600), in F. J. Fisher, *Camden Miscellany* 52, 3d ser. (1936).

20. Cited by Andrew Gurr, *Playgoing in Shakespeare's London* (Cambridge: Cambridge University Press, 1987), 51.

21. Leah Marcus, *Puzzling Shakespeare: Local Reading and Its Discontents* (Berkeley: University of California Press, 1988), 97–98; see also Pearl Hogrefe, "Legal Rights of Tudor Women and Their Circumvention," *Sixteenth Century Journal* 3 (1972): 97–105.

22. See the outstanding collection of essays *Rewriting the Renaissance: The Discourses of Sexual Difference in Early Modern Europe*, ed. M. W. Ferguson, M. Quilligan, and N. J. Vickers (Chicago: University of Chicago Press, 1986).

23. David Underdown, "The Taming of the Scold," in *Order and Disorder in Early Modern England*, ed. Anthony Fletcher and John Stevenson (Cambridge: Cambridge University Press, 1985), 116–36. A valuable survey of the voluminous literature is Lynda Boose, "The Family in Shakespeare Studies; or, Studies in the Family of Shakespeareans; or, The Politics of Politics," *Renaissance Quarterly* 40 (1987): 707–42. See also Hattaway, "Drama and Society," in *The Cambridge Companion to English Renaissance Drama*, ed. A. R. Braunmuller and Michael Hattaway (Cambridge: Cambridge University Press, 1990), 91–126.

24. See Susan Dwyer Asmussen, *An Ordered Society: Gender and Class in Early Modern England* (Oxford: Basil Blackwell, 1988).

25. The standard study is Greenblatt (1980). See also Anne Ferry, *The "Inward" Language: Sonnets of Sidney, Shakespeare, Donne* (Chicago: University of Chicago Press, 1981); Joel Fineman, *Shakespeare's "Perjur'd Eye": The Invention of Subjectivity in the Sonnets* (Berkeley: University of California Press, 1986); Patricia Fumerton, *Cultural Aesthetics* (Chicago: University of Chicago Press, 1991); and Charles Taylor, *Sources of the Self* (Cambridge: Cambridge University Press, 1989).

26. Caroline Lucas, *Writing for Women: The Example of Woman as Reader in Elizabethan Romance* (Milton Keynes: Open University Press, 1989).

27. Barbara K. Lewalski, *Writing Women in Jacobean England* (Cambridge, Mass.: Harvard University Press, 1993).

28. See A. Eccles, *Obstetrics and Gynaecology in Tudor and Stuart England* (Kent, Ohio: Kent State University Press, 1982).

29. See Keith Thomas, "The Relevance of Social Anthropology to the Historical Study of English Witchcraft," in Mary Douglas, ed., *Witchcraft Confessions and Accusations* (London: Tavistock, 1970), 47–79, and Stuart Clark, "Inversion, Misrule, and the Meaning of Witchcraft," *Past & Present* 87 (1980): 98–127.

30. Although Shakespeare had a modern, scientific doctor as a son-in-law, the evidence of the plays (particularly the portrayal of Helena in *All's Well That Ends Well*) leaves open the question of his relation to the conventional terror of female healing practices.

31. See Spenser, *The Faerie Queene*, book 5, canto 9.

32. See John Bossy, *The English Catholic Community, 1570–1850* (London: Darton, Longman & Todd, 1975).

33. See the account of changing attitudes to death in my *Melodious Tears* (Oxford: Oxford University Press, 1991), chap. 1.

34. Ben Jonson was in prison at the time of the Gunpowder Plot in 1605. He was known to have dined with some of those arrested. He wrote to Robert Cecil, King James's chief minister, offering full cooperation with the investigation; that would have involved producing a convincing list of the names of his Catholic friends and associates.

35. See the reproductions in Margery Corbett and Ronald Lightbown, *The Comely Frontispiece: The Emblematic Title-Page in England, 1550–1660* (London: Routledge, 1979); also Knapp 1992, 245–48.

36. See the essays collected in *New World Encounters*, ed. Stephen Greenblatt (Berkeley: University of California Press, 1993).

Chapter Four

1. Modern road numbers are given for readers wishing to follow the journey on a map or in a car.

2. Henry B. Wheatley, "London and the Life of the Town," *Shakespeare's England* (Oxford: Oxford University Press, 1916), 2: 153, describes the route (see also Schoenbaum 1977, 118–19).

3. The most important contemporary account is John Stow, *A Survey of London* (1603). There is an edition by G. L. Kingsford (Oxford, 1908) and an Everyman edition by H. B. Wheatley. In the following pages I have drawn heavily on Stow, on Wheatley's chapter in *Shakespeare's England*, and *The A to Z of Elizabethan London*, comp. A. Prokter and R. Taylor (Lympne Castle, Kent: Harry Margary, 1979). Observations by foreigners are collected by W. B. Rye, *England as Seen by Foreigners in the Days of Elizabeth and James the First* (1865; rpt., New York: Benjamin Blom, 1967). Some are cited in Schoenbaum 1977, chap. 9. An excellent anthology about London in the period is L. Manley, *London in the Age of Shakespeare: An Anthology* (London: Croom Helm, 1986).

4. An example is the complex of buildings in the Blackfriars area where, at the height of his fame and prosperity, Shakespeare would acquire a fashionable residence (as Van Dyck would in the next generation), in the gatehouse of the old friary (whose hall housed his company's indoor theater).

5. For these figures, and for the comments that follow, I have used *London, 1500–1700: The Making of the Metropolis*, ed. A. L. Beier and R. Findlay (London: Longmans, 1986).

6. According to Thomas Dekker, "At every turn, a man is put in mind of Babel, there is such a confusion of languages" (Kay 1992, 75).

7. Details are from *The A to Z of Elizabethan London*.

8. The title pages of books from this period convey some idea of the number and variety of the booksellers and of the colorful signs with which the

stalls and shops were distinguished. To give just a few examples from Shakespeare's works, *Titus Andronicus* was printed for Edward White and Thomas Millington and was "to be sold . . . at the little North doore of Paules, at the signe of the Gunne"; *Venus and Adonis* was to be sold "at the signe of the white Greyhound"; *Richard II*, "at the signe of the Angel"; *Troilus and Cressida*, "at the spred Eagle"; and so forth.

9. See the articles on these military and recreational pursuits in *Shakespeare's England*.

10. From *Essays*, 3 vols., trans. John Florio (1603), Everyman edition (London: Dent, 1910), 1: 18.

11. *The Poems of Sir Walter Ralegh*, ed. Agnes Latham (London: The Muses' Library, 1951), 51.

12. See Steven Mullaney, *The Place of the Stage: License, Play, and Power in Renaissance England* (Chicago: University of Chicago Press, 1988), chaps. 1 and 4, and Marcus 1988, 161–202.

13. *Paul Hentzner's Travels in England, during the Reign of Queen Elizabeth* (1797), 23–24; cited by Schoenbaum 1977, 131. See also E. K. Chambers, *The Elizabethan Stage*, 4 vols. (Oxford: Oxford University Press, 1923), 2: 452–58, and G. B. Evans, *Elizabethan-Jacobean Drama* (London: A. C. Black, 1988), 168–71.

14. In addition to Chambers (1923), I have also followed the accounts by A. Gurr 1987, 10–15, and Glynne Wickham, *Early English Stages, 1300–1600*, 3 vols. (London: Routledge, 1959–81), 2: 161–63, 204–5.

15. The chief proprietors of the Rose (built about 1587) were Philip Henslowe and his son-in-law Edward Alleyn, the great actor. These men were major investors in the bear-baiting stadia from the 1590s on, rising to official positions of control in the sport, which they held from 1603. Henslowe's last major business venture was the construction of the Hope theater, in 1614, designed to double as a venue both for theatrical performances and animal shows. See *Henslowe's Diary*, ed. R. A. Foakes and R. T. Rickert (Cambridge: Cambridge University Press, 1961), and C. C. Rutter, *Documents of the Rose Playhouse* (Manchester: Manchester University Press, 1984).

16. Details from John Stow, *A Survey of London* (1603).

17. Details from Chambers 1930, 2: 88–90; documents reproduced in Schoenbaum 1975, 161–64.

18. For a narrative of the case, see Schoenbaum 1977, 260–64: the documents are transcribed in Chambers 1930, 2: 90–95, and reproduced in Schoenbaum 1975, 209–13.

19. Jackson was related by marriage to Elias James, the brewer who had premises close by at the foot of Puddle Dock Hill. An epitaph on this Elias James—beginning, "When God was pleased, (the world unwilling yet) / Elias James to Nature paid his debt"—has been attributed to Shakespeare. A text is provided in *William Shakespeare: The Complete Works*, ed. Stanley Wells and Gary Taylor (Oxford: Oxford University Press, 1986), and in Chambers 1930, 1: 551.

Chapter Five

1. The standard accounts are E. K. Chambers (1923) and Wickham (1959–81); they are expertly summarized in Andrew Gurr, *The Shakespearean Stage, 1574–1642*, 2d ed. (Cambridge: Cambridge University Press, 1981). See also Robert Weimann, *Shakespeare and the Popular Tradition in the Theatre* (Baltimore: Johns Hopkins University Press, 1978), and Michael Hattaway, *Elizabethan Popular Theatre* (London: Routledge, 1987).

2. A good general account is G. E. Bentley, *The Profession of Player in Shakespeare's Time* (Princeton: Princeton University Press, 1984). The sharers seem to have met formally to hear new scripts; see R. A. Foakes, "Playhouses and Players," in Braunmuller and Hattaway, 45–46.

3. Supposedly Tarleton's ghost; cited in Chambers 1923, 2: 386, and Schoenbaum 1977, 132.

4. See R. A. Foakes, *Illustrations of the English Stage, 1580–1642* (Cambridge: Cambridge University Press, 1985); many of the views are reproduced in Gurr (1981) and in Braunmuller and Hattaway (year).

5. It seems that the Rose, with a diameter of approximately 74 feet, had 14 sides. The Globe, whose diameter was about 100 feet, may have had 20 or 24 sides. See John Orrell, *The Quest for Shakespeare's Globe* (Cambridge: Cambridge University Press, 1983), 160–61, and John Orrell and Andrew Gurr, "What the Rose Can Tell Us," *Antiquity* 63 (1989): 421–29.

6. *Henslowe's Diary*, ed. Foakes and Rickert.

7. As in the opening lines of *1 Henry VI*, "Hung be the heavens with black."

8. See Alan C. Dessen, *Elizabethan Stage Conventions and Modern Interpreters* (Cambridge: Cambridge University Press, 1984); David M. Bevington, *Action is Eloquence: Shakespeare's Language of Gesture* (Cambridge, Mass.: Harvard University Press, 1984); and Hattaway (1987).

9. Evans 1988, 74–75.

10. Evans 1988, 76–77; *Henslowe's Diary*, 319–21. See also Rutter (1984) and Peter Thompson, *Shakespeare's Theatre* (London: Routledge, 1983).

11. Wickham 1959–81, 2: 2, 127.

12. See G. M. Pinciss, "Shakespeare, Her Majesty's Players, and Pembroke's Men," *Shakespeare Survey* 27 (1974): 129–36.

13. Many of their names (Thomas Pope, George Bryan, Kempe, Augustine Phillips, John Heminges, Richard Cowley, Burbage, William Sly, John Duke, and Robert Gough) appear in the plot of *The Seven Deadly Sins*, preserved among Alleyn's papers (Gurr 1981, 34–39). See W. W. Greg, ed., *Dramatic Documents from the Elizabethan Playhouses*, 2 vols. (Oxford: Oxford University Press, 1931), 1: 19.

14. For documents concerning the King's Men, see Chambers 1923, 2: 192–220.

15. See the study of the Globe from 1599 to 1608 by Thompson

(1983), which also considers the repertoire and facilties of the theater as well as the acting and production styles.

16. See Bentley (1984) and M. C. Bradbrook, *The Rise of the Common Player* (London: Chatto & Windus, 1962); on doubling and cast sizes see W. A. Ringler, "The Number of Actors in Shakespeare's Early Plays," in *The Seventeenth-Century Stage*, ed. G. E. Bentley (Toronto: University of Toronto Press, 1968).

17. See Foakes 1990, 43, and David Wiles, *Shakespeare's Clown: Actor and Text in the Elizabethan Playhouse* (Cambridge: Cambridge University Press, 1987).

18. See B. L. Joseph, *Elizabethan Acting*, rev. ed. (Oxford: Oxford University Press, 1964); L.-L. Marker, "Nature and Decorum in the Theory of Elizabethan Acting," *Elizabethan Theatre* 2 (1970): 87–107; and Gurr 1981, 78–112.

19. For two important studies, see W. R. Gair, *The Children of Paul's* (Cambridge: Cambridge University Press, 1982), and Michael Shapiro, *Children of the Revels* (New York: Columbia University Press, 1977).

20. E. Nungezer, *A Dictionary of Actors and Other Persons Associated with the Public Representation of Plays in England before 1642* (New Haven: Yale University Press, 1929), 74; Gurr 1981, 111.

21. "Documents of Control" are conveniently collected in Chambers 1923, vol. 4: they are summarized, with extensive quotation, in Gurr 1981, 71–76.

22. See the edition of *Sir Thomas More*, "by Anthony Munday and Others," in the Revels series by V. Gabrieli and G. Melchiori (Manchester: Manchester University Press, 1990).

23. M. Heinemann, "Political Drama," in Braunmuller and Hattaway, 167–70.

24. G. E. Bentley, *The Profession of Dramatist in Shakespeare's Time* (Princeton: Princeton University Press, 1971), 196.

25. Important studies of censorship provisions include Annabel Patterson, *Censorship and Interpretation* (Madison: University of Wisconsin Press, 1984); Richard Dutton, *Mastering the Revels* (London: Macmillan, 1991); and Janet Clare, *"Art made tongue-tied by authority": Elizabethan and Jacobean Dramatic Censorship* (New York: St. Martin's Press, 1990).

26. See Jonathan Dollimore, "Critical Developments," in *Shakespeare. A Bibliographical Guide*, ed. S. Wells (Oxford: Oxford University Press, 1990), 405–28. Mullaney (1988) and Marcus (1988) are of special relevance to Shakespeare. Two valuable recent anthologies of essays, with full and informative bibliographies, are Richard Wilson and Richard Dutton, *New Historicism and Renaissance Drama* (London: Longmans, 1992), and D. S. Kastan and Peter Stallybrass, *Staging the Renaissance: Reinterpretations of Elizabethan and Jacobean Drama* (London: Routledge, 1991).

27. See Franco Moretti, "The Great Eclipse: Tragic Form and the Deconsecration of Sovereignty," in *Signs Taken for Wonders: Essays in the Sociology of Literary Forms* (London: Verso, 1983).

28. For an excellent overview of the subject with a good bibliography, see the essay by Hattaway, "Drama and Society," in Braunmuller and Hattaway, 91–126.

29. Details in what follows are drawn from A. L. Beier and R. Findlay, eds., *London, 1500–1700: The Making of the Metropolis* (London: Longmans, 1986); Schoenbaum 1977, chap. 11; and Paul Slack, *The Impact of the Plague in Tudor and Stuart England* (London: Routledge, 1985).

30. This and the later passage are taken from F. P. Wilson, ed., *The Plague Pamphlets of Thomas Dekker* (Oxford: Oxford University Press, 1925), 25–26, and Kay 1992, 150–53.

31. Rev. T. Wilcocks, cited by F. P. Wilson, *The Plague in Shakespeare's London* (Oxford: Oxford University Press, 1927), 52.

32. Important early studies are Louis B. Wright, *Middle-Class Culture in Elizabethan England* (San Marino: Huntington Library, 1935), and W. A. Armstrong, "The Audience of the Elizabethan Private Theatres," *RES* n.s. 10 (1959): 234–49.

33. Anne Jennalie Cook, *The Privileged Playgoer in Shakespeare's London, 1576–1642* (Princeton: Princeton University Press, 1981), 93, 272.

34. See the Induction to *Bartholomew Fair* (1614).

35. See Chambers 1923, 4: 322–23; *Henslowe's Diary*, 240; and William Ingram, *A London Life in the Brazen Age: Francis Langley, 1548–1602* (Cambridge, Mass.: Harvard University Press, 1978), 167–96.

36. The passage appears in C. W. Wallace, *The First London Theatre: Materials for a History* (Lincoln: Nebraska University Studies, no. 8, 1913), 278–79.

37. From the postmortem inventory of Sir Thomas Brend (16 May 1599), whose son Nicholas leased the site to the company; cited (translated from the Latin) by Schoenbaum 1977, 209.

38. See Gail K. Paster, *The Idea of the City in the Age of Shakespeare* (Athens: University of Georgia Press, 1985), and J.-C. Agnew, *World's Apart: The Market and the Theatre in Anglo-American Thought, 1550–1750* (Cambridge: Cambridge University Press, 1986).

Chapter Six

1. "Ben Jonson's Conversations with William Drummond of Hawthornden," in *Ben Jonson*, 11 vols., ed. C. H. Herford, P. Simpson, and E. Simpson (Oxford: Oxford University Press, 1925–52), 1: 142–43.

2. These passages come from "Extracts from Paul Hentzner's Travels in England, 1598," in W. B. Rye, ed., *England as Seen by Foreigners, in the Days of Elizabeth and James the First* (1865; rpt., New York: Benjamin Blom, 1967),

104–5, and from André Hurault, Sieur de Maisse, *Journal* (1597), trans. and ed. G. B. Harrison and R. A. Jones (Bloomsbury: Nonesuch Press, 1931), 25–26, 36–37. They are discussed in detail in Louis Adrian Montrose's important study, "'Shaping Fantasies': Figurations of Gender and Power in Elizabethan Culture," *Representations* 2 (1983): 61–94, reprinted in S. Greenblatt, ed., *Representing the English Renaissance* (Berkeley: University of California Press, 1988), 31–64.

3.   Arthur F. Kinney, Preface to *The Historical Renaissance*, ix–x. See the article in the same volume by Jean E. Howard, "The New Historicism and Renaissance Studies," 3–33, esp. 8–12.

4.   E. M. W. Tillyard, *The Elizabethan World Picture: A Study of the Idea of Order in the Age of Shakespeare, Donne, and Milton* (London, 1943; rpt., New York: Vintage Books, 1961).

5.   For a more recent study of Elizabethan political thought, see Stephen L. Collins, *From Divine Cosmos to Sovereign State* (New York: Oxford University Press, 1989), chap. 1. See also Helgerson 1992, esp. 1–18, 105–48, and Quentin Skinner's *The Foundations of Modern Political Thought* (Cambridge: Cambridge University Press, 1978).

6.   Whereas Protestants executed by Mary had been taken to Smithfield to be burned as heretics, Catholics executed under Elizabeth were taken to Tyburn to suffer the fate of traitors—hanging, drawing, and quartering. See L. B. Smith, *Treason in Tudor England: Politics and Paranoia* (Princeton: Princeton University Press, 1986).

7.   M. Hume, *The Courtships of Queen Elizabeth* (London: E. Nash, 1906), is still the standard account of the queen's marriage negotiations.

8.   Thomas Dekker, *Old Fortunatus* (1599), prologue. See Knapp 1992, 83.

9.   A valuable anthology of contextual material of the cult of Elizabeth is Arthur F. Kinney, *Elizabethan Backgrounds: Historical Documents of the Age of Elizabeth* (Hamden, Conn.: Archon, 1975).

10.   The queen's words, to a deputation of Lords and Commons in 1586, are quoted from J. E. Neale, *Elizabeth I and Her Parliaments, 1584–1601*, 2 vols. (London: Cape, 1953–57), 2: 119; they are also cited in, for example, Mullaney 1988, 96 and Helgerson 1992, 145. The observation was quoted with approval by King James in his *Basilikon Doron*; see Jonathan Goldberg, *James I and the Politics of Literature* (Baltimore: Johns Hopkins University Press, 1983), 116–17.

11.   The classic formulation of the doctrine is E. H. Kantorowicz, *The King's Two Bodies: A Study in Medieval Political Theology* (Princeton: Princeton University Press, 1957).

12.   See John King, *Tudor Royal Iconography: Literature and Art in an Age of Religious Crisis* (Princeton: Princeton University Press, 1989), 225–28.

13.   See King, 254, and D. Norbrook, *Poetry and Politics in the English Renaissance* (London: Routledge, 1984), 114.

14.   The standard account is Marie Axton, *The Queen's Two Bodies:*

Drama and the Elizabethan Succession (London: Royal Historical Society, 1977). See also Marcus 1988, 54–55, 228–29, and Louis Adrian Montrose, "'Eliza, Queene of Shepheardes,' and the Pastoral of Power," *ELR* 10 (1980): 153–82.

15. For a study of *The Faerie Queene* in such terms, showing how Spenser was Elizabeth's subject, while she was his, see Montrose, "The Elizabethan Subject and the Spenserian Text," in P. Parker and D. Quint, eds., *Literary Theory/Renaissance Texts* (Baltimore: Johns Hopkins University Press, 1986), 303–40.

16. George Puttenham, *The Arte of English Poesie* (1579), ed. G. Willcock and A. Walker (Cambridge: Cambridge University Press, 1936), 4–5.

17. Cited in Roy Strong, *Portraits of Elizabeth I* (Oxford: Oxford University Press, 1963), 21.

18. Sir Philip Sidney, *The Countess of Pembroke's Arcadia (The New Arcadia)*, ed. Victor Skretkowicz (Oxford: Oxford University Press, 1987), 58.

19. *The Works of John Lyly*, ed. R. W. Bond, 3 vols. (Oxford: Oxford University Press, 1902), 2: 38 (spelling modernized, as in citations that follow).

20. See Jeffrey Knapp, "Elizabethan Tobacco," *Representations* 21 (1988): 26–66, esp. 37–40, and his *An Empire Nowhere*, chap. 4.

21. See Montrose, "'Eliza, Queene of Shepheardes,' . . . etc.," 34–35.

22. Richard Helgerson, *The Elizabethan Prodigals* (Berkeley: University of California Press, 1976), and his more recent study, *Forms of Nationhood*.

23. *The Prose Works of Sir Philip Sidney*, ed. A. Feuillerat, 4. vols. (Cambridge: Cambridge University Press, 1962), 3: 129 (letter to the Earl of Leicester, 2 August 1580).

24. See Jean Howard, "Crossdressing, the Theatre and Gender Struggle in Early Modern England," *Shakespeare Quarterly* 39 (1988): 418–40.

25. Marcus 1988, 97–98, Linda Woodbridge, *Women and the English Renaissance: Literature and the Nature of Womankind, 1540–1620* (Urbana: University of Illinois Press, 1986), 139–41.

26. Gabrielle Bernhard Jackson, "Topical Ideology: Witches, Amazons, and Shakespeare's Joan of Arc," in *Women in the Renaissance, Selections from English Literary Renaissance*, ed. K. Farrell, E. H. Hageman and A. Kinney (Amherst: University of Massachusetts Press, 1990), 88–117.

27. Peter Stallybrass, "Patriarchal Territories," in Ferguson, Quilligan, and Vickers 1986, 123–42.

28. Greenblatt also observes that "the ruling elite believed that a measure of insecurity and fear was a necessary, healthy element in the shaping of proper loyalties, and Elizabethan and Jacobean institutions deliberately evoked this insecurity" (1988, 135–36).

29. John King, *Spenser's Poetry and the Reformation Tradition* (Princeton: Princeton University Press, 1990), 112.

30. Catherine Bates, *The Rhetoric of Courtship in Elizabethan Language and Literature* (Cambridge: Cambridge University Press, 1992), 25–88.

31. See Axton (1977) and her article "Robert Dudley and the Inner

Temple Revels," *Historical Journal* 13 (1970): 365–78; see also David Lee Miller, *The Poem's Two Bodies: The Poetics of the 1590 "Faerie Queene"* (Princeton: Princeton University Press, 1988), 29–67.

32. See Arthur Marotti, "'Love is not love': Elizabethan Sonnets and the Social Order," *ELH* 49 (1982): 396–428. See also two articles by Louis Adrian Montrose, "Celebration and Insinuation: Sir Philip Sidney and the Motives of Elizabethan Courtship," *Renaissance Drama* n.s. 8 (1977): 3–35, and "Of Gentlemen and Shepherds: The Politics of Elizabethan Pastoral Form," *ELH* 50 (1983): 415–59.

33. Francis Bacon, *In Felicem Memoriam* (1608), in *The Works of Francis Bacon*, 7 vols., ed. J. Spedding et al. (London: Longmans, 1858–61), 6: 317.

34. See Helgerson 1972, passim.

35. See Knapp 1992, chaps. 1 and 2.

36. See my article "'She was a Queen, and therefore beautiful': Sidney, His Mother, and Queen Elizabeth," *RES* ns 43 (1992): 17–39.

37. John Nichols, *The Progresses and Public Processions of Queen Elizabeth*, 3 vols. (London: John Nichols, 1823), 3: 612–13.

38. Cyril Tourneur (?? or Thomas Middleton), *The Revenger's Tragedy* (1607), ed. R. A. Foakes (Manchester: University of Manchester Press, 1966), 3: 150. See Peter Stallybrass, "Reading the Body and the Jacobean Theater of Consumption: *The Revenger's Tragedy* (1606)," in Kastan and Stallybrass 1991, 210–20.

Chapter Seven

1. This is the entry for 24–25 March in *The Diary of John Manningham of the Middle Temple, 1602–1603*, ed. R. W. Sorlien (Hanover, N.H.: University Press of New England, 1976).

2. For full accounts of the cult of James, see G. Parry, *The Golden Age Restor'd: The Culture of the Stuart Court, 1603–1642* (Manchester: Manchester University Press, 1981), and Goldberg (1983).

3. Anticipates the words of Macbeth "From this moment / The very firstlings of my heart shall be / The firstlings of my hand" (*Macbeth*, 4.1. 146–48).

4. See Marcus 1988, 111. The standard edition of James's political writings is by C. H. McIlwain, *The Political Works of James I* (Cambridge, Mass.: Harvard University Press, 1918).

5. What follows owes much to the account in Greenblatt (1988). Some contemporary accounts are in Robert Ashton, *James I by His Contemporaries* (London: Hutchinson, 1969); the Newark incidents are recorded on 65–66.

6. James was of course also known as the author of other works—for example, his *Demonologie* (1597).

7. The commentator was either Henri IV of France or Weldon: it is either echoed (if the former) or foreshadowed (if the latter) when Lear's Fool

calls the King a fool and tells him, "All thy other titles thou hast given away" (*King Lear*, 1.4; the passage was omitted from the Folio text).

8. L. L. Peck, ed., *The Mental World of the Jacobean Court* (Cambridge: Cambridge University Press, 1991).

9. From the preface to *Hymenaiae*; for a text of this, as of a number of important masques, see *A Book of Masques*, ed. T. J. B. Spencer and S. W. Wells (Cambridge: Cambridge University Press, 1968). See also the essays collected in D. Lindley, ed., *The Court Masque* (Manchester: Manchester University Press, 1984).

10. *Tethys' Festival* (1610), cited in Samuel Daniel, *Dramatic Works*, in *The Complete Works in Verse and Prose*, ed. Alexander B. Grosart, 5 vols. (London: Spenser Society, 1885–96), 307.

11. See Stephen Orgel, *The Illusion of Power* (Berkeley: University of California Press, 1975), and (with Roy Strong) *Inigo Jones: The Theatre of the Stuart Court*, 2 vols. (Berkeley: University of California Press, 1973).

12. Martin Butler, "Private and Occasional Drama," in Braunmuller and Hattaway, 146.

13. Jonathan Goldberg, "Fatherly Authority: The Politics of Stuart Family Images," in Ferguson, Quilligan, and Vickers 1986, 3–32.

14. Lewalski 1993, 265: see also Paul Salzman, "Contemporary References in Mary Wroth's *Urania*," *RES* n.s. 29 (1978): 178–81; Mary Ellen Lamb, *Gender and Authorship in the Sidney Circle* (Madison: University of Wisconsin Press, 1990); and Helen Hackett, "Wroth's *Urania* and the 'Femininity' of Romance," in *Women, Texts, and Histories, 1575–1760*, ed. Clare Brant and Diane Purkiss (London: Routledge, 1992), 39–68. A text of *Urania*, edited by Josephine Roberts, will appear shortly. A substantial extract is published in Paul Salzman, ed., *An Anthology of Seventeenth-Century Fiction* (Oxford: Oxford University Press, 1991).

15. See Gurr 1987, 145–46, 218. Some scholars have suggested that elements of the *Gowrie* material were reworked in *Macbeth*.

16. See the account in Clare 1990, 111–14.

17. For details see *Eastward Ho*, ed. R. W. van Fossen (Manchester: Manchester University Press, 1979).

18. See, for instance, Margaret W. Ferguson, "The Spectre of Resistance: *The Tragedy of Mariam* (1613)," in Kastan and Stallybrass 1991, 235–50.

19. See L. Tennenhouse, *Power on Display: The Politics of Shakespeare's Genres* (London: Methuen, 1986); Mullaney (1988); Marcus, "Pastimes and the Purging of Theatre: *Bartholomew Fair*," in Kastan and Stallybrass 1991, 196–209.

20. See the chapter on *Bartholomew Fair* in Peter Stallybrass and Allon White, *The Politics and Poetics of Transgression* (London: Methuen, 1986), 66–79, reprinted in Wilson and Dutton 1992, 207–18.

21. See, for example, K. Sharpe and S. Zwicker, *Politics of Discourse: The*

Literature and History of Seventeenth-Century England (Berkeley: University of California Press, 1987); Goldberg (1983); Tennenhouse (1986); Marcus (1988); and the chapter "The Politics of Jacobean Women's Writing," in Lewalski 1993, 309–15.

22. George Chapman, *Bussy d'Ambois*, ed. N. F. Brooke (1964; rpt., Manchester: Manchester University Press, 1979), 1.1.35–36.

23. See D. Kay 1991, chap. 5, also David M. Bergeron, *Shakespeare's Romances and the Royal Family* (Lawrence: University of Kansas Press, 1985), and Roy Strong, *Henry, Prince of Wales and England's Lost Renaissance* (New York: Thames & Hudson, 1986).

24. See my article "'To hear the rest untold': Shakespeare's Postponed Endings," *Renaissance Quarterly* 37 (1984): 207–27.

25. Jill Levinson, "Comedy," in Braunmuller and Hattaway, 279.

26. See Philip J. Finkelpearl, "'The Comedians' Liberty': Censorship of the Jacobean Stage Reconsidered," in Kinney and Collins 1987, 191–206.

Chapter Eight

1. See Schoenbaum 1977, chap. 8; Kay 1992, 58–70; and Honigmann (1985).

2. The best and most amusing account of Shakespeare biographies is S. Schoenbaum, *Shakespeare's Lives* (Oxford: Oxford University Press, 1971). An important recent study of Shakespeare's reputation is Gary Taylor, *Reinventing Shakespeare* (London: Hogarth Press, 1989). See also Graham Holderness, ed., *The Shakespeare Myth* (Manchester: Manchester University Press, 1988).

3. Honigmann suggests that Cottom was asked to find someone for the Houghton establishment and turned naturally to his brightest pupil, whose hopes of university and of social advancement had been dashed by the recent financial misfortunes of his father (1985, chaps. 4 and 11).

4. Ferdinando Stanley, Lord Strange, was the fifth earl of Derby. Some biographers see him as Shakespeare's first patron, and perhaps the man who brought him to London.

5. They may also have been involved with *2 Henry VI* (published as *The First Part of the Contention . . . etc.* in 1594).

6. Two useful studies of the literary profession are G. E. Bentley (1971) and Richard Helgerson, *Self-Crowned Laureates: Spenser, Jonson, Milton, and the Literary System* (Berkeley: University of California Press, 1983).

7. E. A. J. Honigmann, *Shakespeare's Impact on His Contemporaries* (Manchester: Manchester University Press, 1982).

8. They were certainly successful. There were to be at least 10 editions of the poem during his lifetime and a further six before 1636. There is even a record of an individual sale of the book. On 12 June 1593 Richard Stonely, an elderly civil servant who worked in the Exchequer, visited the bookstalls of St. Paul's Churchyard. He bought two books for a shilling and entered the details

into his pocket book. One was Jonn Eliot's *Suruay; or, Topographical Description of France: With a New Mappe*, first printed in 1592 and published in a second edition in 1593. The second, picked up from John Harrison's stall beneath the sign of the White Greyhound, was *Venus and Adonis*. The entry runs, "Books—for the Suruey off ffraunce wth the Venus & Adhonay pr Shakspear—xiid" (Schoenbaum 1977, 175–76).

    9.   Henry Wriotheseley had succeeded to the title at the age of eight in 1581 on the death of his father. The second earl, a Catholic, had been implicated in the early intrigues surrounding Mary Queen of Scots. Since his mother did not remarry for a number of years, Henry was made a ward of Lord Treasurer Burghley and was brought up with a group of similarly circumstanced nobles. Cecil tried, unsuccessfully, to marry the boy off to his granddaughter, Lady Elizabeth Vere. The young Southampton went to Cecil's Cambridge College, St. John's, and received an M.A. in 1589. His early years at court were marked by the queen's favour (he accompanied her on her progress to Oxford in 1592) and by a developing friendship with Robert Devereux, who had taken on Sidney's mantle as the paragon of Protestant chivalry.

    10.   For an account of these matters, see the New Cambridge edition of *Richard II*, ed. Andrew Gurr (Cambridge: Cambridge University Press, 1984).

    11.   The 1608 Quarto is called *M.William Shak-speare: His True Chronicle Historie of the life and death of King Lear and his three Daughters, . . . etc. As it was played before the Kings Maiestie at Whitehall vpon S. Stephans night in Christmas Hollidayes. By his Maiesties seruants playing vsually at the Gloabe on the Bancke-side.*

    12.   See Chambers 1930, 2: 334–35, and Kay 1992, 348.

    13.   Bergeron (1985); Marcus 1988, 121–47.

    14.   From the Introduction to *William Shakespeare: The Complete Works*, ed. Wells and Taylor (1986).

    15.   Some examples: *The Most Lamentable Romaine Tragedie of Titus Andronicus: As it Was Plaide by the Right Honourable the Earle of Darbie, Earle of Pembrooke, and Earle of Sussex their Seruants . . . etc.* (1594); *The Tragedy of King Richard the third. Containing, His treacherous Plots against his brother Clarence: the pitifull murther of his innocent nephewes: his tyrannical vsurpation: with the whole course of his detested life, and most deserued death. As it hath beene lately Acted by the Right honourable the Lord Chamberlaine his seruants* (1597); *An Excellent conceited Tragedie of Romeo and Iuliet. As it hath been often (with great applause) plaide publiquely, by the right Honourable the L. of Hunsdon his Seruants* (1597).

    16.   See G. Taylor (1989) and Holderness (1988). An indispensible work of reference is Brian Vickers, *Shakespeare: The Critical Heritage, 1623–1801*, 6 vols. (London: Routledge, 1974–81).

    17.   Edward Capell, ed., *Mr William Shakespeare: His Comedies, Histories, and Tragedies* (London, 1768), 1.A3^v–A4.

    18.   Martha W. England, *Garrick's Jubilee* (Columbus: Ohio State University, 1964).

19. See Jonathan Bate, *Shakespeare and the English Romantic Imagination* (Oxford: Oxford University Press, 1986).

20. For an account see the chapter "Martial Law in the Land of Cockayne," in Greenblatt (1988).

Selected Bibliography

Given the size and immense productivity of the Shakespeare "industry," this list is necessarily highly selective. Further guides to scholarship and criticism are provided in the Riverside Edition and in Larry S. Champion, *The Essential Shakespeare* (Boston: G. K. Hall, 1986), as well as the numerous annual reviews or bibliographies such as those in *Shakespeare Quarterly, Shakespeare Survey*, and the MLA Annual Bibliography.

PRIMARY WORKS

The Complete Works. Edited by Stanley Wells and Gary Taylor. Oxford: Oxford University Press, 1986.

The Riverside Shakespeare. Edited by G. B. Evans. Boston: Houghton Mifflin, 1974.

SECONDARY WORKS

Shakespeare's Life, Texts, and Reputation

Andrews, John F., ed. *Shakespeare: His World, His Work, His Influence.* 3 vols. New York: Scribners, 1985.

Baldwin, T. W. *William Shakspere's Petty School.* Urbana: University of Illinois Press, 1943.

_____. *William Shakspere's Small Latine & Lesse Greeke.* 2 vols. Urbana: University of Illinois Press, 1944.

Bate, Jonathan. *Shakespeare and the English Romantic Imagination.* Oxford: Oxford University Press, 1986.

Brinkworth, E. R. C. *Shakespeare and the Bawdy Court of Stratford.* London and Chichester: Phillimore Press, 1972.

Chambers, E. K. *Shakespeare: A Study of Facts and Problems.* 2 vols. Oxford: Oxford University Press, 1930.

Dutton, Richard. *William Shakespeare: A Literary Life.* London: Macmillan, 1989.

Eccles, Mark. *Shakespeare in Warwickshire.* Madison: University of Wisconsin Press, 1961.

Fripp, E. I. *Shakespeare, Man and Artist*. 2 vols. Oxford: Oxford University Press, 1938.

Honigmann, E. A. J. *Shakespeare, the "Lost Years."* Manchester: Manchester University Press, 1985.

_____. *Shakespeare's Impact on His Contemporaries*. Manchester: Manchester University Press, 1982.

Kay, Dennis. *Shakespeare: His Life, Work and Era*. New York: Morrow, 1992.

Schoenbaum, S. *Shakespeare: A Compact Documentary Life*. Oxford: Oxford University Press, 1977.

_____. *Shakespeare's Lives*. Oxford: Oxford University Press, 1971.

_____. *William Shakespeare: A Documentary Life*. Oxford: Oxford University Press, 1975.

_____. *William Shakespeare: Records and Images*. Oxford: Oxford University Press, 1981.

Taylor, Gary. *Reinventing Shakespeare*. London: Hogarth Press, 1989.

Vickers, Brian. *Shakespeare: The Critical Heritage, 1623–1801*. 6 vols. London: Routledge, 1974–81.

Historical Studies

Ashton, Robert. *James I by His Contemporaries*. London: Hutchinson, 1969.

Asmussen, Susan Dwyer. *An Ordered Society: Gender and Class in Early Modern England*. Oxford: Basil Blackwell, 1988.

Beier, A. L., and R. Findlay, eds. *London, 1500–1700: The Making of the Metropolis*. London: Longmans, 1986.

Bossy, John. *The English Catholic Community, 1570–1850*. London: Darton, Longman & Todd, 1975.

Collinson, Patrick. *The Religion of Protestants*. Oxford: Oxford University Press, 1984.

Collins, Stephen L. *From Divine Cosmos to Sovereign State*. New York: Oxford University Press, 1989.

Cressy, David. *Literacy and the Social Order*. Cambridge: Cambridge University Press, 1980.

Eisenstein, E. *The Printing Press as an Agent of Social Change*. Cambridge: Cambridge University Press, 1979.

Findlay, Roger. *Population and Metropolis: The Demography of London, 1580–1650*. Cambridge: Cambridge University Press, 1981.

Fletcher, Anthony, and John Stevenson, eds. *Order and Disorder in Early Modern England*. Cambridge: Cambridge University Press, 1985.

Guy, J. *Tudor England*. Oxford: Oxford University Press, 1988.

Hill, Christopher. *Intellectual Origins of the English Revolution*. Oxford: Oxford University Press, 1965.

Ingram, William. *A London Life in the Brazen Age: Francis Langley, 1548–1602*. Cambridge, Mass.: Harvard University Press, 1978.

James, Mervyn. *Society, Politics, and Culture*. Cambridge: Cambridge University Press, 1986.

Kantorowicz, E. H. *The King's Two Bodies: A Study in Medieval Political Theology*. Princeton: Princeton University Press, 1957.

Kinney, Arthur F. *Elizabethan Backgrounds: Historical Documents of the Age of Elizabeth*. Hamden, Conn.: Archon, 1975.

Lee, Sidney, and C. T. Onions, eds. *Shakespeare's England: An Account of the Life and Manners of His Age*. 2 vols. Oxford: Oxford University Press, 1916.

Manley, L. *London in the Age of Shakespeare: An Anthology*. London: Croom Helm, 1986.

Morrill, J. S. *Seventeenth-Century Britain*. London: Longman, 1980.

Parry, Graham. *The Golden Age Restor'd: The Culture of the Stuart Court, 1603–1642*. Manchester: Manchester University Press, 1981.

Peck, L. L., ed. *The Mental World of the Jacobean Court*. Cambridge: Cambridge University Press, 1991.

Prokter, A., and R. Taylor. *The A to Z of Elizabethan London*. Lympne Castle, Kent: Harry Margary, 1979.

Russell, Conrad. *The Crisis of Parliaments: English History, 1509–1660*. Oxford: Oxford University Press, 1971.

Skinner, Quentin. *The Foundations of Modern Political Thought*. Cambridge: Cambridge University Press, 1978.

Slack, Paul. *The Impact of the Plague in Tudor and Stuart England*. London: Routledge, 1985.

Smith, L. B. *Treason in Tudor England: Politics and Paranoia*. Princeton: Princeton University Press, 1986.

Stone, Lawrence. *The Crisis of the Aristocracy, 1558–1641*. Oxford: Oxford University Press, 1965.

_____. *The Family, Sex, and Marriage, 1500–1800*. New York: Oxford University Press, 1977.

Strong, Roy. *Henry, Prince of Wales and England's Lost Renaissance*. New York: Thames and Hudson, 1986.

Taylor, Charles. *Sources of the Self*. Cambridge: Cambridge University Press, 1989.

Thomas, Keith. *Religion and the Decline of Magic*. New York: Scribners, 1971.

Tillyard, E. M. W. *The Elizabethan World Picture: A Study of the Idea of Order in the Age of Shakespeare, Donne, and Milton*. London, 1943; rpt., New York: Vintage, 1961.

Underdown, David. *Revel, Riot, and Rebellion: Popular Politics and Culture in England, 1603–1660*. Oxford: Oxford University Press, 1985.

Williams, Penry. *The Tudor Regime*. Oxford: Oxford University Press, 1977.
Wrightson, Keith. *English Society, 1580–1680*. London: Hutchinson, 1982.

Shakespeare and the Elizabethan and Jacobean Theater

Agnew, J.-C. *Worlds Apart: The Market and the Theatre in Anglo-American Thought, 1550–1750*. Cambridge: Cambridge University Press, 1986.
Bentley, G. E. *The Profession of Dramatist in Shakespeare's Time*. Princeton: Princeton University Press, 1971.
_____. *The Profession of Player in Shakespeare's Time*. Princeton: Princeton University Press, 1984.
Bevington, David M. *Action is Eloquence: Shakespeare's Language of Gesture*. Cambridge, Mass.: Harvard University Press, 1984.
Bradbrook, M. C. *The Rise of the Common Player*. London: Chatto & Windus, 1962.
Chambers, E. K. *The Elizabethan Stage*. 4 vols. Oxford: Oxford University Press, 1923.
Dessen, Alan C. *Elizabethan Stage: Conventions and Modern Interpreters*. Cambridge: Cambridge University Press, 1984.
Evans, G. B. *Elizabethan-Jacobean Drama*. London: A. C. Black, 1988.
Foakes, R. A. *Illustrations of the English Stage, 1580–1642*. Cambridge: Cambridge University Press, 1985.
Gair, W. R. *The Children of Paul's*. Cambridge: Cambridge University Press, 1982.
Greg, W. W., ed. *Dramatic Documents from the Elizabethan Playhouses*. 2 vols. Oxford: Oxford University Press, 1931.
Gurr, Andrew. *The Shakespearean Stage, 1574–1642*. 2d ed. Cambridge: Cambridge University Press, 1981.
Hattaway, Michael. *Elizabethan Popular Theatre*. London: Routledge, 1987.
Henslowe's Diary. Edited by R. A. Foakes and R. T. Rickert. Cambridge: Cambridge University Press, 1961.
Orrell, John. *The Quest for Shakespeare's Globe*. Cambridge: Cambridge University Press, 1983.
Shapiro, Michael. *Children of the Revels*. New York: Columbia University Press, 1977.
Thompson, P. *Shakespeare's Theatre*. London: Routledge, 1983.
Weimann, Robert. *Shakespeare and the Popular Tradition in the Theatre*. Baltimore: Johns Hopkins University Press, 1978.
Wickham, Glynne. *Early English Stages, 1300–1600*. 3 vols. London: Routledge, 1959–81.
Wiles, David. *Shakespeare's Clown: Actor and Text in the Elizabethan Playhouse*. Cambridge: Cambridge University Press, 1987.

Essay Collections

Brant, Clare, and Diane Purkiss, eds. *Women, Texts, and Histories, 1575–1760*. London: Routledge, 1992.

Braunmuller, A. R., and Michael Hattaway, eds. *The Cambridge Companion to English Renaissance Drama*. Cambridge: Cambridge University Press, 1990.

Dubrow, Heather and Richard Strier, eds. *The Historical Renaissance*. Chicago: University of Chicago Press, 1988.

Farrell, K., E. H. Hageman, and A. F. Kinney, eds. *Women in the Renaissance: Selections from English Literary Renaissance*. Amherst: University of Massachusetts Press, 1990.

Ferguson, M. W., M. Quilligan, and N. J. Vickers, eds. *Rewriting the Renaissance: The Discourses of Sexual Difference in Early Modern Europe*. Chicago: University of Chicago Press, 1986.

Garber, Marjorie, ed. *Cannibals, Witches, and Divorce: Estranging the Renaissance*. Baltimore: Johns Hopkins University Press, 1987.

Greenblatt, Stephen, ed. *New World Encounters*. Berkeley: University of California Press, 1993.

_____. *Representing the English Renaissance*. Berkeley: University of California Press, 1988.

Holderness, Graham, ed. *The Shakespeare Myth*. Manchester: Manchester University Press, 1988.

Kastan, D. S., and Peter Stallybrass, eds. *Staging the Renaissance: Reinterpretations of Elizabethan and Jacobean Drama*. London: Routledge, 1991.

Kinney, Arthur F., and Dan S. Collins, eds. *Renaissance Historicism: Selections from "English Literary Renaissance."* Amherst: University of Massachusetts Press, 1987.

Lindley, D., ed. *The Court Masque*. Manchester: Manchester University Press, 1984.

Parker, Patricia, and David Quint, eds. *Literary Theory/Renaissance Texts*. Baltimore: Johns Hopkins University Press, 1986.

Sharpe, K., and S. Zwicker, eds. *Politics of Discourse: The Literature and History of Seventeenth-Century England*. Berkeley: University of California Press, 1987.

Wells, Stanley, ed. *Shakespeare: A Bibliographical Guide*. Oxford: Oxford University Press, 1990.

Wilson, Richard, and Richard Dutton, eds. *New Historicism and Renaissance Drama*. London: Longmans, 1992.

Other Studies

Altman, Joel B. *The Tudor Play of Mind*. Berkeley: University of California Press, 1978.

Axton, Marie. *The Queen's Two Bodies: Drama and the Elizabethan Succession*. London: Royal Historical Society, 1977.

Bates, Catherine. *The Rhetoric of Courtship in Elizabethan Language and Literature*. Cambridge: Cambridge University Press, 1992.

Bergeron, D. M. *Shakespeare's Romances and the Royal Family*. Lawrence: University of Kansas Press, 1985.

Bevington, David M. *From "Mankind" to Marlowe*. Cambridge, Mass.: Harvard University Press, 1962.

Clare, Janet. *"Art made tongue-tied by authority": Elizabethan and Jacobean Dramatic Censorship*. New York: St. Martin's Press, 1990.

Dutton, Richard. *Mastering the Revels*. London: Macmillan, 1991.

Ferry, Anne. *The "Inward" Language: Sonnets of Sidney, Shakespeare, Donne*. Chicago: University of Chicago Press, 1981.

Fineman, Joel. *Shakespeare's "Perjur'd Eye": The Invention of Subjectivity in the Sonnets*. Berkeley: University of California Press, 1986.

Fumerton, Patricia. *Cultural Aesthetics*. Chicago: University of Chicago Press, 1991.

Goldberg, Jonathan. *James I and the Politics of Literature*. Baltimore: Johns Hopkins University Press, 1983.

Greenblatt, Stephen. *Renaissance Self-Fashioning from More to Shakespeare*. Chicago: University of Chicago Press, 1980.

_____. *Shakespearean Negotiations: The Circulation of Social Energy in Renaissance England*. Berkeley: University of California Press, 1988.

Helgerson, Richard *The Elizabethan Prodigals*. Berkeley: University of California Press, 1976.

_____. *Forms of Nationhood: The Elizabethan Writing of England*. Chicago: University of Chicago Press, 1992.

_____. *Self-Crowned Laureates: Spenser, Jonson, Milton, and the Literary System*. Berkeley: University of California Press, 1983.

Jones, Emrys. *The Origins of Shakespeare*. Oxford: Oxford University Press, 1977.

_____. *Scenic Form in Shakespeare*. Oxford: Oxford University Press, 1970.

King, John N. *English Reformation Literature: The Tudor Origins of the Protestant Tradition*. Princeton: Princeton University Press, 1982.

_____. *Spenser's Poetry and the Reformation Tradition*. Princeton: Princeton University Press, 1990.

_____. *Tudor Royal Iconography: Literature and Art in an Age of Religious Crisis*. Princeton: Princeton University Press, 1989.

Kinney, Arthur F. *Humanist Poetics: Thought, Rhetoric, and Fiction in Sixteenth-Century England*. Amherst: University of Massachusetts Press, 1986.

Knapp, Jeffrey. *An Empire Nowhere: England, America, and Literature from "Utopia" to "The Tempest."* Berkeley: University of California Press, 1992.

Lamb, Mary Ellen. *Gender and Authorship in the Sidney Circle*. Madison: University of Wisconsin Press, 1990)

Lewalski, Barbara K. *Writing Women in Jacobean England*. Cambridge, Mass.: Harvard University Press, 1993.

Lucas, Caroline. *Writing for Women: The Example of Woman as Reader in Elizabethan Romance*. Milton Keynes: Open University Press, 1989.

Marcus, Leah. *Puzzling Shakespeare: Local Reading and Its Discontents*. Berkeley: University of California Press, 1988.

Moretti, Franco. *Signs Taken for Wonders: Essays in the Sociology of Literary Forms*. London: Verso, 1983.

Mullaney, Steven. *The Place of the Stage: License, Play, and Power in Renaissance England*. Chicago: University of Chicago Press, 1988.

Norbrook, David. *Poetry and Politics in the English Renaissance*. London: Routledge, 1984.

Orgel, Stephen. *The Illusion of Power*. Berkeley: University of California Press, 1975.

Paster, Gail K. *The Idea of the City in the Age of Shakespeare*. Athens: University of Georgia Press, 1985.

Patterson, Annabel. *Censorship and Interpretation*. Madison: University of Wisconsin Press, 1984.

_____. *Shakespeare and the Popular Voice*. Oxford: Basil Blackwell, 1989.

Rackin, Phyllis. *Stages of History: Shakespeare's English Chronicles*. Ithaca, N.Y.: Cornell University Press, 1990.

Stallybrass, Peter, and Allon White. *The Politics and Poetics of Transgression*. London: Methuen, 1986.

Tennenhouse, L. *Power on Display: The Politics of Shakespeare's Genres*. London: Methuen, 1986.

Woodbridge, Linda. *Women and the English Renaissance: Literature and the Nature of Womankind, 1540–1620*. Urbana: University of Illinois Press, 1986.

Index

The Author

Since 1980 Dennis Kay has been a fellow and tutor in English at Lincoln College, Oxford, and university lecturer in English at Oxford University. He is the author of *Sir Philip Sidney: An Anthology of Modern Criticism* (1987), *Melodious Tears: The English Funeral Elegy from Spenser to Milton* (1991) and *William Shakespeare: His Life, Works and Era* (1992). In 1995 he will take up the Russell M. Robinson Distinguished Chair in Shakespeare at the University of North Carolina at Charlotte.